REGGIE JACKSON

BECOMING MR. OCTOBER

Reggie Jackson was inducted into the Baseball Hall of Fame in 1993. He hit 563 home runs and drove in 1,702 runs over the course of his twenty-one-year career. He played three World Series–winning seasons with the Oakland Athletics and two with the New York Yankees. He is a special adviser to the Yankees.

www.reggiejackson.com

Kevin Baker is the prize-winning author of the historical novels *Dreamland*, *Paradise Alley*, and *Strivers Row*; the baseball novel *Sometimes You See It Coming*; and, most recently, *The Big Crowd*. He served as chief historical researcher for the nonfiction bestseller *The American Century*. His writing has appeared in *The New York Times*, *The Washington Post*, the *Chicago Tribune*, the *Los Angeles Times*, and *Harper's Magazine*, among other publications.

BECOMING MR. OCTOBER

BECOMING
MR. OCTOBER

~

REGGIE JACKSON

with Kevin Baker

ANCHOR BOOKS
A DIVISION OF RANDOM HOUSE LLC
NEW YORK

FIRST ANCHOR BOOKS EDITION, SEPTEMBER 2014

Copyright © 2013 by Reginald Martinez Jackson

The Cataloging-in-Publication Data is available at the
Library of Congress.

Anchor Books Trade Paperback ISBN: 978-0-307-47680-7
eBook ISBN: 978-0-385-53312-6

Book design by Michael Collica

www.anchorbooks.com

Printed in the United States of America
10   9   8   7   6   5   4   3   2   1

To my daughter, Kimberly, who has never seen me play baseball but has seen me as Dad. Enjoy your journey, love God, family, and friends.

I'd like to dedicate this short story of mine to some who have had similar things happen to them. Jackie Robinson and his family, who have dealt with far more than I. Negro players of the past, the great Josh Gibson, Satchel Paige, and many more who have endured so much more than those of us who came through the 1960s and 1970s. It was a different time a hundred years ago, fifty years ago, twenty-five years ago. From Jackie to Hammerin' Hank, Larry Doby, Willie, Mickey and the Duke, Sandy Koufax and his commitment, Ernie Banks, Roberto Clemente, Willie McCovey, Bob Gibson, Frank Robinson, and more. Our great game has continued to evolve.

I remember the dinners in Arizona with Billy Williams, Fergie Jenkins, and Stretch McCovey, educating me on how to stay in the background, what to say, and what not to. I heard and listened to their teachings and those of others as we ate together.

I learned to respect and understand that it takes a "we" attitude to make the changes that can make our world a better place.

As Jackie played and maintained his composure, he fought for his and all our dignity, both blacks and whites. With help of his family and of whites, such as Walter O'Malley, Branch Rickey, some of his teammates, and other players who stood by him, to help him through our (America's) issues at that time.

As we move forward in time, some of us forget the difficulty that those before us went through. Please remember and give thanks for them and what they gave to pave a road that didn't exist just a short time ago. Many do not remember, and they can't because they weren't born fifty years ago, thirty years ago. Hopefully, we will have reminders to help us to continue to be *careful* with each other—and we should translate that word with the thought of "*being full of care*" for our fellow man or woman.

This book has been written because I wanted to set the record straight regarding what the 1977–1978 seasons of the Yankees were like from my side. The miniseries *The Bronx Is Burning* thoroughly embarrassed me the way the story was told. So I was lucky enough to have my friend David Black connect me with a great writer, Kevin Baker, and a great publisher, Doubleday, where Bill Thomas, Coralie Hunter, Bette Alexander, Ingrid Sterner, Lawrence Krauser, and others helped me tell my story the way I saw it.

I tried to get almost all who were mentioned in the book to have their say. Some did and others declined, as is their right.

As you read my rendition please remember, as a nation we have been selected as the leader in our world of so much. It's our responsibility to set standards that are admired around the globe—to "do the right thing," not always what "I" want. To allow our faith to lead is our duty, wouldn't you think?

Contents

BECOMING MR. OCTOBER

Bull in the Ring

I never intended to play professional baseball.

After high school, I had gone down to Arizona State on a football scholarship, playing for Frank Kush, who was a great coach. He knew my high school football coach, John Kracsun, from the Pittsburgh area, and Kracsun told him I would be a good college player.

I was a much better football player than I was a baseball player at the time. I was maybe a better basketball player, too. I could do everything. I was a great shooter, played guard, but also jumped some center, even though we had a guy, Alan Tractenberg, who was six eight while I was five eleven. I was a great jumper, a high flier.

In football, I was a running back on offense and a safety on defense. There were several schools interested in recruiting me—Syracuse, Penn State. Oklahoma—but you had to be in at ten at night, for your own safety. Duke—but I was a little afraid to go to school in the South then; I didn't know what to expect at the time. I didn't want to be the first black player to go anywhere. Notre Dame and Michigan were interested in me, but I wanted to play baseball, too, and they were schools in cold-weather climates, where you couldn't get enough time in to play much baseball.

John Kracsun was a father figure to me, so I listened to him. I saw Coach Kush much the same way. I was eighteen years old, but Frank Kush was going to make me a man. Football started at Camp Tontozona, up in the hills near a little town called Payson. We went there for two weeks in mid-August, and it got up to 105 degrees during the day, five thousand feet above sea level, but cooled at night.

We had two workouts a day. Lots of running, mostly sprints. If you couldn't make it, or you were dragging, you had to run "Mount Kush" at the end of the workout, which was this rocky hill, this Prudential rock, where you'd be sliding, slipping, and falling. Lots of one-on-one drills, to see who's tougher than the next guy.

We had this drill called "bull in the ring." There would be a big circle of the entire team, anywhere from eighty to ninety guys, out there in full pads and helmets, with numbers on the jerseys. To test our mettle and see who was tough enough to play Frank Kush football, Coach Kush would call out a guy's number. If you were the "bull" in the circle, another player would run at you full speed. You had to find out where he was coming from—if he was behind you or on one side—and defend yourself in a one-on-one, head-on crash.

I felt like I was in the middle more than anybody, and I wasn't the best at it. The best at it was a guy named Curley Culp, who was the NCAA heavyweight wrestling champion when he was a freshman in college and who would go on to make the Pro Football Hall of Fame as a great, great defensive lineman with the Kansas City Chiefs.

Curley and I bunked together at camp. His number got called when I was in the circle, and he took it easy on me. Coach Kush said, "Oh, taking care of your buddy, huh? Okay, *you* become 'bull in the ring'!" Curley broke the next guy's face mask and helmet, and that ended the drill.

In those days, you couldn't play varsity ball as a freshman. I played on the freshman team, played both ways as a safety and a running back and did well. I remember I gained a lot of yards running behind Curley Culp. But I wanted to play baseball, and my dad wanted me to play, too; he had been a professional player with some of the old Negro Leagues clubs.

I had been a center fielder, a first baseman, and a pitcher in high school. At the plate I hit about .500. I had one of the best arms on the team, so I pitched a lot, but I threw a lot of curveballs and ended up hurting my arm. I did pitch a couple no-hitters. I could pitch a no-hitter, strike out fifteen—and usually walk ten or twelve.

When he came to recruit me, I asked Coach Kush if I could play baseball as well. That would be almost unheard of today, a top recruit playing two sports, but he told me I could play baseball as well as football if I kept up a B average, and I had a 3.0. Freshman year at Arizona State, spring of 1965, we had spring football practice, but the baseball season was starting at the same time. A couple of guys in my dormitory, Joe Paulson and Jeff Pentland, who became a major-league hitting coach for many years, bet me that I couldn't make the baseball team.

Much as I wanted to play, I was leery about going out for the team, because the baseball coach was Bobby Winkles. Winkles was a legend, but he was from Arkansas, and Arizona State had never had a black player on its baseball team. They'd had one guy, Sterling Slaughter, who was a mulatto and later pitched for the Cubs, but he really wasn't recognized as a black player. But Joe and Jeff bet me $5 I couldn't make the team, and $5 was a lot of money to us then. After football practice one day, I went over to the baseball field and told Coach Winkles, "Boy, I'd like to try out one day."

Winkles had already heard from the major-league scouts who watched me in high school that I had really good tools, and he said in his southern drawl, "Well, come over here and take some batting practice." I still had my football gear on at the time. I was wearing a pair of Riddell football shoes, had my football pants on still, my shoulder pads and shirt. I was still wearing my helmet. But he said, "Take some batting practice," so I just took off my shoulder pads, set my football helmet down, put on a baseball helmet, and started swinging. After a couple pop-ups and grounders, I started hitting line drives and fly balls over the fence.

Bobby Winkles said, "Would you like to try out for the team?" And I said, "I would love to"—and thought of course of my $5 payday. It also meant I got to miss Frank Kush's spring football practice, which was a big plus!

I played on the freshman team, and everything went fine. We had ten games, all of them at home or within a day-trip away. The next year, in the spring of 1966, I was on the varsity. We played a fifty-game schedule and traveled around the Western Athletic Conference to the states in that region. The team had decided to have a vote, to see who would room with me when they traveled. I had to wait outside. When I look back on that, it just made me feel so small, so insignificant. I don't know how many people actually objected to me, but it was a different thing for the team, having a black player, even in 1966—nineteen years after Jackie Robinson broke the color line in major-league baseball.

It never went to a vote, because the captain of the team, Jan Kleinman, said, "I'll room with Reggie, no worries."

Jan and I are friends to this day, and we got along very well. Later, after he went to play in the Phillies' organization, I roomed with a country kid from Kansas named Glenn Smith, and we had a blast together. Glenn was just a real salt-of-the-earth person with a great midwestern twang who went on to play in the Minnesota Twins' system for a few years. He used to call me a "yearling"—said I ran fast like a yearling deer—and we had some great times together.

We ended up having eight players from that squad who were drafted by major-league teams, and four of them made it to the show: Al Schmelz and Duffy Dyer, who played with the Mets, and Rick Monday, who was the top prospect in the country, and Sal Bando—both guys I would play a lot of games with as a professional with the Oakland Athletics.

I did well, I led the team in everything. I got along great with Bobby Winkles. He really treated me like a son. He helped break me of some bad habits, helped kick some of that chip off my shoulder I had then. He ran me to death, taught me to play up to my potential. He taught me discipline and sacrifice—on and off the field.

It was Bobby Winkles who taught me to hustle *all* the time. He taught me to control my emotions, learn the right way to play the game. Don't throw your bat and helmet when you strike out. Keep learning and getting the best of your ability. Be more responsible. He helped start me on the road to becoming an adult.

It also helped that I was in great shape. They still used to tell baseball players in those days, don't lift weights too much, you'll get muscle-bound, you'll get too tight. But I was already a football player, so I knew about working out, I went to weight-lifting classes, and I was pretty muscular and thick. I believe weight training in football helped me in baseball.

At Arizona State, because it was a great baseball school, the major-league scouts were all over the place. I was considered the number one draft pick in the country. Danny Murtaugh, who would manage the Pittsburgh Pirates to two world championships, was taking some time off for his health, scouting amateur players for the Pirates, and he came to see me play. He was asked, "What do you think about this year's draft?" and he said, "It's a pretty good crop of players. But there's this kid at Arizona State who's built like a blacksmith. And his name is Reggie Jackson. He's head and shoulders above everyone else."

You can imagine how excited I was when I read that in the *Arizona Republic*. Danny Murtaugh! At the time the Pirates had an amazing lineup: Willie Stargell, Donn Clendenon, Matty Alou, the great Roberto Clemente. "*The Lumber Company.*" I would've loved to have played with those guys, but Murtaugh didn't think there was any way the Pirates would ever get to me in the draft, that I'd be taken first by some team with a higher draft pick.

The team that had the first pick in the draft that year? The New York Mets. They had never finished out of last place, so they had the first pick, and everyone figured they would pick me.

I think about that sometimes. If I had gone to the Mets then, my career would've been in New York from the very start. I would've been coming up just as that team was finally improving. They had all those great arms: Tom Seaver, Jerry Koosman, Jon Matlack, Nolan Ryan, Tug McGraw. Oh, boy! They had Cleon Jones and Tommie Agee in the outfield, Jerry Grote behind the plate. A little later they acquired Rusty Staub and Felix Millan, brought up John Milner. They brought back Willie Mays—I could've learned so much if I'd got to play with him, my boyhood idol.

As it was, they would win two pennants and a World Series. Add me, and who knows what the Mets would have done? I played against them with the A's in the 1973 World Series, and I was the MVP. We won in seven, and I drove in half the runs in the last two games. Maybe they could've won that Series if they'd had a guy who could hit thirty home runs and drive in a hundred. Maybe they would've pushed across a couple more pennants if I were there with all those other great players. Oh, well . . . and, oh, that pitching.

It would've meant that I would have been in New York about a decade earlier than I was. But with the Mets, that would've meant playing with very different personalities. It would've meant playing for Gil Hodges, who nobody ever said a bad word about anyone and who played with all those great black players on the old Brooklyn Dodgers. It would've meant playing for Yogi Berra, who got along well with everyone. Unlike Billy Martin, Yogi didn't need to be the star all the time. He already was the star; he didn't need to prove it to anybody. Tom Seaver and I were always friendly; he introduced me to my agent Matt Merola in 1969.

It's intriguing to think about. I think it would've gone very well.

But then, a day or two before the draft, Bobby Winkles sat me down and told me, "You're probably not gonna be the number one pick." He said, "You're dating a Mexican girl, and the Mets think you will be a problem. They think you'll be a social problem because you are dating out of your race."

"*Wow, really?*" I said.

I didn't know what he was talking about. I said, "Well, she's Mexican, and I'm part Latino, so what's that?" My father's mother was from a little town outside San Juan, Puerto Rico. I mean, my *middle name* is Martinez. And he said, "No, you're colored, and they don't want that. It may hurt your draft." I told him, "Everyone says that I'm the best." And he said, "Yes, but the Mets think you're gonna maybe cause a problem, socially." I said, "But I think we're gonna get married." Her name was Juanita Campos.

But that didn't matter. It turned out Bobby Winkles was right. I heard it was Bob Scheffing, who was the Mets' director of player development then—the same guy who traded Nolan Ryan a few years later, after Scheffing became general manager. He saw to it they drafted a guy named Steve Chilcott, a high school catcher who would become one of only two first picks in history to retire without ever playing a single game in the majors.

Scheffing denied it later, said there was nothing racial about it. Then he tried to blame it on Casey Stengel, who was about seventy-five years old at the time and doing some scouting for the team. Can you believe that? I couldn't. I know I never saw Casey Stengel when I was being scouted—and how could you be in a ballpark and not know if Casey Stengel was there?

Ten years later, when I was a free agent, the Mets *still* didn't even try to sign me. After the free-agent draft, Bob Scheffing told a reporter from the St. Petersburg *Evening Independent*, "Jackson wasn't the best ballplayer available, Joe Rudi was. Jackson was the best press-agent around." He said I was "a pleasure to talk to" but that I was "not an outstanding offensive ballplayer."

This was the sort of thing that put that chip on my shoulder, when I was a young man. It had a lot to do with what went on with the Yankees, when I finally did get to New York.

It's hard for many people to understand what a different place the world was when I was young. And it's hard for them to understand the ways in which it still hasn't changed.

I wasn't raised in the Deep South. I grew up in Pennsylvania, in a nice town outside Philadelphia called Wyncote. I was in a nice neighborhood; the people were nice. The neighbors were wonderful. But it was 95 percent white. Not far away, across the Mason-Dixon Line, there were regular Ku Klux Klan meetings that went on in Maryland, maybe sixty to eighty miles from my home. There were certain towns down there where you didn't go.

Pennsylvania was considered the North. But there were often reminders that color was a social issue, and I was colored. I went to a white school, and being black, you were a second-class citizen. The *n*-word was overheard from time to time. Socially, in those days, the world was different. You weren't allowed to (or, it was *preferred* you didn't) swim in the community pool in Glenside if you were colored. You weren't allowed to go to the country club in Elkins Park and play golf, because you were colored!

The parents of a lot of kids I knew didn't want me to play with them. I was in Glenside one day and was riding a buddy of mine's bicycle back to my house. I had been hanging out with him all day, and rather than make me walk the two or three miles back home, he lent me his bike. On the way home, I got maybe a mile, and his step-dad saw me. I can still remember he was driving a '57 yellow Chevy, with a Continental kit. And when he saw me, he stopped that beautiful car, and then he stopped me. He made me get off his stepson's bike and walk it back to his house—*walk it back!*

How's that for a memory? I don't know if I felt embarrassed, small, humiliated . . . I don't know how I felt, except bad. I knew exactly what was going on. He did not want a colored kid riding his son's bicycle, and we were best friends. I know the guy—my friend—to this day. Still a great guy, and one of my longtime elementary school, junior high, high school buddies. I'm sure it broke his heart, just as it broke mine. We were thirteen, fourteen, and we didn't know what to say. I just felt like the sole of a shoe.

Call it a petty humiliation, but there was nothing "petty" about it. "Mountainous" would be a better word. Those humiliations become scars. They become wounds—and then they get opened up again, on another day. And then before the scab heals, someone else opens it up. You wind up getting in a fight with someone because of something else you've had on your mind for two years.

And dating—there was a girl in our neighborhood, her name was Helen S. She was cute, and we wanted to be friends. We were, you know, thirteen, fourteen, but her parents wouldn't allow it. Because I was colored. There was another girl in high school, a few years later, named Sandy H. I had a friend, George Beck, a white guy. He had a '55 Chevy and I had a '55 Chevy, so he would pick her up at her house when it was light out. Then, when I drove her home, I'd have to hold the interior light button down with my hand when I dropped her off, so the inside of the car would stay dark and her parents couldn't see who it was. Then she could get out in the dark and run in the door.

Meanwhile, things were going on all around us. You know, I was thirteen years old when they held the first sit-in at the Woolworth's counter in 1960. Negroes weren't allowed to vote in much of the United States until 1965—we were still physically kept from voting when I was already in college! All that stuff that went on, all the murders in the South, the burning of the churches, the murder of Martin Luther King—that all went on when I was a teenager or in my early twenties.

It's hard to get across to some people—what that does to you. Many think of it as ancient history: "Oh, my gosh, that was so terrible.

Forty years ago, I can't believe it! That's the way it was? My, my, what a terrible thing. That's really too bad!" is what people would say.

But my brothers and sisters, the six of us? We were raised in that era. Our youngest is sixty-two, my older sister is seventy-five, my brother is seventy-three. We were *raised* in that America. So it's not something that you easily forget. *It's part of who we are.* Part of who I am. You don't just forget! You work at forgiving.

As a kid, you tend to just accept that that's how things are. But it still hurts. Growing up, all through my teens, I was raised as a second-class citizen. You'd have to be a psychologist to know all the different ways that impacts someone. I'm just a human being who felt the hurt in mind and heart.

People ask you, "How did you feel about that?" and you almost want to say to them, "How do you *think* I felt?" I'd want to start swearing or something, because it's hard to find the words, it's not comfortable even to think about that again. You just want to get away from it emotionally. Invariably, though, something happens to remind you of the ugliness.

My father used to tell us, "If you ever get in a race, if you ever get in a contest, make sure that you're clearly the winner. Make sure that there's no photo finish. Because if there's a photo finish, you won't win the race."

So now it's 1966, and here I was, I had won going away. Danny Murtaugh said it. A white guy, been around baseball all his life, a great judge of talent. He said I was head and shoulders above the rest. And then the Mets drafted Steve Chilcott. I don't want to disrespect Steve Chilcott, he got hurt. I'm sure he was a good ballplayer and a good guy.

But that wasn't why he was drafted first. He was drafted first because I was dating a "white" girl.

I suppose I was surprised and I wasn't surprised when I heard that from Bobby Winkles. The ironic thing was, the Mexican girl I was dating, her uncle—his name was Ferdie—told Frank Kush that he didn't want me dating his niece.

I married Juanita in the end. It didn't work out; we were only married for about a year and a half. But it wasn't because she was this much Mexican or I was that much black. It was because I wasn't a good husband. I wasn't from an institution of successful marriage, my parents were separated by the time I was six. I never knew much about marriage, never lived in the environment of marriage. I wish I had—at least I think so.

If the Mets had only been willing to wait, or sign me because of my ability, I would have played with Seaver—and later maybe Strawberry and Gooden. That would've been fun. But what it came down to was, I wasn't going to New York yet. I was going to Kansas City.

Birmingham

The great thing about Bobby Winkles was, as soon as he broke it to me that I wasn't going to be the number one draft pick because the New York Mets disapproved of my dating habits, he also told me, "But there's a guy, Bob Zuk, who's a scout with the Kansas City A's, and he loves you. He signed Willie Stargell a few years ago, and he's gonna recommend that the A's draft you with their first pick."

The A's had that pick because they'd been the last-place team in the American League in 1965. The next year, the last-place team in the league was the Yankees, and they had the very first pick in the draft. I knew that Tom Greenwade, the great scout who signed Mickey Mantle and Bobby Murcer and a lot of other players for the Yankees, was looking at me, and he liked what he saw. Never mind the Mets. Who knows, if I'd stayed in college another year, I might've come to the *Yankees* ten years before I did.

But whoever drafted me, Bobby Winkles told me, "I'd recommend that you sign and leave college. It's gonna be a lot of fun. And the money, Reggie, I'm sure will help your family."

Which was a very fatherly thing for him to do. His teams were always contenders for the national title. He won the title in 1965, 1967, and 1969 as it was, and who knows, if I'd stayed, maybe he would've won five in a row. But he was looking out for me first!

I went ahead and signed with the Kansas City Athletics. Or rather, I signed with Charlie Finley, the A's owner. That was the best part of all.

He was a special character. I flew into Chicago with my dad (also my agent!), and we went directly to Mr. Finley's office there, at the insurance company he had on Michigan Avenue. I can still remember the address: 310 South Michigan Avenue.

Finley could be a funny-looking guy, with those little Bear Bryant hats and those loud jackets he always wore. (He was from Birmingham.) But he was very impressive when I first saw him, sitting at a big desk in his big, mahogany office. The biggest office I'd ever been in before was the principal's office. You could look out the window from the twenty-something floor, and you could see out over Lake Michigan. To me, it felt like I could see the North Pole, or maybe California.

Finley sent his secretary, Rebecca, who was very nice as well as very attractive, out for lunch, and she brought back this amazing meal, oysters, and shrimp, and crabs. I remember he cleared his desk of all its papers and put the seafood right on it, in a very large plate. Then he mixed up this sauce himself, Tabasco sauce with ketchup and vinegar, touch of mayonnaise, and we ate the cracked crabs, and the oysters, and the shrimp right there with his special sauce. We drank whatever we wanted, water, soda, tea, lemonade. Charlie rolled up his sleeves and ate with us. My dad and I were in heaven.

He was a hard man to figure sometimes, Charlie Finley. Thinking about it now, quite frankly he might've had us eat like that in his office because he didn't know of a good restaurant that would seat my dad and me. This was still 1966, after all. Or maybe he just wanted to put on a show, which he always liked to do. We had a great time.

We were in his office for three or four hours, talking about baseball and about finishing my college education. He volunteered to manage my signing bonus and guaranteed to make me money, and he was true to his word. He invested $37,500 of my bonus, and he got it all back to me, with profit. He also put aside $12,000 for me to go back to college. I did for a couple of semesters, even though I never quite graduated, ending up twelve to fifteen hours short of graduation. I was an education major, with a minor in biology. I was a good student, sat up front, never missed class. It got to be too much once I became a professional ballplayer.

I should have taken the few remaining courses and graduated. I have since connected with Arizona State University to finish the remaining courses I need online. Once I do, I'm going to finally go to graduation.

After the meeting in his office, Charlie flew us over to his house, in La Porte, Indiana. We flew across Lake Michigan in a private plane. I thought, "Wow!" I had never been in anyone's private plane before. He had this whole compound in La Porte. There were lots of different buildings and houses. We met his wife, Shirley, and his kids, five or six kids; they were a great family. He had animals, too; it was something of a working farm.

The next day my dad and I had breakfast with Charlie and his family. Boy, that was a treat. We had eggs and bacon, sausage and ham, pancakes, waffles, and fruit—I remember eating cantaloupe à la mode. I'd never seen so much food in my life, and I ate until I was about to burst.

We talked about the contract for maybe thirty minutes to an hour. It was so much money that we started out happy and only got happier as the talks went on. I was going to sign, and I was excited. I couldn't really relate to that much money, nor could my dad. We just knew our bills would be paid. Finally.

The next day I signed the contract. My dad wanted to make sure we slept on it, just to show we weren't going to do this without considering it—though it was hard to sleep after all that food. To this day, I like to think about things overnight before I pull the trigger.

In the end, Charlie gave me a signing bonus of $95,000. That was more money than I'd ever heard of. I mean, this was at a time when the best players in the game, men like Willie Mays and Henry Aaron and Mickey Mantle, still made about $100,000 a year. That was big money. My father must've had about $1,000 to his name at the time, including what he kept in his mattress.

I gave part of that bonus money to my mom, and some of it went to my brother who was going to college. Gave some of it to my dad and paid off all of his and Mom's bills.

To clinch the deal, Charlie Finley offered me a new car. We all know I love cars. It took me about a month to make that decision. I finally settled on a new four-speed Pontiac, 421 cubic inches, 375 horsepower, burgundy with a black hat—a vinyl top. It was the first new car I'd ever owned. My dad didn't even have a new car. Nobody I was friends with had a new car. But now I had one. I was in high cotton.

I went back to my dad's house in Wyncote for a few days, and then I went down to my mother's in Baltimore to help her out, give her some money. Then, on June 13 or 14, I went out to report to Lewiston, Idaho, to play for the Lewiston Broncs in the Northwest League.

I was there two weeks. It was a short-season, Single-A league, mostly for college and high school rookies just out of school. I stayed in the Lewis-Clark Hotel. I hit a home run in one of my first games in Lewiston. I remember hitting two home runs in a night game in Yakima, Washington, while it was snowing. In June!

Then I got beaned, and the A's minor-league manager, Bill Posedel, took me to the hospital in Lewiston. They said they wouldn't admit me because I was colored—in Idaho! Bill Posedel was a great guy; we were friendly for many years before he passed. Bill got on the phone to Charlie Finley, and Charlie said, "Get Reggie out of there. Get him to Modesto, in the California League."

So all of a sudden there I was in California. And it was there that it felt like my professional career really began. It was in Modesto, for me, that it all came together—that the great A's dynasty was born.

Guys look back and tend to think about the bad parts of being a minor leaguer. The low pay, all the long bus rides, the lousy fields. Not me. I was making $500 a month, $3 a day meal money on the road—and I felt I was in the penthouse! That was a great year. We were good—no, we were *great*. We had fun and we were young.

I shared a room at the team hotel with this older pitcher, Stan Jones. He was twenty-six—and I thought that was *old*. I thought he was ancient—I used to ask him when he was going to be getting his pension. He had all the stories, you know, and he showed me around. It was all fun. All the clothes I had were new because I didn't have anything as a kid. I bought three, four pairs of pants, four or five new shirts, a couple of sweaters, and a sport coat. My share of the hotel room was all of $3 a day, I think. We ate just around the corner, at this chain restaurant called the Hofbrau. They served good food, and it was cheap. You could get a whole meal, sauerkraut, mashed potatoes, turkey and gravy, and dessert, for a couple bucks. We'd eat there pretty much every day, then we'd go over to the ballpark, which was nearby as well.

The Modesto Reds, that was our name, even though we were an A's farm team. We were monsters. We *destroyed* teams. We went 88–53, won the league by eleven games. I had twenty-one homers, drove in sixty runs in a little over two hundred at-bats, and just missed hitting .300, finished at .299. But we were all good.

We had twelve future major leaguers on that team. Guys like Tony LaRussa, who's going to be a Hall of Fame manager, Syd O'Brien, who played some third base for the Red Sox, Ossie Blanco, Skip Lockwood, who became a closer for the Mets. The manager was Gus Niarhos, the old Yankees catcher, who knew how to win and make it fun. He loved his job, the kids, the game, and life. Gus has always been a good memory for me.

But most of all, we had the core of the dynasty the A's were going to eventually have in Oakland. We had two future Hall of Famers, myself and Rollie Fingers, who would become the best relief pitcher in the game until the great Mariano happened along. Rollie was still a starter then, and a good one. He used to come pick me up in his car and take me to the park every day. We had Joe Rudi, who was to be an all-star left fielder; he hit twenty-four home runs that year. And we had Dave Duncan—big, tall, blond-haired guy from California, who would be our catcher.

I remember, the first time I met him, Duncan had his own bonus car: a white Corvette with a red interior. I was like, "*Wow!*" He was the catcher that year and missed four weeks with a broken hand but still managed to hit forty-six home runs. Rudi broke his hand, too, he missed time as well, but he came right back. That's how good we were; that's how tough we were, even as kids.

After that season, we were all moving up another level or two, to Double- or Triple-A. I reported to spring training the next March in

Waycross, Georgia—Deep South!—where I had to live in a barracks ten to twelve miles outside town.

That's right. That was what moving up meant for us in 1967. You had a great year, you got promoted . . . but being black, you had to go live in an old army barracks for your own safety.

They had most of the A's black minor-league players there—maybe fifteen, twenty of us at the peak. We ate right there in the barracks. The team told us, "You guys shouldn't go into town at night. Not so safe." It was just like one of those old southern towns, with the signs saying, "We Don't Serve Niggers." At the time, it was a Jim Crow town. We didn't test that much, and to be honest, I don't remember ever going into town. It was 1967, man.

But we were young; we had a good time. We had a black-and-white TV we all would watch. We'd get back from the park, eat, tell stories a little bit, eat again, tell some more stories, and go to sleep. We went to bed most nights at ten o'clock. It was isolated, but it was our home, and we liked it.

We were playing ball, eating for free. Being black back then—the other things were just part of the deal. We did the things we could do, didn't complain about the things we couldn't do, and looked for our opportunities. We stayed together and supported each other—and nobody from the team, at least, treated us as anything less than equal.

Charlie Finley looked out for his players. There were some white owners and general managers like that, then and later—men like Finley, like George Steinbrenner—who helped their players along. It was paternal in the best sense of the word. Sometimes it felt like they were plantation owners, because they had the right to trade you at their whim. I had heard about the O'Malley family and August Busch caring about their black players back then, and there were others who looked out for your welfare, who made sure the players came first.

I got paid around $47 a week that spring training. They wanted me to sign a contract for $800 a month, but I didn't want to sign. It wasn't the money. It was because if I signed, it meant they were going to assign me to the Birmingham farm team, in the Southern League.

That was a big step up; it was Double-A ball. But I did not want to go to Birmingham, Alabama. Last week of spring training, they finally had Charlie Finley himself come down and make a special appeal to me. He wanted me to sign and go to Birmingham because it was his old hometown and he really wanted to have a good team there.

He told me, face-to-face, "Reggie, I want you to go there." He said it nice, but there wasn't any choice. In those days, the owners had that kind of authority. They spoke, you went.

When I started playing ball in the South, the idea of race hit me like a sandbag coming from the blind side. I had never been in the Deep South before, and Birmingham was a tough, tough town for a colored kid. It was just four years before that they'd blown up those four little girls in Sunday school, dynamited a black church with the people in it.

My reaction was more one of shock than of anger. I didn't know what to do. I didn't know where I was allowed to eat, where I was allowed to live. It's tough to take, suddenly dropping into an environment like that. There was a black section of town, but I didn't know anything about Birmingham, and the team didn't provide any help.

Think about that one. Here you are, a promising talent for a big-league ball team, and they make you stay in an army barracks during spring training and don't help you to get housing in Alabama.

If all those big-league teams had really used their influence, really exerted some pressure, they might have helped open up the South years before it did. But it seemed to me that wasn't on the top of the list. For years, black players stayed in segregated hotels, until the Cardinals in St. Petersburg and the Dodgers in Vero Beach bought their own hotels in which to put their players. In 1965, the last minor-league team in Birmingham, the Barons, was forced to move out of town because Bull Connor closed the ballpark rather than let blacks and whites play together. He closed sixty public parks, all over the city, rather than let them be integrated.

I was there just two years later. You can imagine how uncomfortable it was. Charlie Finley was bringing back organized ball to the city, which was nice, but not for me. I didn't have anywhere to live. It's hard, being part of a social experiment. The first month, I slept on the couches of white friends, Dave Duncan, Joe Rudi, Rollie Fingers. Their landlords didn't like it; they would threaten to make them move out. Joe Rudi's wife, Sharon, she had a brother who was a lawyer, and every other day she would get him to call up their landlord and insist that I was legally entitled to be there. She just insisted that I was going to be able to stay.

Finally, I left anyway, because I was afraid that something was going to happen. I moved into the Bankhead Hotel, which was a big, beautiful old hotel that was a little tired, but it seemed great to me. It beat Joe Rudi's couch. My only problem was a little blond girl, the owner's daughter, who was hanging around there and was always very nice—but I wanted to get out in one piece!

On the road, it was a whole other story again. By the time the season opened, I was the only African American on the Birmingham A's. We had Gil Blanco, who was Mexican American but "looked white," and then we had George Lauzerique, who was Cuban and looked Latino. But that was it, at least until a little later, when a couple more Latino guys joined the team.

I was really the only black guy on the Birmingham A's. The wonder, of course, is that there weren't more. I mean, that had been the same situation for Henry Aaron, when he was with Jacksonville in the Sally League, back in 1953. He was the only black guy on the team, the only black guy in the *league*. And here it was fourteen years later, and I was *still* the only black guy on my team—and the A's were one of the more liberal organizations around. They were bringing up all sorts of players of color then—Bert Campaneris, Blue Moon Odom, Ramon Webster, George Lauzerique, Tommie Reynolds, and more.

Luckily, my manager was John McNamara, who was great about it. The Southern League in those days, every other team was below the Mason-Dixon Line except for Evansville, which was in southern Indiana. We'd go to Montgomery, Alabama; Macon, Georgia; Charlotte, North Carolina; Knoxville, Tennessee.

Every city we went to, McNamara would send somebody in to check the hotel, see if they'd let me stay there. If not, we would drive the bus to another hotel. This was three years after the Civil Rights Act passed, it was supposed to be against the law, but they'd just ignore it. I remember he sent Gil Blanco into a hotel in Knoxville, and he came back and said, "They won't let Reggie stay here." McNamara just said, "Well, let's go on down the street to another hotel."

Same thing with restaurants. Driving all the way to Charlotte, Knoxville, Macon—those were *long* trips. But if we stopped at a restaurant and I couldn't eat inside, he'd have the food brought out to the bus. For *everybody*. Everybody ate together; everybody stayed together. Major-league baseball couldn't make that happen? John McNamara made that happen.

I was so young, so new to the South, I didn't know what it was like. My father would talk to me on the phone and try to explain, but I didn't really understand. But I found out fast! Back in Birmingham, I tried to eat in some local restaurants, but in some places it wasn't meant to be. That just wasn't part of the deal. You were in Birmingham, buddy.

Then I got off to a great start, and the A's promoted me to the big-league team. I got to skip Triple-A and go right up to Kansas City, where I played left field for Alvin Dark. But it was too soon. I played about a month there, hit maybe .170-something. I was nervous, and the team was doing poorly. I wasn't ready yet.

They sent me back to Birmingham. I've always believed that if you go up and catch on and take off, great. If you don't, you go back down and try again. A lot of guys will say about a prospect, "You shouldn't rush him, he'll never develop." But I think if you can't recover from being overmatched and having a bad month or two, then you're not going to make it anyway.

However, at the time, I felt crushed. I remember going to see my manager and feeling so bad, because I had failed. Johnny McNamara was waiting for me with open arms, like a father figure. He told me I hadn't failed at all and I was going to be back in the majors in no time. Johnny Mac was always perfect at all times. I needed a "dad" at that time; he was that for me. As usual.

I remember everybody was very supportive. Guys like Joe Rudi, Bando, Duncan, Fingers. We all came up together, we all sort of got there at the same time, and we all looked out for each other.

After that, I just tore up the league. We all did. We had another great team, twenty guys on that roster who had been in the big leagues or who would be. I finished second in home runs, had sixty extra-base hits, even though I missed a month. We finished about thirty games over .500, took the league title.

It even worked out best for me in a way that I didn't stick in Kansas City that first time. That was the year the A's kind of imploded. There was a big fight between Finley and Dark, who got fired, and Hawk Harrelson jumped the team. It wasn't a good situation. The A's had been fielding bad teams for years, and Finley was getting on the fans in Kansas City for not showing up.

He was starting to take the team apart and rebuild it for the future with his money and new talent. Say what you want about Charlie Finley. He knew how to build a team, and he knew talent.

By the time I was with the big club again, Finley had moved it to Oakland, which was a whole other story. All of a sudden we were in California, in a town with a lot of minorities, and all the guys I'd come up through the minors with were on the team. I was very comfortable there. And we were going to make some big things happen.

GUNSLINGERS

OAKLAND, CALIFORNIA, 1968. Our home opener was a night game, and we drew more than fifty thousand people. To give you an idea, the A's had been drawing fewer than ten thousand a game back in Kansas City. But here it was, our first game in a new city, and the atmosphere was electric.

I was the right fielder, batting second. Bob Kennedy, our manager, told me in spring training, "You're gonna be the right fielder." I was nervous. I said to myself, "Gosh, I don't know if I'm ready. Maybe I should do Triple-A first." And then I went out and got four hits against the St. Louis Cardinals late in spring training and boom! I was the right fielder. That was it!

That first night, there was so much excitement. It was against Baltimore, and Dave McNally beat us. Rick Monday hit a home run. I think Lew Krausse started for us.

The next day, we were back down to about five thousand fans, and it rarely got much better than that. As well as we played, Oakland was going through some hard times, and we could never get that many people out; sometimes we couldn't even fill the ballpark in the postseason.

But still, we had this excitement about ourselves, because we knew how good we were with such great talent. I came up for good that year along with Joe Rudi and Rollie Fingers. Dave Duncan was already up, and so was Bert Campaneris, who was a great shortstop, maybe even a Hall of Famer. Catfish Hunter, who *is* in the Hall. Johnny Odom, Blue Moon Odom. A couple of other guys, like Dick Green, who was a terrific fielder down at second. Sal Bando, our third baseman, was such a solid citizen, from a great family, and our spiritual leader on the team. I've always had much respect for Capt. Sal. I thought he could've been a manager, and I wasn't surprised that he became a general manager.

We won twenty more games than we had the year before, went from last place to sixth—almost the first division in the old ten-team league. Never mind Kansas City. It was the first winning season the A's had had since they were back in *Philadelphia*, in 1952! *Two* cities earlier!

And every year, we just kept getting better, kept bringing guys up, and adding guys in trades—both stars and great role players. Vida Blue came up and won the Cy Young *and* the MVP his first full year with us. He went 24–8 that year, with a 1.82 ERA, 301 strikeouts in 312 innings, 8 shutouts, and 24 complete games. Gene Tenace, the first baseman and catcher. A veteran at first base named Don Mincher, Mike Epstein, a good player, a tough guy and a tough player. Ted Kubiak, Billy North. Paul Lindblad, Darold Knowles, and Bob Locker in the pen. Felipe Alou, Angel Mangual, George Hendrick, another great player. We traded Rick Monday, but we got Ken Holtzman for him, who was a terrific, underrated lefty pitcher. It seemed like he could pitch a game in less than ninety minutes.

It was a tremendously well-balanced team. Built like the Yankees of the late '90s, to go long or go short. We could win a pennant race, and then—with baseball breaking the leagues into divisions for the first time and adding another level of playoffs—we also had the starters and the deep bullpen to win a short series. Dick Williams, our manager, was managing a game years ahead of his time. He got criticized sometimes for overspecialization, but we had the tools to play that way, always bringing guys in to pinch-hit, pinch-run, as defensive replacements. Bringing in four, five relievers in big postseason games.

We were one of the great dynasties in the history of baseball. We won five straight division titles, 1971–75. No one else did that, back in the old, six- or seven-team divisions. No one. We won three straight World Series, 1972–74. Only the Yankees have ever done better than that, in the history of the sport.

What's more, we were a show. We were entertainment. Charlie

Finley saw to that, in part, with the outrageous, flashy uniforms, and the mustaches, and the nicknames. But it was more than that. We were the baseball equivalent of "Showtime."

It was the attitude, the swagger we had. We believed we were good and could play like a great team together. Fran Healy called us a team of gunslingers, which was a pretty good description. There was a lot of publicity about the fights we used to get into with each other.

But that was about the passion we played with. We were a band of young renegades, playing hard and having fun. We were just following the lead of our owner, who was always getting himself involved in spats, whether it was with the commissioner or the community, or the city or the league.

There was no real tension; there was no ill will building up. We had spats, and we talked about them openly. Sometimes there were tussles as well. It would have been called insanity if we hadn't won championships. I remember Blue Moon Odom got into a fight with Vida Blue in the locker room one day after the two of them *won* a playoff game against Detroit. Odom cut open Rollie Fingers's head just before the start of the 1974 World Series, supposedly after Odom said something about Fingers's wife. Rollie needed six stitches to close the cut, and Blue Moon walked away with a limp.

Didn't matter. Rollie was the MVP of that Series; Odom picked up a win and a save. Bert Campaneris got fined and suspended for throwing his bat at Lerrin LaGrow of the Tigers, after LaGrow hit him with a pitch in the 1972 playoffs. Didn't matter, we won the playoffs and the World Series that year. We were the Swingin' A's.

I got into a wrestling match myself with Billy North. Billy was a scrappy little player, terrific outfielder, a terrific base stealer. He got into a few fights. I remember once he ran out to the mound and started punching Doug Bird after Bird threw him a *strike*. Dick Williams said it was the first time he ever saw a guy go after the pitcher when he threw him a strike. That was Billy. Bird hit him with a pitch in the ear three years before, back in the Midwest League, and Billy never forgot it. Walked out to the mound and dropped Bird with a right to the jaw, then just started banging away on him.

Billy North came to Oakland in '73 from the Cubs. He brought with him some great skills, and he helped our team tremendously, until injuries got in the way. From the beginning, he was a tough, scrappy kid for us, who knew what it would take for him to be productive in the lead-off spot, and who played the outfield as well as any center fielder in the game at that time. He hit line drives, led the league in both putouts and stolen bases twice, and was a dependable player, year after year.

Talk about someone who had your back. During our playing days together, his attitude was "Whatever—just don't bring it to me or my boys." I think he was right, and I think he was underappreciated as a player and a friend. He was real good at protecting himself and his teammates.

He did seem to have a chip on his shoulder, and a lot of guys, including Billy, I think, felt like he was capable of exploding if the wrong situation happened. What did not come out when you talked to Billy was how much he'd had to overcome to make the major leagues, and how he had been treated by various teammates and management as a black player who was a smart, independent guy—but who happened to date white women when he hit the bigs in Chicago.

He was a very proud guy, and he saw the same things I saw as a black man in professional baseball, and spoke up about them in a way which no doubt rubbed management and other players the wrong way. He waited until well after he retired to express openly the racism he experienced in the game, and I don't need to quote him. The point here is that it wasn't just in any one city that guys were feeling this. It was all over, and it was not about who we were on the field, but rather, who we were as people.

It was not a surprise that the two of us, coming up the way we had, playing as hard as we did, would butt heads over the course of a long season. But we made it up, put it behind us, and went back to playing great ball. I appreciated the spirit that Billy brought.

What made him so feisty was what made him such a good ballplayer. Dick Williams said he was the only guy he ever saw strut onto a championship team, and it was true, he made us better, we won the World Series again.

We'd have fights. And when we got done, we'd play baseball. We played together, we played hard, and we played as a team. We pulled it together when we had to. And in the end, we always bonded together against our owner, Charlie O., and the rest of baseball, as a team.

Once you played for Charlie Finley, you could deal with anything. At least I thought so before I came to New York.

There was always something going on with Finley; he was always fighting with somebody, always pulling some stunt. Always trying to save money. The craziest was probably when he hired M.C. Hammer to be vice president of the club. He was just Stanley Burrell then, a poor young kid growing up in Oakland. Finley saw him dancing for money with a boom box in the stadium parking lot. He hired him to be a clubhouse assistant and batboy because he liked his style. That was Charlie, he went with his instincts.

Stanley was just eleven years old at the time. I was the one who first gave him the name Hammer, because he looked so much like "Hammerin' Hank" Aaron. Rollie Fingers started calling him Pipeline, because Rollie believed he was a clubhouse snitch for Charlie Finley. Charlie made him his executive vice president, this eleven-year-old kid. He was running around with a hat that read "Ex VP." You'd see him sitting up in the owner's suite, watching the game while he was on the phone with Finley, who was back in Chicago or somewhere. Finley would call him on the speakerphone and have Hammer tell him what was going on. How's that for 1970s technology?

Hammer would report back on everything he heard in the clubhouse. But we didn't really care. You know, that was life with Charlie. If the manager didn't win the pennant, or do what Charlie wanted, he was fired. Mike Andrews, he made those errors in the World Series in 1973; Charlie put him on the disabled list, claimed he was injured. Stuff like that went on all the time.

He traded Dave Duncan in spring training 1973, a deal I didn't like because Dave and Joe Rudi were close to me in the minors. Dunk was my close friend, and it just broke my heart. I cried; we were close as kids in the minors. Dave was a very dear friend, and he helped me. I remember Dick Williams giving me a dad's hug during some tough times like that. He gave me the day off; it helped me get through it.

But mostly, we just let it roll off us. If I didn't do something at home my father wanted done in some way, I got whupped. In baseball, the owners couldn't whip you in public. Maybe they wanted to, but all they could do was make it tough for you or trade you. It didn't scare us.

We were a bunch of kids who didn't know much about the big money; we didn't know anything about the media. We didn't know much about anything. We were all twenty-three, twenty-four, twenty-five. Nothing bothered you at that age. You just lived your life, helped your family, and played good baseball, and everything was all right.

It's pretty much the same as baseball is today. If you play well and win, everything is fine. People think it's a happy clubhouse that makes a winner, but it's not. It's the other way around. You win, *then* you have a happy clubhouse. You're not winning, the owner's not happy. The general manager's not happy; the manager's not happy. Nobody's happy.

That's what life is. That's the sociology of sports. It builds on itself. You're winning, the clubhouse gets happy, everybody's having a good time. Everybody stays loose. What's the saying Al Davis had? "Just win, baby." But if you're *not* winning, and you have a happy clubhouse, you're accepting losing. If you're a losing team, the clubhouse *needs* to have unrest. That's proof that you care. It sounds crazy, I know, but that's how it is.

In Oakland, we didn't *let* ourselves lose. Nineteen seventy-five, we won more games than we had in four years. We lost the league championship series in three games to the Red Sox, but they were all close games most of the way, and Boston had a great team that year. The core of our team was still pretty young. We were still in our twenties, save for Campy and Bando, who were in their early thirties. And every year, we were adding terrific young players—guys like George Hendrick, and Phil Garner, and Claudell Washington, who would go on to become stars.

We could've gone on winning for years and years. The only trouble was that free agency was here—and Charlie Finley didn't have any money to keep up with the "haves."

4

Leaving Charlie O.

I REMEMBER IT was in spring training when I knew it was all going to change. The first couple years I was with the Athletics, we had our training camp in Bradenton, Florida, but starting in 1969 we moved to Mesa, Arizona, which was great. I always loved it down there, that big sky, the dry heat, the Superstition Mountains in the distance. I had a house down there at the time; I'd liked it ever since I first went to Arizona State, just one town west in Tempe.

It was a nice lifestyle there, lots of nightlife, plenty of restaurants. I would meet and have dinner with Willie McCovey, Billy Williams, and Fergie Jenkins—three Hall of Famers. I always enjoyed being with them. We would go and eat out in Scottsdale, usually at a place called the Fig Tree restaurant, on Indian School Road. One of those guys would pick up the check, because they were older, they were making more money than I was then. They were always schooling me in what to say, how to act. They always told me to be careful what I said in public—and they were right!

I remember picking up Willie McCovey to go out to dinner one night, and I was driving a 1973 Pontiac T-top—a brand-new Pontiac I'd been given. McCovey and Willie Mays would get a free car from Chrysler every year. But I had this Pontiac, and it started raining buckets from above, and the T-tops started leaking. It was coming inside, dripping on McCovey's pants, and he was saying, "What're you doing, driving this car? This ain't no star's car! It's raining inside!" I'll never forget that. LMAO.

I had a condo there, and it was closer to home than what I had in Oakland. I liked it more than Florida.

What I didn't love was spring training. I never much liked to go to spring training; it was too long. Unlike most ballplayers of the time, I knew how to take care of myself. I worked out all year long. I didn't go to spring training to get in shape. I showed up in shape. I was ready to play ball for real a couple days after I arrived.

I especially didn't want to go that year, 1976. That off-season, I'd been in arbitration with Charlie Finley and lost. I was making $140,000 a year at the time, which is what now? About a third of the minimum major-league salary?

I thought I'd had a pretty good year in 1975. I tied for the American League lead in homers with George Scott. Had 104 ribbies, led the league in extra-base hits, was second in total bases. We won the West Division for the fifth straight season, and I'd been an all-star every year since 1971.

I asked for a raise from $140,000 to $168,500. A raise of $28,500.

Nowadays, you don't even hear about raises like that. Nowadays, that's what you tip the clubhouse guy for a year.

I lost.

The team's argument in arbitration was that I struck out too much. And that we'd only won the division title, not a fourth straight World Series.

After that, I just didn't have it in me to go to camp on time. I was berated so much in that arbitration case I was harboring bad feelings. I showed up about a week late; that was my protest. And when I did, Charlie Finley comes up to me, and he gives me a check for $2,500. He tells me, "I know you lost in arbitration, but here's $2,500." He didn't want it on my official salary, because if we wound up in arbitration the next year, he didn't want me starting off with $142,500.

That was Charlie O., nickel-and-diming you on something all the time. Back in 1969, my second full year in the majors, I hit forty-seven home runs. I was twenty-three years old, making $20,000 a year. When I asked for more money, he offered me a $10,000 raise. I held out to get more for six weeks, until April 2, while he leaked his side of negotiations to the papers, turned the writers and the fans against me.

I had no idea of how to handle the fact that whatever was said to the papers, they would write it as the truth. I had no idea what to do.

In the end, I got him up to $40,000 for 1970, plus a rent-free

$750-a-month apartment on Lake Merritt for the year—big money for those days. But I had to go in cold, no spring training at all, missed the first week of the season; the fans were on me all the time. There were threats of sending me to the minors and numerous belittlings by the owner. I had a bad year in 1970, hit .237 with twenty-three homers—and Charlie cut me $2,000 for 1971.

I was shocked and hurt that Finley turned out not to be the father figure he had presented himself as. But anytime you get ready to sign a contract, everybody's in love. Five, ten years later, you're ready for the divorce. It can get bitter, contentious; things turn sour. With Finley by then, it was "My way or the highway."

You had to put up with that then, because we still had the reserve clause, which had applied to all players in the majors since the 1890s. Under the reserve clause, you had a choice. You could take what they offered you, or you could stay home. Whoever owned your contract controlled you for as long as you chose to play organized baseball, unless they decided to trade you or sell you to another team, like a piece of property. It didn't matter when the contract expired. Your "owner" still held the rights to you. Forever.

That began to change once the Players Association hired Marvin Miller as its executive director, just before I came up to the majors. He helped us to build the Major League Baseball Players Association (MLBPA) into one of the strongest unions in history. You could tell things were changing because we *had* an impartial arbitrator. For the first time in the history of the game, we could take contract disputes to an independent outsider. The players' union was changing things for the better for the players.

But the owners still fought us every step of the way. We had to go on strike for two weeks in 1972, just to get arbitration and additional pension money, among other benefits. As a business, baseball was doing well. Attendance was going up; TV money was going up. But the average ballplayer was still making less than $45,000 a year.

Then came the Messersmith case. Near the end of 1975, Peter Seitz, the independent arbitrator, ruled that the contracts Andy Messersmith and Dave McNally had with their teams had expired and that they were now free agents, eligible to sign with any club they wanted.

Naturally, the owners took it to court, forget about the independent arbitrator. They'd been fighting every case like it for more than fifty years. They ran Curt Flood out of baseball, rather than give in when he sued. He never got the credit he deserved for challenging the reserve clause all the way up to the Supreme Court. He stepped up years before everyone else. His timing wasn't right, and he paid a terrible price for that. He got kicked to the curb, died a broken man. It was really a tragedy, and nobody came to his rescue. He just didn't get the support from his own fraternity, us players.

But now, in 1975, the owners lost. I remember it was right before we reported to spring training a federal judge upheld the decision by Seitz. McNally retired, but Messersmith signed a three-year deal with Ted Turner and the Braves, for a million dollars. Ooh—one million clams!

The owners couldn't believe it. They had no choice; they had to deal with us now. For the first time in more than eighty years, ballplayers had the same right that every other American citizen enjoys. That is, when his contract expires, he can go and work for whoever he pleases. It's as simple as that—some still can't accept it!

Of course, the owners appealed again. It wasn't until July 1976—mid-season—that we had a new agreement in place, setting up exactly how the free-agent system was going to work. But once that court ruling came down, we knew the world had changed forever.

Under the agreement, you had to have six years in the majors to become a free agent. Marvin Miller put that in himself. Charlie Finley wanted to let everyone become a free agent every year. He was the smartest guy on the owners' side at that time, because he knew that would have driven the price down. It would have been like Rotisserie baseball every season!

Marvin was afraid the owners would go for that, but they didn't. That meant Charlie Finley and the A's just didn't have the money to compete with the really deep-pocketed owners, people like the O'Malleys in Los Angeles, or Bronfman in Montreal, or Tom Yawkey up in Boston—or George and his Yankees. Charlie had a small-market team that didn't draw well even when it won, and small cash reserves—hardly any local TV or radio revenues. He couldn't keep the team together any longer.

You knew intellectually what would change, but still you weren't prepared. I knew what the arbitrator's ruling meant; I knew what the court decisions meant. I knew what getting rid of the reserve clause meant. But I still didn't expect it to change anything for me. I was in spring training; I was still ticked off at losing in arbitration and Charlie Finley giving me that $2,500 off the books, like he was tipping the groundskeeper. I was preoccupied with that and getting ready for the season.

Then, a week from Opening Day, it came down. I remember it was the first or second day of April. I was driving in my car, and I heard it first on the radio. Me, Kenny Holtzman, and a young pitcher named Bill VanBommel were traded to Baltimore for Don Baylor, Mike Torrez, and Paul Mitchell.

Finley had started unloading his players, and Kenny and I were first. Before two more seasons had passed, we were all gone—Rudi, Campy, Sal Bando, Vida Blue, Tenace, Garner, Washington, Billy North. And almost every one of us went to teams that went on to win still more rings, or that at least became contenders overnight. It was like we were the magic A's.

But we would never play together again. Just like that, everything we'd done, everything we built, was over. It broke my heart. I was still in the prime of my career, didn't know what "traded" meant! You can still see it in the pictures of me at the time. I had no idea what was going to happen; Finley never said a word to me. I was walking around in shock.

As I look back, I can see he was trying to protect his investment. But ultimately, Charlie still wasn't able to hang on to his team—and it still didn't make me feel any better.

I wasn't an old man yet. I wasn't thirty-five or forty, I was still twenty-nine, and I thought, "What's the matter with you, trading me away?" I drove over to my agent's office, Gary Walker, who was also one of my best friends at the time and still today, and we just sat and talked. I didn't know what to do. I'd been with the A's since I was twenty years old. I had played together with all those guys, and now we were all leaving. And I was going first.

I was so upset that I just went and hid out for a while. I went to Hawaii, stayed at this hotel I liked on Waikiki, the Rainbow Hilton, where I used to go and do the commentary for the old *Superstars* sports shows they used to have. I wanted to get away, and I didn't want to go back. Nothing against Baltimore, it was just that the A's were the only team I ever played for. I knew nothing else. I was depressed or in shock, take your pick!

And it was there that I figured, "Well, if that's how it's going to be, that's how it's going to be." I knew then that I had them in a bind. They had just traded two pretty good players for Kenny Holtzman and me. And I took a cold, calculated attitude, just as I felt their attitude had been toward me.

Charlie Finley got some good young players instead of just losing us to free agency. The Orioles got Kenny and me to help them make a pennant run. It worked out all around, and everybody's happy— except for the players. Nobody asked us what *we* wanted. So I just felt, "Okay, you're gonna trade me and not tell me about it beforehand, and do whatever you feel like doing? I'm good with that. If you're going to do it this way, here's how I'm going to do it. I'm gonna stay out here in Hawaii until you feel like doing what I want to do. Now we all good!!" I was okay with that.

The Orioles wanted me to report right away, but I drew a line in the sand. I told them right up front I wanted the money I lost in arbitration. And more. I wanted a contract for $200,000. I knew that was what Dick Allen was making with the White Sox. He was the highest-paid player in the game at the time. I felt I deserved the same. I was going to either make that or sit out. Gary Walker listened to what I wanted, and he said I could get it. It would take time. But I could get what I wanted if I held out. He said to just stay out of the papers.

So he started talking to Hank Peters, who was the Orioles' general manager at the time. He was a good man—and if I had talked to him, I would probably have given in. But Gary kept me away, and kept the pressure on him, and kept me informed.

I hung out in Hawaii, and Gary negotiated. They had never dealt with a player this way before. Nobody had in baseball, at least not since Sandy Koufax and Don Drysdale held out together on the Dodgers, back in the mid-1960s.

I came back from Hawaii, stayed around the neighborhood where I was living in Berkeley. Worked out, stayed in shape, made a couple of trips down to Arizona to talk to Gary there. He kept negotiating with Hank Peters, who was a wonderful man, and in the end they got the deal done. I got the $200,000, minus the time I missed. That came out to $190,000, so I was the second-highest-paid player in baseball.

I flew into Baltimore on May 1, 1976. Held a press conference, suited up, and took batting practice that night. They put the lights on in the stadium for me, and I hit until 11:30 or midnight. Dave Duncan was on the Orioles, too, by then, he gave me his number 9 so I could wear it. That's the kind of guy he was. Next day, I started the second game of a doubleheader against the A's, drove in a run, and we won.

I still felt like I was behind on the season. I just plunged in and kept taking extra batting practice until my hands bled.

The only thing was, I didn't understand the consequences of what I had done. I was still twenty-nine years old, and I didn't pay attention. I thought, "If you're tough enough to trade me, then I'm tough enough to do this," and that would be the end of it.

But there were articles; there was a negative reaction from the fans. Nobody understood how this would work out yet. Nobody understood how baseball was a business, because the owners didn't want the fans to look at it that way. Nobody published what *their* revenue was every year—the owners—but they published our salaries, and sometimes more, to exaggerate. I didn't know, *nobody* knew how the fans were going to react to our treating this like a business, too, and getting the money we could.

After all, the American pastime was a game that we got to *play.* The focus was on how we got paid to play this *game.* It wasn't thought of as our job.

Once I got to Baltimore, I had a good year. I stole twenty-eight bases, my career high. I knocked in ninety-one runs, hit twenty-seven home runs. I could've been a thirty-thirty man—thirty home runs, thirty stolen bases—if I hadn't missed that first month of the season. Back then, that was something that only three men in baseball history had ever done.

At the time, numbers like that weren't emphasized as important. So you didn't take the chance of getting injured to pad your stats. I remember on two occasions meeting Mickey Mantle and Willie Mays in 1988, when José Canseco became the first "forty-forty" man. Both Mickey and Willie said, "Gee, if I'd ever known it was such a big deal, I'd have done a fifty-fifty season."

We came in second, but you knew we were going to get better. I loved playing for Hank Peters, loved playing for Earl Weaver, the Orioles' manager. Weaver told his front office, "If you sign him, we can win pennants."

He was right, too. The next year, Eddie Murray came up to the big leagues with Baltimore. A few years later, Cal Ripken came up, and they were already a contender. They always had good pitching. They had Jim Palmer still, and Mike Flanagan, and Denny Martinez. They would pick up Steve Stone a couple years later, and Scott McGregor and Tippy Martinez came over from the Yankees in 1976—all those arms. That gave you a Hall of Famer for your number one pitcher, in Palmer, and four other number two pitchers behind him, with Flanagan and Denny Martinez probably being number ones on most other teams.

I loved playing for Earl Weaver. He was just an East Coast Tommy Lasorda. Just a lovable guy who loved the game. All his players loved playing for him. He was one of those characters who would get so mad that he was almost funny. Cussin' like a sailor. As coarse as it is, Lasorda's swearing sounded like a poem. He's a YouTube star today because of it. Earl Weaver was the same way. When he cursed, it was like a melody.

I liked Baltimore, too. It was a great baseball town. My family was living there, including my sister and my mother. Baltimore was a city that didn't *feel* like a city. It was a city that felt like a community. It was in the South, but it had lots of Middle America in it. It was more of a plain, folksy kind of place, full of a lot of country folks. Because of that it felt a little more comfortable to me. They didn't have a lot of newspapers, didn't have a lot of skyscrapers, more two-family homes. I liked Baltimore and its fans.

I loved playing there with Jim Palmer, who was a longtime friend. I loved playing with Brooks Robinson, who was still in the organization. I loved playing with Lee May and Bobby Grich, who were both outstanding players. We all worked well as a team—good history, good record of success. It was all very comfortable.

Hank Peters, the general manager, was like a dad to me. Jerry Hoffberger, who owned the team, nice man, nice family. Lou Gorman was there, as the assistant general manager. Tom Giordano was there, as the director of scouting and player development. These were great baseball people, who had built a great baseball organization.

I liked it so much I would just as soon have stayed in Baltimore.

I even made them an offer in August 1976. I'd spoken to Gary Walker and we came up with an idea of taking care of my future like any other businessperson. The first move I made wasn't greedy, wasn't full of demands. I made the Orioles a very reasonable offer: a $1.5 million contract, for five years. Thirty thousand of that would go to my father every year, another twenty thousand a year to my mother. Break it down, that would've come to just $250,000 a year for me, personally, and I was already making $190,000 a year. All I was really asking for was a good raise, without ever testing the market.

They turned it down.

Knowledgeable as the men running the Orioles were, no one had the foresight to see around corners and understand where salaries were going. Just like Oakland, the Orioles didn't have the capital to compete for most players in the open market. They weren't going to sign free agents; they were going to lose them, guys like Bobby Grich and me.

Baltimore was a great team and could have been a better team than the Yankees in that period of 1977–81. The clubs were close enough that there were any number of players on both teams—maybe Jim Palmer, Eddie Murray, Mike Flanagan on the Orioles, or on the Yankees, maybe Thurman Munson, Rich Gossage, Ronnie Guidry, or *me*—who might have changed the history of the American League in those five years if they had changed teams. They were *that close*.

It wasn't just me who could have made the difference. But I *was* the only one of those players who switched teams.

5

"Like a Guy Trying to Hustle
a Girl in a Bar"

I KNOW ALL the stories about how I said they'd name a candy bar after me if I played in New York. How I was longing to come and play on the big stage and become Mr. October.

Most of it is just that—stories. I was already a star before I came to New York, and I was going to take my star with me anywhere I went. In fact, New York was about the last place I thought I would end up.

The way they did free agency that first year was different from how it is now. They set up a draft where up to twelve teams could draft you—plus the team you were already on. I was one of only twelve players who were selected by the maximum thirteen teams. And as it turned out, I was the very first player picked, in the very first free-agent draft, by the Montreal Expos.

The number one pick—at last! And nobody asked about what color my girlfriend was. I guess that was progress.

In a quiet moment, after this all went down, I mentioned to my agent, Gary Walker, how I could only laugh inside. It did feel good. It was symbolic of how slow the social progress was in our country and in our game. But at least the social mores were forced to adapt.

If a team hadn't drafted you, it wasn't allowed to negotiate with you. But that still left me with a lot of choices. I've read all kinds of things telling me where it was that I wanted to go. But my real first choice was the Dodgers.

To me, the Dodgers made perfect sense. They were a good team. I played in the World Series there in 1974, and the ballpark felt small to me. I hit a ball out of there to left field off Andy Messersmith, hit a couple doubles to right center off Don Sutton. I always hit very well there. I always loved the environment there. It was a beautiful, attractive facility—and it still is today, almost forty years later.

They had a manager who was full of energy in Tommy Lasorda. They had a great farm system, great ownership in the O'Malleys. I always admired the family: They were minority conscious, and they had always been community conscious. They were the team that signed the first black player, Jackie Robinson—they had a great history. Their values were something you wanted to be around.

On the field, they always had great pitching, guys like Tommy John and Don Sutton and Messersmith. And they had a lineup that was almost all right-handed. Davey Lopes, Steve Garvey, Dusty Baker, Ron Cey—all right-handers—and then Reggie Smith, who was a switch-hitter. It would have been perfect—for them and for me. They were going to get right-handed pitching coming at them all the time. I could have feasted!

Los Angeles was a good spot for me in many ways, on and off the field. It was just three hundred miles from my home. My mother had moved to California by then, two of my sisters were there, my brother was there. And I knew the Dodgers wanted me. Al Campanis, their general manager, was always trying to get me in a trade. A small ballpark, in a fastball league. It was the place, dude!

Los Angeles picked me in the free-agent draft. But then they didn't make an offer. I don't know what they were waiting for, but they moved late. They had Maury Wills make the first call to my agent, but by that time it was too late. Things were moving too fast for them. They laid back—I never did find out why.

By then, I already had a big offer from Montreal. On behalf of the Bronfmans, John McHale, their general manager, offered me $5 million—$1 million a year for five years, with the possibility for that to go up with bonuses, incentives. They made mention of me wearing number 7, because they owned Seagram's 7.

It would have been interesting to go to Montreal, too. The Expos already had some terrific young talent and more on the way, guys like Tim Raines, Steve Rogers. They were an expansion team, but they wound up being a contender within another couple years. Hitting between a couple of righties like Andre Dawson and Ellis Valentine, I might've made the difference, and they had just hired my old manager from Oakland, Dick Williams, who I always got along with and respected.

But I don't know, I just wanted to stay in this country. America just seemed . . . more like major-league baseball. I just thought it was important for me to play in the United States. And while I was considering the Bronfmans' offer, my agent, Gary Walker, told me, "There's a lot more money in New York than in Montreal." He said, "With your career, and your skills, you should play with the Yankees. It's a franchise with a great legacy. Ruth, Gehrig, DiMaggio, and Mantle. Yogi and Whitey. You should play in New York."

New York. Gary also told me, "I don't know if you'll *like* New York, but . . ."

Because I was a small-town kid. I'd grown up in a small town in Pennsylvania, lived in a small city in Oakland, lived in Berkeley. Oakland had one newspaper. There were a few others, like the *San Francisco Chronicle*, the San Francisco *Examiner*, the *Berkeley Gazette*, the *Sacramento Bee*, the *San Jose Mercury News*. But that was about it—and sometimes the San Francisco papers didn't cover our games.

New York was something else. I wasn't sure I was interested. And they weren't interested in me.

I wasn't the Yankees' first pick in the free-agent draft. The one they went right out and signed first was Don Gullett, the pitcher for the Reds who'd just shut them down in the World Series. After that, Joe Rudi was Billy Martin's choice. George Steinbrenner and Gabe Paul, the Yankees' general manager, wanted to sign Bobby Grich and move him from second base back to shortstop, where he'd played in the minors.

I couldn't blame them. I came up with Rudi. I played with him for years and saw how great he was. An underrated player, but a great player. Good hitter, played well in the field both at first and in left. A complete player. He would've fit in very nicely with the Yankees.

Bobby Grich, I played with him in Baltimore, then later with the Angels. He was a terrific player, very athletic. He was one of the best defensive second basemen in our era. The Orioles only moved Grich out of shortstop because they already had Mark Belanger. He was also a great offensive player, and hit for power.

Some people thought neither Rudi nor Grich was a good fit because they were both right-handed hitters, in a Yankee Stadium that still tilted toward lefties in those days. That was still a huge park back then, even after they made over the original Stadium—430 feet to left-center, I think, 417 to center.

I think they still would've been fine, but as it worked out, both of them got hurt with the Angels in 1977 and missed most of the season. Grich came back strong; Joe was never really the same player again. But if they'd signed one of them instead of me, who knows what would have happened?

Whatever the Yankees decided, it seemed like it would have nothing to do with me. That was another rule that first year of free agency: You could only sign a maximum of two players—unless you had lost more than two free agents yourself.

The Yanks had already signed Gullett, which left them with room for just one more, Grich or Rudi, they had to choose. But the Angels were allowed to sign three guys because they'd lost that many free agents, and they snapped up Joe Rudi very quickly. Then Don Baylor, who'd been traded for me just the year before, got out of Oakland and signed with them, too. That decided it for Bobby Grich, who George Steinbrenner was courting very heavily. Grich had been friends and teammates with Baylor since their minor-league days with Baltimore, so once Don went to the Angels, Bobby wanted to go there, too.

I later found out that Steinbrenner did everything he could to sign Grich. He even told Bobby the Angels had manipulated the market, and he was going to file a protest with the league commissioner, maybe go to court. He told Grich he'd win the protest, and then Bobby would be left out in the cold.

The Boss bluffed a lot, but he wasn't very good at it. Bobby Grich signed with the Angels. The commissioner, Bowie Kuhn, turned down the protest, and George didn't bother to take it to court.

All of a sudden all the guys the Yankees had been looking at were off the market.

All that was left was me.

I'm not sure who it was who first advised George to take a good look at me. I don't know just how important Gene Michael was with the team at the time, but I know later, when he was very influential in the makeup of the roster, he always loved left-handed power for Yankee Stadium. So did Birdie Tebbetts, the former catcher, who had become another one of George's "baseball people."

Or maybe it was George himself. George Steinbrenner always said he wanted to bring a big name to the Yankees. What he understood was marquee value, showbiz value. He saw the full potential of having a name in New York. He saw the potential with me.

I said it at the time: George Steinbrenner went after me like a guy trying to hustle a girl in a bar.

He went after me just the way Charlie Finley did, more than ten years earlier. Even though I was aware of what he was doing, the game he was playing, I have to admit I was flattered. I was charmed. He just made me laugh.

He flew me into New York, had me to his apartment at the Carlyle hotel, and asked me what kind of money it would take to sign me. I laughed at him trying to get around my agent like that.

I told him right back, "I just wanted to meet you, see what kind of money *you're* talking about."

So then he told me, "Well, we don't want to spend more than two million. I don't think we can do business."

That was the nerve he had, right there, trying to lowball me already. He laughed, too. That was George. He loved to compete, loved to negotiate.

When he saw I was onto him, he took me to the '21' Club for lunch.

And once we sat down at the table, we really got along pretty well, not like adversaries in a business deal. He really tapped a chord with me on certain ideas and philosophies he had. I could relate to all of it. His desire to win, his desire to build the franchise into a perennial champion. It might sound like "win at all costs," but he also spoke about some of the players on the team with great affection, guys like Thurman Munson, who was the captain, Lou Piniella, Sparky Lyle, the new kid Willie Randolph, Chris Chambliss. I was very impressed by his commitment.

George also made sure that most of his closest business friends and advisers were there or came by to meet me: Tony Rolfe, Larry and Zach Fisher, Bill Fugazy, Mike Forrest. The one gentleman who wasn't there that day, who he relied on heavily, was George's wealthiest partner. I had to meet Lester Crown before he signed me, because George had such great respect for him. These were all men who became friends and supporters during my time in New York, and they were some of the most successful businessmen in New York City.

The '21' Club was a revelation for me. There were all these business cards and items that hung from the ceiling and these older businessmen in suits and ties there. I quickly understood it was a fraternity for the men who ran the business of New York City. I looked around and said, "There isn't even a carpet on the floor! I have to wear a tie to get into this place, and they don't even have wall-to-wall carpeting!"

After we ate and met everyone, George did this very smart thing. He sent his driver on, and we walked back to the Carlyle. And as we walked to his apartment, all along the way people in the street noticed. They came up to us, saying, "Mr. Steinbrenner," or "George, bring Reggie to New York. Get him signed to a contract." Or, "We love you, Reggie. We want you here. This is the place for you."

I mean, all these kinds of comments from cabdrivers and the people on the street. Bus drivers stopped in the middle of the street to call out to us. The passengers opened their windows to call out to us, people waved. It was like a movie.

I don't think he had it planned. I think it just went that way. I *think* he didn't have it planned. Or put it this way: Maybe George already knew his city that well. Maybe he just knew exactly how it was going to go. This was really my first time walking around New York like that. For all the times we'd played there before, I just stayed at the team hotel with the team and went to Yankee Stadium and back.

I just felt I was here to play for a good team and win a few games. To take care of myself, Mom and Dad, and my family. New York was a great place to do it, and the Yankees were a great team with an owner who wanted to win. But when I thought about it later, about everybody coming up to us on the street . . . yeah, it was exciting. It was exciting for sure. Yes, it certainly influenced me.

In the end, George just outhustled everybody else for me. I felt he dealt with me as a young man and a person, and I respected that. I also recognized something of myself in him. I knew even then he was a little crazy and a hustler to get it done. And the city acted as an assistant agent for him. It was easy to see he wanted to win, and win in New York for the fans!

He knew how to close the deal, too.

The day before Thanksgiving, Gary and the other people I had advising me in my free-agent negotiations went and camped out at the Hyatt near the Chicago airport. We told anyone who was still interested, come and make your final offer.

I just wanted this done. I wanted to know where I was going to play in 1977 and who I was going to play for.

George was out in Culver, Indiana, visiting his son Hank at the military academy he went to there. He made us promise he'd be the last person we talked to, no matter what.

Then, early that morning, he chartered a small plane and flew into Chicago to make his offer to us. He flew back to Indiana to spend the rest of the day with his family, then came back out again that night to nail down the deal.

I have to admit I felt a little nostalgic, thinking of the way that Charlie Finley had my dad and me out to his office in Chicago, then flew us to his farm in Indiana, a little over ten years before. I have no idea if George Steinbrenner knew anything about that. Probably not. But here he was, just as ready and willing to close the deal.

He paid attention. You grow up black in this country, in the time I did, people did not pay attention to you unless you did something they didn't approve of. They didn't *want* to see you. Except if you were doing something they found abhorrent, like dating their daughter or riding their son's bike. You want someone to pay attention, to want you. To take you for the content of your character, not the color of your skin, as Dr. King said. It makes a nice change.

We reached agreement on most of the deal that night. George stayed over in town, and we had breakfast on Thanksgiving morning and agreed to the rest of it. I told Mr. Steinbrenner I would be a Yankee, and we wrote out the deal on a table napkin.

Right after that, I heard back from the Dodgers. They offered $3 million, just for openers. The Yankees' final offer was $2.96 million, with a portion of it deferred or in bonuses. George told me they could only pay me $200,000 a year in up-front salary, because he'd told Thurman Munson, the captain, that nobody on the team would be paid more than he was—and he'd have to give him a raise as it was. The rest of my money would be deferred, or bonus money for signing.

That was fine with me. I was fine with getting that money later. But then here were the Dodgers, offering me $3 million *to start*, to play in the park and the city where I really wanted to be. There had already been an offer from Montreal for $5 million, and then the San Diego Padres came in with a late offer that was for $3.4 million. These were all starting offers.

I didn't have anything signed, but I had a handshake deal with George, and I wouldn't break it. I couldn't get out of it morally. My dad taught me better. I shook his hand. He made a big effort to fly to see me, to bring me to New York and introduce me to his friends and the organization—to tell his crowd that I was going to be a Yankee. He put his hand out, I shook it, and I gave him my word. We wrote the basics of the deal on a restaurant napkin. That was it.

I thought later about how it all might have turned out. The different teams I could've signed with. Baltimore was a place where I was very comfortable, a wonderful franchise, good people involved; a lot of my family was there. Certainly, in Los Angeles, I would have had a wonderful time.

Now, I know it's true: I don't think you ever get the fanfare and the recognition and the support that you can create in New York with the media and the fans there. It's just not the same anywhere else. But there've been players who have done it other places. Look at what Michael Jordan did in Chicago, what Willie Mays and Joe Montana did in San Francisco, what Jim Brown did in Cleveland, or what Tiger Woods did worldwide for himself. If you're great, it doesn't matter where you are.

You think about the other teams. Baltimore, even after the free agents they lost, when I went to New York, we beat the Orioles out by just a couple games every year. And when we met the Dodgers in the World Series, I would've been on the other team. I would've been there with them, instead of doing my best to beat them with the Yankees.

I'm not saying I was the balance of power or that I would've made all the difference. But I represented a final piece at that time for a few different franchises. Things might've been very different if I had been on the Dodgers or the Orioles.

I gave my word to George. So I signed with the Yankees, and he brought me back to New York for a press conference.

Now, I had already played in two World Series. But I had no idea what a big press conference was until I got to New York. I mean, in Oakland, we had two or three regular beat writers. In Baltimore, there was the *Baltimore Sun* with Phil Hersh and Jim Henneman, I think, the *Washington Post* with Tom Boswell. That was it.

In New York, there were thirty-plus beat writers. Thirty-plus. From three different states. And a lot more of them at that first press conference. New York, New Jersey, Connecticut, and occasionally Washington, D.C., and Philly scribes came to New York as well. It was—*is*—the media capital of the world.

They had the press conference in the Versailles Terrace Room of the Americana Hotel. The room was full of reporters; there were TV cameras everywhere. Thurman Munson was there for it. I really appreciated that; I thought we were getting off on the right foot. Everywhere you looked was plus. George was there, Roy White was there, the media were there, my mom and dad were there. Everything was just wonderful. How could it not have been?

But I had no idea that you had to be so aware of everything you said (and still have to). You had to really listen to what you said before it came out and in print. You had to understand that certain words projected different connotations, certain words were inflammatory. I had to learn on the spot how to say things. And I didn't do a very good job of that my first year in New York.

I tried to be honest, open. But you have to be guarded in what you say. I needed to learn to read what I was saying, when I was saying it.

Look at someone like Derek Jeter, he's got it down to an art. In addition to being a great ballplayer, he knows how to say exactly what he wants to say. And nothing else, nothing that somebody can take and twist. He's the best, always has been remarkably mature for his years. He knew how to do that from the beginning as a Yankee. He knew how to say a lot and give nothing.

I'm still learning.

I didn't understand how the media would take things. That very first day, in the Versailles Terrace Room, somebody asked me if I was afraid my star would get lost somewhere else, and I told him, "I didn't come to New York to become a star. I brought my star with me."

That got some people started right away. But what was wrong with that? I *was* a star. I'd been a star for eight to ten years. I'd already been an MVP in the regular season, I'd already been an MVP in the World Series, I had won three World Series titles and a couple home run titles playing for Oakland.

Somebody asked me then, "But wouldn't your star have got lost if you'd gone to Montreal or San Diego?"

I told him, "Fort Knox is in Kentucky. But Fort Knox isn't lost. Everybody knows where Fort Knox is."

It got a lot of laughs. I honestly didn't understand what they were getting at. I thought it was some kind of put-down of me. I mean, I'd been a star in Oakland, a small city. People knew who I was, even though I played in Oakland. Why wouldn't they know me if I went somewhere else?

I didn't know yet how the media thought of New York. I didn't get it yet, how the *awareness* of New York is so all-encompassing compared to anywhere else. I found that watching everything I said was a very difficult thing to do and still be me—but, oh boy, I was going to get a crash course in how to do it.

But at that press conference, everything still seemed fine, everything seemed good. George was there. Thurman was there. Billy Martin didn't show up, but that was all right. I'm sure he had places to be. Everything seemed perfect.

There was just one thing that happened a little later, one thing that, thinking about it now, maybe should've rung some alarm bells.

Someone put it out to the papers that when George first spoke to me on the phone, he told me, "I want you more than anything in the world. What do you want more than anything in the world?"

He claimed that I told him, "A Corniche Rolls-Royce." That was the top of the Rolls line then, went for $63,000.

Supposedly, George told me, "It's yours. All I'm asking in return is the right to be the last person to talk to you before you make up your mind."

Nice story, right?

Only trouble was it didn't happen. George never offered me anything to be the last person to speak to us. Only at the end of the negotiations did he throw in some more money to clinch the deal, another hundred thousand or so in bonus money. I used that money to buy the Corniche. And a Corniche Rolls-Royce was never "what I wanted more than anything in the world."

And that's not how George told it to the press.

Instead, it became a different story. One where he looked all the more generous, and daring, and smart. But I was someone who knew cars very well and was perfectly capable of taking his money and going out and buying what he wanted. Which is what I did.

Not a big deal. I didn't say anything at the time. I knew George didn't mean anything much by it, that was just him trying to be the showman.

But when I thought about it later, it was an early warning signal. I missed it. So many times, the headline is an eye-catcher but the real story is completely different.

6

"ANY SPECIFIC PLAYER"

THE FIRST WARNING I got that things might not go so smoothly in New York was out in Hawaii.

I was a broadcaster for the *Superstars* competition they would have in the off-season. You remember those, where they'd have top athletes—people like Pete Rose, Tony Dorsett, Bruce Jenner, O. J. Simpson, Walter Payton, and others—compete against each other in things that weren't their sport, usually stuff like track and field, different events like a tug-of-war, sprints, volleyball. Then they started bringing in "SuperTeams"—the two teams that went to the Super Bowl and the World Series.

I know it seems almost unimaginable now. That's how different things were, back before free agency. In fact, right after that year, I believe George Steinbrenner put a clause in every Yankee's contract prohibiting him from doing anything like it in the off-season. The talent just got too high-priced to risk on Sunday afternoon sports filler.

That winter, they were having a SuperTeams competition out in Hawaii between the Yankees and the Reds, the two teams that had just been in the World Series. It was a great chance for me to be out there with all the guys who were going to be my new teammates. There were ten Yankees altogether, guys like Chambliss, Graig Nettles, Sparky Lyle, Roy White—I don't remember if Munson or Piniella was there.

They really didn't give me the time of day. I was a little stunned, but I was trying to be cool about it. Afterward, I was asked how it was being in Hawaii with my new teammates, and I said it was uncomfortable, and I tried to be diplomatic. I don't remember being welcomed to the team by any of the Yankees. It was awkward.

"When I walk outside, and it's thirty degrees, I'm not comfortable," I said. "Do you feel comfortable in a bathtub filled with cold water?"

I thought that would be the way to brush it off, make light of it. But instead, that just set things off. Once what I said got published, another writer asked the Yankees who were there what they thought of it, and that started a whole back-and-forth thing.

"What were we supposed to do? Take him out to dinner?" one of them said.

And I read that and I thought, "Well, that wouldn't be horrible, would it? That would've been a normal thing to do."

I didn't understand that. I was going to be their new right fielder, and it didn't seem they wanted much to do with me. And if you don't feel welcome, then you don't reach out. I had friends there because I'd been with ABC for a few years, I was broadcasting with Keith Jackson and Bruce Jenner, so I had plenty to do, places to go. I didn't need people to hang out with. I just thought that a friendly visit would have been nice. I guess I could have asked them to go out as well.

To me, once it was over, it was over. I didn't think too much about it. I didn't *let* myself think too much about it. But looking back, I should have picked up on that for a sign of how things might go.

It became a pattern: I would say something to the press that I didn't think was a big deal, didn't think that much about. And then the reporters would run off to quote me—with a slant—to someone else, and see if they could get a response from the person. That someone always wanted to remain anonymous, I would notice. I was out there saying what I thought, putting my name on it, standing behind my words. And then somebody else on the team would take some shot without being man enough to put his name behind it—coming out as "an unnamed source"!

Who knows if the person really said it that way? Who knows if he really said it at all? I don't see how that's journalism. Or if someone *did* say it, how's that being a teammate?

But that's how it was, right from the beginning. There were negatives before I even played a game.

Some of it was understandable. *Some* of it. The Yankees were a proud team. They'd just had a great year in 1976, got into the World Series. They had a right to be proud. I don't think many of them liked the fact that so much attention was on me, all the stories about how I was going to "save" them. I could certainly appreciate their views.

But you know, that wasn't me so much as it was the press reacting to me—and a story. I was going to help the team. They had some terrific hitters, but they didn't have that much power.

Graig Nettles was a great defender; a very good power hitter, he'd led the league in home runs the year before. Chris Chambliss had power.

But as a left-handed power hitter in Yankee Stadium, I would bring an additional dimension.

To give you an idea: My best home run year in the Bronx, I hit forty-one in 1980. I was told that was the first time any Yankee hit more than forty homers in a season since Mickey Mantle and Roger Maris did it in 1961, the year Maris set the record. The *next* time any Yankee did it was Tino Martinez, when he hit forty-four in 1997. That really surprised me, considering the short porch in right field at Yankee Stadium and all the great hitters the team had.

In other words, almost twenty years each way. That was a big difference. And I don't think people fully understood it. They didn't understand the power game the way they do today with things like sabermetrics and all these new statistics. They didn't understand that I was good at getting on base. They didn't understand all the ways one could make a difference.

So yes, I was coming to a very good team. But I was bringing something with me. I was bringing something rare. I was a left-handed power hitter with the ability to get on base, a pretty good, seasoned pressure player.

What was wrong with that? When I was on the A's, we had guys joining the team all the time. Almost all of them made a real contribution, either as starters, or as platoon players, or off the bench.

We accepted that. We were glad to have them. Willie McCovey, Billy Williams, the Alou brothers, and others. We didn't act like we didn't need them.

People still didn't get how free agency was going to work, and it would take time to evaluate it. The sportswriters didn't get it; the fans didn't get it. The players didn't get it. Some teams got it; some refused.

Nobody had a complete understanding yet, with the new system, with free agency, that the players would get their shots at their big payday every few years or so. In that way, baseball now was almost like any other business: Your contract's up, you put your skills on the market.

People didn't get that—many fans, players, and even some owners. Some embraced it, and some didn't. Most thought it should have stayed the way it was, where if you had a good year or the team won, you asked for more, hoping the general manager or the owner would *grant* it to you.

Everyone thought every player should be measured against every other player on the team, *every year*. So when I came to the Yankees with the biggest contract in the game at the time, it wasn't like everyone understood, i.e., "Okay, when it's my turn, when I can declare for free agency, I'll have my payday." Instead, many players on the Yankees and other teams wanted to be paid right away, forgetting they already had a contract.

When I got to camp in 1977, it seemed as though everyone was holding out. Checking back on it, I know several guys were unhappy with their contracts: Sparky Lyle, Roy White, Dock Ellis, Oscar Gamble, Chambliss. Even Fred Stanley, our shortstop, who hit .238 the year before. It was the situation that free agency was creating, but it was made to seem that I was the catalyst.

I sympathized with all these guys, many of whom had been terrific players, and some of whom were probably too old now to get what they deserved. They had helped the team win the American League pennant. But it wasn't my fault that they didn't get paid what they felt they should, or what they could get on the open market. Some guys have the makeup to play out their option and some guys don't. It's not easy for some guys to deal with the pressure. I had played out my option. I took some risks. But somehow, part of the resentment these guys had was directed at me.

It was reported that Mickey Rivers was deliberately not playing hard. He wanted a raise because he was having what he called "personal problems," and that was his way of holding out.

We all loved Mickey—but can you imagine what the reaction would've been if I'd done that?

"I signed my contract because I thought it would be best at the time, but I didn't really like it," he said. "I'm sorry I signed it."

Can you imagine if I said that?

Dock Ellis got into it with George Steinbrenner in the locker room, yelled at him, called him names. Before they traded him to Oakland in the spring, he told reporters that he hoped we'd lose more, because "the more we lose, the more often Steinbrenner will fly in. And the more he flies, the better chance there will be of the plane crashing."

Now, I do believe he meant that as a joke. Dock would never truly wish anybody's death. Who would pray for someone's plane to crash? That would be insane. But they went and printed it as if he was serious.

It was just locker-room humor. The writers never should've printed it.

But can you imagine if I had joked like that?

It was reported that Oscar Gamble, when Gabe Paul told him he'd been traded in the Bucky Dent deal, said, "Mr. Paul, you've made a big mistake. You know I'm a better ballplayer than Reggie Jackson."

Huh? How did I get into this? Neither Oscar nor I was a shortstop.

It went on and on. Graig Nettles was making $140,000 a year, but he was unhappy that Sal Bando, who was our third baseman with the A's, had just signed a free-agent contract for $1.4 million with the Brewers. So Nettles jumped the team one day without saying anything to anybody.

"It seems the only way to make money with the Yankees is to play for another team," he told the writers later. "It seems the guys who make more money are the flamboyant, controversial guys."

Gee, I wonder who he was referring to.

Sparky Lyle held out, too. He said he wanted $500,000 for three years, guaranteed, "even if the club goes defunct.

"I'm not using any specific player as an example but as soon as a good player becomes available, there goes $2 million or $3 million to him," he said. "But the guys who won for him [George] see very little of it."

Uh-huh. Wonder who he was talking about. I should've had "Any Specific Player" put on the back of my uniform. But I guess I should have been pleased. At least I had moved up to being a good player now.

Nowadays, guys wouldn't think twice if somebody came on the team after getting a big free-agent contract. Today's player understands the timing, of having your option year and getting the money in your turn. Back then, many guys didn't understand that.

Just like every other free agent, I had played out my option and taken my risk. If I had blown out my knee or something before I signed a new contract, that would have been too bad for me. I would have been out of luck. That's just the risk I took—and that's just how a marketplace works.

Reporters would write things about how I was a lightning rod, or I was always the center of controversy, but I don't really understand that. Why, because I took the opportunity any ballplayer—or any writer—would have taken?

What's more, almost everyone on the Yankees got a raise when I came on the team. Almost all of the holdouts, George ended up giving them bigger contracts. So you could say in the end I helped every one of them get more money. How did that make me the bad guy?

The situation with Thurman was even more tricky, thanks to the press.

When I came on the team, Thurman reminded Mr. Steinbrenner that he'd promised him he would always be the highest-paid player on the club. George was as good as his word: He raised his salary to the same as I was getting in straight salary.

But Thurman thought he should get the deferred money and the bonus money I was getting, too. He was even upset that I got a Rolls-Royce and he didn't. He had his reasons and his promises.

When George wouldn't pay him the extra money, he started talking about buying out his contract or wanting to be traded. Then George got mad and wouldn't go to a dinner in Thurman's honor. It got to be a tangled situation, and I could sympathize with both men. But again, I was uncomfortable that I should be in the middle.

I felt it was the press that kept me there. Right from the beginning, all they wanted to write about was how Thurman and I weren't getting along—when they weren't writing about how Billy Martin and I weren't getting along. And if they couldn't find enough to write, it seemed they would drum up things to create controversy.

The very first day I was in camp, they asked me how I got along with Thurman. I told them, "I don't know him." I told them, "Why do you want to write about that?"

I could see what they were trying to do, but I didn't see why they should. What did they mean, how did I get along with Thurman? We'd never played together. When Gene Tenace came on as a catcher on the A's, nobody asked me how we got along. Why wouldn't we just get along like two great pros on the same team, trying to win a championship?

In fact, from what I knew, Thurman was one of the guys very much in favor of me coming to the Yankees. What I heard was that he told the Boss, "George, if you're going to get a free agent, go get the big S.O.B. in Oakland. That's what we need."

Thurman wanted the power. He understood it. He wanted a player he thought could get the team over the top and help win a World Series. George talked to his players, especially Thurman and Lou Piniella, and that's what they both told him.

But right from the start, the writers were trying to make something between us. They wrote a story that was in *The Bronx Is Burning*. That first day of spring training, I wanted to go hit in the batting cage before I did my running, and Thurman came in as the captain and said, "Hey, you have to run first, that's how we do it here."

And then, supposedly, I went over his head and appealed to Dick Howser, our third-base coach at the time, and asked him if I could hit first. And Dick supposedly said yes, and that made Munson mad, and it was all downhill from then on.

Makes for a nice story, doesn't it? Matches with what my personality was—or, I would say, what they *made* my personality out to be.

Thing was it never happened. It couldn't happen. You don't do anything on your own on a team. You can go out early and work on things. But if the team runs, everyone runs.

If the team does exercises, everyone does exercises.

And you don't hit first. You always do your stretching and your exercises first, before you hit. You hit in groups, too. And I never hit in the first group anyway.

That was just a conversation that Thurman and I never had. It was just a way of clowning me.

But that wasn't going to be the worst of my worries on the New York Yankees.

7

BILLY

I DIDN'T KNOW Billy Martin. I didn't know much about him. I didn't know who he liked and what he didn't. I just think Billy was out of control.

I know that Billy was a drinker. I really think that if he didn't drink, he'd have been a different person. But what his motives were, why he disintegrated at different stops along the way, I don't know. I never knew him, is how I'd say it.

Later, I heard a lot of things about what he was going through back then, when I came to the team. His marriage had broken up; his daughter was in jail down in Colombia. But I didn't know any of that at the time. I don't think many on the team knew that about his daughter—ever. Billy never *let* anybody know that. (I do know he was lucky to have had a great son, Billy junior.)

I don't even think that Billy Martin had any personal dislike toward me. At least I didn't know why he would. I heard he was very upset that he wasn't part of my acquisition—that he didn't get to be part of the decision. But that's just not how it's done with most teams; it wasn't done that way with the Yankees—especially with the Boss running things. It was going to be mostly his decision.

You see it with the Yankees today. The manager has some input; his opinion's respected. But it's the front office, it's the general manager, who makes most of the final decisions as to who's the best fit. That's just the way it is . . . The final say belongs to the owner of any team. That's one plus one equals two—that simple. That's the golden rule.

Billy didn't want me on the team. He wanted Joe Rudi, or maybe later Bobby Grich, because they needed a shortstop. I could respect that. They were great ballplayers. He wanted somebody who fit into his idea of the team, and I could respect that, too.

The teams that always fit best for Billy were the ones where it was about him. He always wanted teams that ran a lot, bunted a lot, so he could direct that. They called it "Billy-ball" for a reason.

Throughout his career, he was always best with young teams, unknown teams. Underperforming teams. He would turn them around. The minute those teams were expected to win, the minute they had some other big personalities, he had problems. Remember what he did to the incredible young pitching staff he had in Oakland from 1980 to 1982? All those great young arms: Mike Norris, Matt Keough, Rick Langford, Steve McCatty, Brian Kingman. He had them throw all those complete games . . . and by 1982, their careers were all but finished. He just chewed up their arms.

The spring of 1977, Billy had a problem with lots of players. Somehow, everything seemed to involve me.

Billy Martin was mad at Gabe Paul and George Steinbrenner because they didn't get who he wanted and because he felt George was interfering with the team. All spring training, Billy was feuding with them. He'd yell at Gabe. He had a screaming match with George because the Boss wanted Billy to travel on the team bus. They had a fight because George wanted him to play every spring training game to win, especially against the Mets. Billy ripped his office phone right off the wall one time because George called down to yell at him after a bad loss. (George could never understand why we didn't win every game!) "We're the best team, why don't we win every game?"

Billy told the writers that spring, "Without me [Billy], they could win, but there would be a lot of problems." Billy was going to be the mediator of all of our problems?

Uh-huh.

I admit I had misread Billy. In October 1976, after my offer had been turned down by Baltimore and I became a free agent, I did some broadcasting work for ABC Sports during the playoffs and the World Series, which the Yankees were in. I enjoyed watching them play, and I said, "I could play for that man"—meaning Martin.

He just looked like a scrappy kind of guy who you would want on your side. We had the same sort of mentality, I thought, in terms of being willing to do anything we could to win a ball game. I related to him socially, because I understood that he was part Portuguese. His middle name was Manuel, and his father came from the Azores, part of the nation of Portugal, which made him part Latino, like me. He even grew up in Berkeley, not far from where I lived and played for so many years for the A's.

It befuddled me that we never had an alliance. It looked to me like it would be a good fit in those 1976 playoffs. Martin looked to me like a scrappy guy in the mold of a Weaver or a Lasorda, and he had the reputation of being a player's manager. I thought we would get on well. I never had an inkling, before I signed with the Yankees, that he might have a problem with me.

You see, the whole winter after I signed, in 1976–77, I never heard from Billy Martin. Not a phone call. Not the standard thing a manager says: "Hey, Reggie, welcome to the team. I look forward to seeing you in spring training. We have a chance to win. Last year we got close. This year, with some new acquisitions, we can go a little further down the road. Be in shape when you get there, and I look forward to seeing you."

Wouldn't have been so hard. That would have been a nice scoop of ice cream to serve to the new kid. But all right, I didn't really care.

But then I heard that he expected *me* to call *him* when I signed, and he was offended that I didn't. I surely missed that side of it. It seemed like he could work anything up into an insult.

He didn't come to the press conference when my signing was announced in New York. George was there; Thurman was there. But that was all right, too. I didn't really even notice that Billy wasn't there, with all the commotion and thinking about how the Jackson family was going to be better off.

I mentioned at the press conference how George was so positive and how he was the reason, along with my agent, Gary Walker, that I came to New York. Billy decided to take that as a slight, too. I heard he said to Fran Healy and to a couple of his friends, "I'll show him who's boss." When I heard that, I thought, "Wow."

I don't know where that came from, but I didn't think too much about it. Then I started to hear he was telling people, "We won without him. We don't need him"—meaning me, of course. He was telling people that he thought Nettles and Munson and maybe some other guys would be disturbed by my presence.

Later, I was told that he was in the Hotel St. Moritz coffee shop in New York the same time I was or something like that and that he didn't come over to say hi. I don't know—I certainly don't remember being there when he was. I didn't assume anything about that. To me, that was just the papers stirring up trouble. But somehow all the stuff they played up in the press started to become reality.

Before I came to New York, I never thought much about Billy Martin as a manager. I never thought about him being a good guy or a bad guy. I only knew what I thought watching him manage in the 1976 playoffs, that he was a scrappy-type guy.

What I overlooked was that he got into a fight with a couple of players and sucker punched a couple of guys. Dave Boswell in Minnesota. I heard Billy hit him when he had his hands in his pockets. I heard that Boswell's pockets were torn when they picked him off the floor. But I never thought about any kind of confrontation with him. Just didn't enter my mind.

I didn't think of him much as a field manager. In my career, I played for some of the great managers of the time. Dick Williams. Earl Weaver. Tony LaRussa. I played for Gene Mauch, I played for Dick Howser, Bob Lemon. And Billy Martin would not come up ahead of any of those guys. Not as a clubhouse leader, not as a field manager.

The trouble was that he lied to people. That was his history. He lied to the general manager; he lied to the owner. He lied to players all the time, which was a big reason why he wore out his welcome. That first spring I was on the Yankees, one of the writers, Steve Jacobson, told me he saw Billy in his office telling Fred Stanley, "Don't worry, you're my shortstop." The very next day, Steve said, he was up in the front office, screaming at Gabe, "You gotta get me a shortstop!"

Every stop he made, he'd bring along his combination pitching coach and drinking buddy, Art Fowler. Goose Gossage said he didn't think he ever saw a day when Art's eyes weren't bloodshot. The pitchers didn't like him. Most of the pitchers thought he was a second-guessing guy, always second-guessing the pitches they made once they got back to the dugout.

Billy was much the same, though he used different tactics. When I first came over to the Yankees, I was told that Billy was the kind of manager who would crucify you in the dugout when you made a mistake on the field but then wouldn't say anything once you got back in the dugout.

That would change.

I know it will sound crazy now, but when I got to spring training, I still thought I was going to get along well with Billy. Wow, I thought that! We were both a little *outspoken.*

But there was a big stumbling block with that right from the start.

I was standing near the bat rack early in spring training, and I heard some of the worst anti-Semitic remarks and jokes directed at one of our own players. This went on far too often. When this player was pitching and doing well, he was "the great lefty." When he wasn't, it was the name of his ethnic group and religion, "the Jew."

I was raised in a Jewish community in Pennsylvania, Cheltenham, and I was very comfortable with Jewish people. My whole life, I gravitated toward them, because I thought that as minorities they had an experience with bigotry and social ostracism similar to what blacks went through in the United States—one that was just as severe.

I was upset because first of all these remarks hurt my teammate, who knew about them but didn't want to cause a distraction that might hurt the team. Billy Martin wouldn't pitch him if he had any other choice. When we look at the records, it was pretty obvious. He didn't pitch. I always wondered why. He just sat there and accumulated rust.

What really hit me over the back of the head, all the way to my heart, was the fact that I knew if they were willing to say the sorts of things they did in my hearing range, they were no doubt willing to make black and Latino jokes.

I was left with an uncomfortable feeling in my stomach. A dose of Pepto-Bismol, please. They had to have known I was close enough at the bat rack to be in earshot. It was a problem that stuck inside me.

As a black man who had played all around the country, I had heard every kind of racial epithet from the stands. I had heard some things in clubhouses, too. But I had never heard anything of this duration or this magnitude from my teammates before.

Coming from where I did, the social inequities I had grown up with, I found the anti-Semitism awkward at this juncture. It was ugly. Because I knew, if that's what they were saying about one ethnic group, then they felt the same thing or worse about black people.

It made me uncomfortable, I wasn't on the team more than three weeks, and I went upstairs and talked to Gabe Paul, who was Jewish, about it. I said, "I'd like to be traded away from here."

Gabe gave me a long story: "This is a great place for you, you'll be fine." What was he going to do, trade the highest-paid player in the game after three weeks? I didn't think about how that could happen. I just wanted out.

All that season, it made me feel awkward. Out of place.

I had no idea it would be so blatant. You just didn't get that in Oakland; you didn't feel the prejudice. You didn't get that in Baltimore. Scorn from someone because of your religion, race, beliefs, or looks.

I still hear these sorts of racial jokes and insults. I'm in New Jersey today, and as I speak and breathe, yesterday I had several experiences of people talking of other ethnicities with no regard for who was around. It's who we are, sadly, as a people and a nation. 2013. I heard comments at breakfast about Latinos. I heard comments at the ballpark, about Italians. And I heard comments about Asians later on in the evening, before I went to bed. And everyone does it! It ain't cool! And we need to improve.

I liked the multicultural society of New York, lots of different ethnicities and mixed people. I liked the melting pot of New York. I'm from a mixed background, and the mix of people made me comfortable.

Overall, New York had such broad social bandwidth. But it was still a city that was controlled by the corporate world. Still is today, in many ways. And while I have tremendous respect and love for what the city is, there was still a wide separation between its different ethnic communities. There was a social conflict that is still there, in pockets. New York still is the greatest city in the world. But there was and is still a need for change. We are still not all on equal ground. It still needs alteration. And many people in that era weren't ready to hear that.

I said at the time that I was used to a much more liberal place like Oakland, Berkeley, and the Bay Area. People didn't know what I was talking about, but it was true. As much as New York maybe thought of itself as liberal, it wasn't the same thing. Berkeley is liberal—the Left Coast, man!

California's dress is not nearly like it is here, in the East. It's more T-shirts and jeans. Whereas New York is still suit and tie. California is more laid-back. New York is hustle-bustle; it's in your face at all times. "Hurry up, move on." But even so, as laid-back as California is, African Americans and others forced their way into power in places like Berkeley and Oakland the way they still have not quite done in New York and other places.

Long after I retired from baseball, I saw the first episode of *The Bronx Is Burning,* which I then stopped viewing due to my disgust at how I was portrayed. The look they gave me, the way they had the actor play me, how I supposedly thought of myself—the whole way they portrayed "Reggie Jackson in New York" was a huge disconnect for me. I was coming from a place where racial attitudes were very different than they were in New York.

Oakland, California, and the entire Bay Area were at the epicenter of the social revolution and the civil rights movement that took off in the 1960s and '70s. The student riots in Berkeley, the Free Speech Movement, and the founding of the Black Panthers had all taken place shortly before I arrived there. I played my very first game in Oakland less than two weeks after Martin Luther King was assassinated, and not two months after that came the death of Bobby Kennedy. Dissent over civil rights and the Vietnam War continued to grow. People were afraid and society was in turmoil.

This was all strange to me, but I understood the frustrations and anger that were behind it all. It was the first time that I had first-hand experience of what it was to be a black person at a time when people were speaking out about what it meant to be a black person in America—something that was long overdue. The trend that had started with Jackie Robinson and progressed through the civil rights movement had by now evolved into a demand for dignity and respect. These words had long been on the minds of all black people, but unfortunately, that is where it ended for many of us. What we thought and what we said were two different things.

I was never a very political guy, and I was not involved with what was going on around me politically. But I was showing up every day doing my job while people were getting beaten by police within a few miles of the A's ballpark, going to jail, starting fires in the streets, and being told by Black Power advocates that there was a new day coming and that they should get guns. I could not help being affected by it, no matter how much I tried to look away. At the time, sports in general had always been oblivious to politics and social unrest, but it was hard to avoid these things in Oakland in the late '60s and during what turned out to be our terrific run in the early to mid '70s.

I started to grow my hair and was probably one of the first black ballplayers to wear a mustache and an Afro. I thought I was just keeping up with the times. But I was surprised to learn from some of my friends that other people read more into my looks and my actions than I did. They saw me as speaking out as a black athlete when that was not done by black people and, especially, black athletes—the example of Tommie Smith and John Carlos in the 1968 Mexico City Olympics notwithstanding.

Oakland's racial scene started stirring the pot inside of me, and I think my consciousness about being black in a white man's world was rising. Apparently, people read into what they were seeing on the field and reading in the press about me and concluded that I was starting to act like I "wasn't going to take it anymore." I think that when

I left Oakland, this perception might have come with me—perhaps not consciously, but I think it was there. I was developing the reputation among certain segments of society as someone who was willing to speak out and say what other black athletes were merely thinking. The way I carried myself on the field, the way I looked in my uniform when I was at the plate, the results I got—it felt to them as if I was there to challenge everyone I faced. I think people were so charged up, and, at the same time, confused with what was happening around them, that some folks saw me as a leader in the black community for things I had nothing to do with.

That never really went away. In fact I was, at one point, so influenced by this that when Muhammad Ali retired in 1981, I truly believed that it was an obligation to take my turn and continue the move forward for people of color, African American and Latino American.

Even before that, this perception that I was some kind of racial firebrand or agitator became attached to me. As I look back now, I can't think of one time when I said anything political in the press, but I think that this misperception of me as some kind of revolutionary was picked up by the press, and that it perpetuated this image of me, which I am sure did not go unnoticed in other parts of the country. I was branded with something I really did not understand, but it was certainly something I felt.

There was at the same time a confluence between all the social revolutions going on in our society at large, and the labor revolution going on in baseball. "Dignity" and "respect" were now also something that black athletes, especially, were demanding be applied to them by management and white players—something that I know shaped some of my attitudes. I think that, as a result of our demands to get rid of the reserve clause and restore our rights, many current players of all ethnicities and backgrounds have an entirely different concept of themselves than players of my time had. We were just meat then, and some of us were lower than that. Now we're all men. I think it all started in the era that coincided with my coming to New York, and, for me, in my own way, it came to a head there.

I am now starting to realize that part of my experience in New York in 1977 might have been shaped by how New York players and fans perceived me, based, in part, on what they had read about me, the way I looked, and what I had to say. Take a look at the pictures of me in '77 before George made me shave. Yeah, sure, I was young and brash. But I did not look like other black ballplayers in New York. Couple that with statements like "bringing my star with me" and POW! I'm someone who *should* be ostracized. Things like the article in *Sport* magazine that would cause so much ill will just confirmed what people were already feeling about me.

I was not the revolutionary these people perceived me to be. But in retrospect, I was clearly a new breed of black player in New York. Everyone else had acted like they were lucky to be there, but I was seen as someone who *expected* to be there, too cocky for my own good. I was seen as a black athlete who felt that he did not need to respect authority, Yankee history, or even his new Yankee teammates. I was seen as making my own rules in a town where that was just not what black people did or what black athletes ever would have thought about. And, most of all, I was seen as someone who did not appreciate the opportunity I was being given to play on the big stage. And here I was coming *with attitude* from the radical Left Coast.

So, now I have to ask myself: Was it *really* all about me coming to New York with my star—or was it about me coming from a place where black people were starting to act differently, like they weren't going to take it anymore—and that I was bringing some of that *attitude* with my star? I guess I looked the part, and many people felt that I acted the part, even though I did not really feel the part and may have not really understood it. Lots to think about, especially when I look back on my relationships with my white teammates when I arrived in New York—very few of whom saw me as I saw myself. Becoming a Yankee was a childhood dream come true—and, in my mind, I was the furthest thing from an "angry black man" coming to New York to "put it to the man" or show people up.

Others, though, saw me as exactly that. They conflated the idea of a black man who was comfortable in his own skin, who knew his own worth and ability, who was able to shape his own destiny in the game, with their stereotype of the angry black radical. So much of the controversy that surrounded me in New York came from their inability to forget their preconceived notions of what I was, and see the reality.

One of my major disappointments was that in New York they didn't want to hear about the anti-Semitism or prejudice on the ball team. At least not from me. Nobody in the media ever really stood up for the Jewish player on our team. I was disappointed and hurt that the press wouldn't defend him, and I believe he was as well. To this day, I don't know if he has gotten over it. The media were there when Billy and other people said what they said, but they never really asked questions about it. The newspaper guys never put questions to Billy or anyone else about whether he was anti-Semitic. I still can't get past that. The media are supposed to report. They sure as heck did report on me—but not on this.

Many of our writers were Jewish. They were on the same side that I was—I thought. They were the victims of the same prejudices. I was so disappointed that they wouldn't talk about it. Not only wouldn't they stand up for this player, but the writers didn't defend *themselves*. I lost respect for them, because of the fear that they had. They were more interested in getting their stories than in standing up for their own beliefs.

I know that Henry Hecht said a player called him a "backstabbing Jew c———er," when he reported that the player went out a window in a hotel once to break curfew in spring training, and he did write about that. But there was so much else they did not report.

Some of those writers were as bright a bunch of people as I've met in my baseball life. Bright, sensitive people. But they would not write about so much of what went on.

I understand they didn't want to interject themselves into the story. But I will always believe that they did not do what they should have done. It's not whether or not you put yourself in it; you just do what's right and report what should be reported to the public. You're supposed to do the right thing. You're supposed to report what's happening. They would write about everything else. But they wouldn't write about the social inequities they themselves felt and experienced.

I do wish, too, that I had been more forthcoming and better able to explain the double standard that I felt I saw here. It was *all* of our responsibility to do something about it, and I blame myself as well for not finding a way to get across what I knew.

Part of the problem, I think, was that they didn't want to hear it from me. I was always good for a quote, but they didn't want to hear anything from me that didn't fit in with some preconceived image.

I was raised to be honest; I was raised to be straightforward. I was too straightforward. You couldn't be direct with the writers in New York. No one ever spoke their feelings—especially if they were black. It didn't matter. You didn't count. We were supposed to be glad we were allowed to play—period.

It was a touchy social time. It was 1977; there were very few black players who spoke out. Muhammad Ali. Henry Aaron, Kareem, Bob Gibson, Frank Robinson, who said what they thought. Jim Brown spoke out, and he was considered a militant. You were labeled a clubhouse lawyer if you spoke up. You were a troublemaker. You were considered unappreciative if you had any comment that didn't fit in with a "good ol' boy" way of thinking.

Henry Aaron was not considered the social giant that he is now when he was breaking the record. He was a colored man who shouldn't have been breaking a white man's record. He was supposed to feel lucky to be here.

Your great black athletes at the time were considered "gifted athletes." However, if a white athlete was a great athlete, he was "a general on the floor." He was "a coach on the floor" or in the clubhouse. He was bright, analytical, and calculating. Rather than the black athlete just being physically talented. Thank goodness for Branch Rickey, Walter O'Malley, Red Auerbach, Vince Lombardi, Jerry Buss, Phil Jackson, and other white coaches, owners, and general managers in sports who were able to see beyond these stereotypes.

Nonetheless, it went on for a long time. Magic Johnson was just "gifted." Jordan was "gifted." It wasn't that he had great leadership skills or great communication skills or a superior philosophy. He was just gifted.

That's where we were, socially, as a nation at the time—that's where we still are, sometimes. So any comment from me about what I thought was right or wrong came off as "Yeah, who's this colored kid, colored man, black man," whatever you want to call it, "who is *he* to be making a comment about what is right or wrong?"

And so I became "arrogant" and "egotistical," rather than "sensitive" or "bright" or anything that was complimentary. I was tooting my own horn or trying to sound smarter than I was.

If I ever took out my billfold and counted how much I had left in it, I was "flashy." There was a company in New York that gave me a couple of fur coats—I didn't even wear 'em. They gave them to me; I still have them in storage. But I was "flaunting a fur coat." Joe Namath was "cool" when he had his.

I felt the connotation at the time was, "What's this black guy doing with all this money? What's this black guy doing in a fur coat?"

On anything that had to do with color, or a different viewpoint in the game of baseball, or a different view about society—if a black person spoke out and said something truthful, he was either a loudmouth or trying to cause trouble. It always had to be about "Here's a black man speaking." It was always, "Where's he going with that? He should just be glad to be here."

I was just supposed to shut up and play ball. When you were born in this country in that era, you were black first, a boy or a girl second.

The frustrations I had came from the things I saw happening in the clubhouse, the things I saw happening in the game of baseball at the time. They were legitimate frustrations. I saw all this blatant prejudice in this city that was supposedly the great melting pot of the world. But it was always *my* problem—not anyone else's problem, telling Jew jokes around the batting cage.

I had another disappointment. It was with many of the black players on the team who sided against me.

I had some friends on the team. Ken Holtzman. Catfish Hunter. Lou Piniella was always good; Ron Guidry was a great friend. Fran Healy became my best friend on the team when he came over from Kansas City. Mike Torrez. But Willie Randolph was the lone black player who reached out to me. He was a good friend from the first day I was there.

The rest . . . I felt they were always supporting the other side. I couldn't understand it. Mickey Rivers was always in the middle, Roy White and Oscar Gamble were somewhat friendly, but always managed to stay in the middle.

I looked for support. However, I never understood the fact that I didn't get that support! Looking back, I would have tried to be more involved with them. "They aren't giving, so I'm not giving," was not the way to do it. I should have still given.

The Yankees at that time probably had more black players than they've ever had, before or since. There were other black sports stars in New York at the time, such as Willis Reed, Walt Frazier, and Earl Monroe with those great Knicks teams of the era. But I was the first black baseball star in New York who spoke out since Jackie Robinson.

Still, most of the black players on our team did not support me, and that hurt. I must make a note here. How many of us have been in situations where we've heard something that was a negative comment, that was contemptuous or even racist, and didn't say anything? We've all been there. We've all said to ourselves, "Why didn't I say something?" Even then, things were volatile, and most of us stayed away from a confrontation.

I don't know if it was about the money, or them resenting me because they won the year before, or if it was about Billy. Certainly, he did enough to make guys take sides. To test me. To push me to my limit.

That whole spring, he kept putting me in the lineup anywhere from second to sixth. That is, anywhere but fourth. It was prestigious to hit cleanup for the New York Yankees. Almost my whole career, I came to the park knowing I was going to hit fourth. That was where I hit as one of the premier power hitters in the game; that was where it made sense for me to hit. That was where Mr. Steinbrenner wanted me to hit. But Billy was out there telling the writers I struck out too much to hit cleanup, or whatever came to mind that day.

That whole spring, my left elbow, my throwing arm, hurt like crazy. When I reported to camp, it felt great, I was in great shape. Then the elbow. I'd never had arm soreness like that before; every time before when I had some soreness, it was in my shoulder. At first I didn't say anything about it. I didn't want it to be a problem. I kept my head down and kept playing.

But the elbow kept getting worse. It got so I couldn't throw with it, and it bothered my swing. Late in the spring, I hit a ball off the end of the bat, and the pain shot right up my arm to my elbow. It hurt so bad I couldn't even run; it just took my breath away. But I stayed in the game.

In fact, I was still in that same game in the bottom of the tenth inning, against the Cincinnati Reds. The tenth inning! In a spring training game—and I'm still in the game! As I think about it now, in 2013, I don't believe I was in there. The score was tied, the ball gets hit out to me in right, on a hop, and they sent the runner from second. I couldn't even make a throw. I just put the ball in my pocket and ran in.

That was made into a huge deal, that I didn't make a throw and we lost the game. But I kept playing, pretty much every day. Play all nine innings, play ten innings. Even after I told them about the arm. In those days, they didn't even take you to the hospital. They just iced it. Ice, ice, ice everything. And put you back out there. That would be unheard of today.

I didn't get any relief until almost the end of spring training when Gene Monahan, the trainer, diagnosed it as tendinitis and gave me a cortisone shot. After that, it got better. But they kept playing me the whole time. I thought it was that they wanted me on the field, to draw the fans. That's what I thought—"Play that old horse," you know?

Late in the spring, Phil Pepe, one of the writers, asked me about it. He said, "What're you doing, playing every day? What's the purpose?" And I told him, "Don't ask me, I don't know what he's trying to prove"—talking about Martin.

So he goes back and tells that to Billy, and Martin curses me out to Pepe and says I asked to play. He says I told him at the start of spring training I liked to play a lot of innings to get in shape.

I don't know where that came from. I didn't say it. I never told him that.

I was one of the few ballplayers at the time who worked out all year. I would lift weights, work out on those old Nautilus machines we had. I was into maintaining a proper diet, the way guys do today. Most guys didn't really start showing up in shape until the 1980s. It was only then that they started paying attention to what they ate, understood diet better, because they could see how that would help. Some started having their food prepared for them.

Then the teams got into it. The Yankees were one of the first teams to be concerned about their diet inside the clubhouse, started eliminating the candy, sugar, and the ice cream. The alcohol went away soon thereafter. Now the Yankees even have a chef, and our front office promotes a better, more healthy environment.

But when I was coming up, there was nothing like that. Spring training was usually where you got yourself in shape. There were a few guys, men like Willie Mays, who would just come to camp with great bodies. (Mays always took care of himself, never drank or smoked.)

In the off-season, I would run Lake Merritt in downtown Oakland three or four days a week; a little over three miles around. I'd run it once around, until the last week before spring training, when I'd run it twice. I did sprints there as well. I truly enjoyed it. I was young, energetic. I came to camp in shape my entire career. I could have played a game a couple days after being in camp.

But whatever I told Billy, I didn't tell him I wanted to keep playing until my arm fell off. I didn't tell him I wanted to keep playing in the field and play all the innings when I couldn't even make a throw. My first year there with the Yankees, I played every spring training game. I played every spring game all five years I was with the Yanks, until the last year, when I got hurt and missed a couple games.

The way things would go, it was easy to get paranoid. I mean, you never knew just what was going on beneath the surface. Was Billy putting me out there hurt to show me up? Did he just misunderstand? Was he lying to Pepe because it was really the front office who told him to put me out there and Billy didn't want it to seem like he wasn't in charge? What?

I thought, I'm playing hard for you, why don't you like me?

The wheels just went round and round. And nothing ever stayed in the clubhouse. It always leaked to the media in some way.

When I think back on that time, that's what went on in my head. Now I understand that it was Billy showing me he was the boss—and showing me up.

Back in Oakland, in Baltimore, I never paid attention to the media and what they might do. I never worried about remembering what I said or didn't say. Trying to outwit someone. I just tried to speak the truth and be honest.

But in New York, people went to the press with everything. Billy told us to stop talking to the media. Then, just before Opening Day, he holds a team meeting, and afterward he goes and tells a writer, Milt Richman, that I said in my twelve years in baseball, it was the best meeting I—Reggie—had ever been in. What was that?

Nothing was ever confidential. You had to learn to speak in riddles. You had to tell the press something. But the truth? Let's see, the whole truth? The partial truth? Some of the truth? This was a crazy movie.

I had to just let it go. You can't get into a contest of wits with the media. Just tell the truth, let the chips fall. If you tell the truth, you don't have to worry about remembering anything.

I couldn't take it any further than that, because after a while it just became decay. There was no upside to it. You harbor resentments and you get miserable, and where are you going to go with what's eating you?

You feel that. And you don't let it penetrate. You don't let it get to you. All the racism, the anti-Semitism that was around then, I didn't really want to get involved in that. But how does anyone stay away from that. All the stories about what I said to Martin, or Thurman, or whoever . . . it just kept going on and on.

I never put myself in the class of a Mantle, an Aaron, a Mays, a Clemente—any of the greats. But I hit cleanup for a world championship team for three years in Oakland. And it was too hard to do what I was doing—to try to drive in runs, try to help win a game, try to hit the ball out of the park—it was too hard to do that and care or worry about whatever kind of nonsense was going on or to try to discern the truth. I couldn't understand why people spent so much time on the negatives. Lies, stories, trying to one-up people all the time . . .

I know I was very religious that year. I first became a Christian in 1974 with Oakland. I didn't live like it yet. But I accepted Christ as my Savior, through our chapel service, in Oakland.

Being a Christian is not easy; it's hard work. But the benefits are remarkable.

Baseball still has a great chapel service going on every Sunday, in every ballpark, home and on the road. There are two services, one in Spanish and one in English, and I enjoy going to both. I've enjoyed playing with and watching so many other players, like Sal Bando and Joe Rudi, men like Mariano Rivera, Andy Pettitte, Dave Robertson, Mark Teixeira, and many more—a long list of great people—walk the walk, with Christ. The Yanks have great attendance every service.

I don't think ballplayers are more religious than other people. With some of the teams I've been with, there is a lot of participation in chapel. With the Yankees, it was as much as 50 percent. Oppression and difficulty in life bring you closer to God. The church gives you something to hold on to when you have nothing. It gives you a closer attachment with God. That has been my experience with people of color.

Most of us, when we're players, we're very young and insecure. Very few players have the maturity, just like very few people in general who are under thirty. They tend to come to Christ when they're a little older—or a little more in need. Most of us are like that. I got close to God because I was hurting.

You learn through difficulties, through problems and issues. I learned from Mike Singletary, the Hall of Fame linebacker from the Bears, to always carry a prayer book. He talked to me about how I had to learn to let *my* rules go. I've been fortunate to have a few people help me with my relationship at special times. Even an ex!

What I learned from him, too, was that the Bible is really like a guide. I say to people, "The Bible is like a map." I would say to someone, "Go down to the third stoplight and make a right turn. I really don't know the address, but when you go down a little ways, you'll see it. I don't know the address. I don't even know how far it is. But you just go down the road. When you get there, the light'll be green. You'll see it. You'll know it when you see it." That's how you come to grace and salvation.

I remember praying a lot in 1977. Praying with my agent at the time, Gary Walker, who was and is very close to Jesus. Gary always preached about Christ, and I really thought I was insulated from a lot of the worst of the strife because I prayed.

That was another underappreciated talent of Billy Martin's. He could bring a man to God.

8

The Hole in the Doughnut

"You know, Reggie, you have to look at the whole doughnut, not just the hole in the doughnut."

That's what Gabe Paul told me when I asked him for about the second or third time in spring training if he would please trade me to anyone. Gabe had a million little sayings like that. He also liked to say, "One man's . . . crap is another man's ice cream." I was about to find out what that meant! LOL!

I had a kind of unwritten agreement with the Boss that he wouldn't keep me in New York if I didn't like it or I didn't want to be there. So I went to Gabe and asked to be traded during spring training. Later, during the year, I insisted. I was always going to Gabe and his assistant, Cedric Tallis, and trying to get myself traded.

But it didn't work. I was in New York and I couldn't get out.

The talent we had was impressive, I have to say that. I read in the paper that on Opening Day the umpire looked into the dugout of the team we were playing, the Milwaukee Brewers, and said, "Time to play ball—if you dare."

You could see what he meant.

We had Thurman behind the plate. He was the MVP the year before, and he was about to have his third straight season hitting over .300 and driving in at least a hundred runs. I'm told that nobody in baseball had done that since Bill White, more than ten years before.

Chris Chambliss at first base, a great team guy, played every day.

Was a good RBI man and an outstanding hitter, hit .290 to .300, fifteen to twenty homers. And he drove in runs when they counted. Very steady, a great defender, Gold Glove winner. His nickname was "Snatcher." If he could get anywhere near a ball, he'd snatch it.

Second base, you had Willie Randolph. He was a great young man, a real pro at a young age. He lockered near me. Randolph was a great defender, best second baseman in the league at the time. Only Bobby Grich had as much range. Willie became and still is a great friend.

Third base, you had Graig Nettles, power hitter, home run champ, hit thirty-seven homers for us that year. Best fielding third baseman in the game, one of the best I ever saw—and I played with Brooks Robinson. Bucky Dent, we got in a trade just as the season was starting; he was a great glove, too. If you hit it to Bucky, you were out.

In the outfield, we had depth. We had Mickey Rivers in center, who hit .320-plus and could cover the ground like Bambi. Lou Piniella, who hit .330, Roy White, me. We had Jimmy Wynn, Carlos May, Oscar Gamble. We brought over Cliff Johnson to catch and play first, and he crushed balls, great pinch hitter. We had all-stars backing up all-stars, with Paul Blair, the best defender of his era, behind Rivers in center.

The pitching staff had Catfish Hunter, Ed Figueroa, Don Gullett, Holtzman. Mike Torrez came over in a trade a little later. We had a young "Louisiana Lightning," Ron Guidry. He was supposed to relieve for us, but instead he had his first great year as a starter. In the bullpen, we had Sparky Lyle, who won the Cy Young in 1977, and Dick Tidrow, a great versatile arm. He could start and pitch long or short relief.

It was a great team—though I thought the teams we had in Oakland were better. Easy now! That's just my opinion. But I thought they were better, and they would have been even better still if we'd got to play in Yankee Stadium. With the great pitching we had on those teams, they would've really used the massive center field they still had in the Bronx. When I got there, it was still 430 feet to left-center, close to the dimensions of the original park, which had been 457 to left and 461 to center. You needed a sandwich to just walk to the fence at 461 feet from home plate.

It hurt me, because I was never really a pull hitter. So I hit a lot of balls to center field and left-center field that just became long outs. Shoulda, woulda, coulda. But that was all right. After everything, all the crap that happened in Florida, I was just happy to start the season.

Before Opening Day, I was still wearing Terry Whitfield's uniform, with his name on it, after he was traded to the Giants. Back in Oakland, I wore number 9, but Graig Nettles already had that, so I wore number 20 in spring training, honoring my friend Frank Robinson. He had mentored me in the winter of 1970–71, when I was playing winter ball in Santurce, and he was the manager. He taught me how to control my temper, focus, and become a team leader.

I had worn number 9 because that was the number the A's gave me. I just said, "Hey, Ted Williams wore number 9, that was good enough for me!" (What not too many people know is that Williams was also the first great Hispanic ballplayer in the majors. His mother had Mexican, Spanish, and Basque roots, as well as American Indian.)

I finally decided on number 44 because of the great "Hammerin' Hank" Aaron, of course, who wore that number. So did my great friend Willie McCovey, so did a lot of great black ballplayers because of the Hammer, Mr. Aaron.

Opening Day at Yankee Stadium, I saw already how things were going to be very different than they were in Oakland. Like the ad says, it was a "whole 'nother ball game." The Stadium was only a year old then, bright, shiny, and new. The crowd was over forty-three thousand.

It had been a long time since I'd played before so many people. That used to be a week's attendance, where I came from. We didn't have fans in Oakland.

We had a good day, that day, and everything went right. Jimmy Wynn hit a ball 420 feet into the center-field bleachers. Catfish, who had been having arm troubles all spring, pitched a great game. He threw seven shutout innings before he got hit in the foot by a line drive hit by Von Joshua, I think. He had to leave the game because of it, and later he tried to come back too fast and hurt his arm, many believe, the way pitchers sometimes do when they're throwing a different way. Some think because of the injury he was never really the same again.

But we didn't know that at the time. The sun was out, and it was a great day. I had a walk and two singles. I went first to third on a headfirst slide, then scored on a squeeze play when I slid under the catcher. Couple innings later, I hustled in on a wild pitch and ended up scoring two runs. We won, 3–0.

When I came up in the eighth inning, that's when I started to hear it for the first time. That whole Stadium, chanting, "Reg-gie! Reg-gie!"

For a few years, starting back in the late 1960s, they had a thing called Reggie's Regiment in Oakland, out in the right-field bleachers. I used to give away tickets to kids—they were like fifty cents, a dollar—and they'd sit out in the bleachers and call themselves Reggie's Regiment, and root for me and the team. That was pretty cool.

But it wasn't anything like this.

You hear that sound, "Reg-gie! Reg-gie!" and it turns on your adrenaline. You feel welcome, like the fans have their arms wrapped around you, and you feel comfortable. It makes you feel loved. It makes you feel you can do anything. You know, when you're a major-league hitter, you never pay too much attention to the crowd. You can't pay too much attention to it. But you do hear the support and the chants—and oh, yeah, the boos, too, when they come!

I always liked that sound in the background. It always felt good to hit to that sound. "Reg-gie! Reg-gie!"

So the team played great, I had a good day, and Billy got to play Billy-ball. He had me batting fifth again, but so what. He had me run in on a squeeze play.

When was the last time you saw a team's best power hitter score on a squeeze play? Billy must have remembered how I stole home against his Tigers team five years before in the American League Championship Series—but that was a double steal, and, more to the point, I tore a ligament right off the bone, and missed the World Series.

But we won; we had a great team. The schedule was on our side.

Most of our early games were against Toronto, which was an expansion team that year and finished last in the division, and Milwaukee, which finished next to last.

What could go wrong?

Then we lost seven of the next eight.

Two weeks into the season, we're 2–8 and dead last. The team's playing terrible. I was playing bad. Next game against Milwaukee, I dropped a fly ball in the outfield, led to all three of their runs. We lost, 3–2. Game after that, I got picked off first in the ninth inning, and we lost, 2–1.

Oh, man.

First game of the season, it was "Reg-gie! Reg-gie! Reg-gie!" By the third game, it was "Boo! Boo! Boo!"

Well, that's why they play 162 games. You never like to make a mistake. I never liked to screw up. Who does?

As major-league players, though, we knew it was a long season. We all knew you can't dwell on one mistake.

What I was learning, though, was that in New York everything gets magnified. Billy Martin jumped all over me for dropping that fly ball. He even called me a "bad defender" in the press.

I'd always been a pretty good outfielder in Oakland. I played center field in the 1973 World Series and was the Series MVP. I played some center field in 1972, and I would've started the Series there if I didn't rip up my leg.

But here in New York, I make one bad play and he's calling me out. In the second game of the year. And the media picked up on it. I was having a little trouble out there, with the new park and everything. Great as it was to play before all those fans, it was loud. It was louder than I'd ever heard before. It just required some adjustment, but after two games I make an error and I become a "bad defender," according to my own manager.

That was part of Billy at times. He tried to undermine his own players when he didn't like them. He did it to Ken Holtzman whenever he got a chance. Tried to do it to Elliott Maddox. I tried not to pay attention to that kind of stuff, but he did it to me, too.

So there we were, 2–8, in last place. Must be one of the worst starts the Yankees ever got off to, and the Boss was freaking out. He'd come to town and raise hell in the locker room. Go on for ten minutes at a time. It was pretty funny, but you couldn't laugh. Get all over us for not concentrating enough, not trying hard enough. You had to hold it in sometimes; you couldn't look at another player sitting near you, or you might lose it. George thought that with the talent we had, we should be 162–0. But he was "the Boss," so . . .

You know, he felt if he owned the team, he had the right to say what he wanted when he wanted to say it. He'd come down and give us his pep talks. Just kind of rah-rah stuff, "go out and beat 'em" stuff.

George meant well, but he didn't understand. He was a football guy, and he didn't realize baseball doesn't work that way. Twelve and oh, 16–0, is not 162–0. No one gets close to that. He was a fan as much as an owner. All in all, you had to admire his relentless desire.

We knew we were too good a team to stay down, though. And Billy had a good idea to break up the tension. He had us pick the lineup out of a hat, an old baseball tradition. That's what you have to do in baseball: stay loose, stay within yourself over the long season. I was the one who picked the names out of the hat.

I had no idea how I got the honor. I couldn't believe I was going to be the player. You would have thought I'd have been the last guy. You'd think it would be Thurman, as the captain, or somebody who Billy loved. But how the hell he ever picked me . . . Clearly, he must have been going for the *opposite* of what he usually did.

As luck would have it, I picked my own name for the third spot.

I guess that was the only way I was going to hit that high in the lineup with Billy as manager. And as it happened, we won the next six games in a row, and I had eleven hits in those games. You'd think that might have told him something.

After that, we played better. We got up maybe five or six games over .500. Going into May, we moved into first place for a little while. It was already obvious it was going to be a three-way race between us, the Red Sox, and the Orioles. We split a couple short series with the Sox, won a game in Fenway when Mickey Rivers made a great throw to the plate in the ninth and Munson just hunkered down and flipped Butch Hobson right over him in the collision at home plate.

We knew we could play with anybody. We all knew it. But we were still treading water. I don't know how much it had to do with how we were playing, but there was a bad atmosphere around the club still. From how anxious Billy was, from all the fights in spring training. This was the feeling around the league. Even other teams could feel it.

There was so much inner strife on the team, with the situation with myself, with Billy pinch-hitting for Bucky Dent all the time. Other players were grumbling, and cliques were forming. We did not have a good social atmosphere.

I still didn't realize how much it was going to be about the money. Late April, we went down to Baltimore for the first time, and there was a really bad reaction from the fans. Throwing darts at me out in right field, throwing containers of ice cream, anything else they could find.

They even hanged me in effigy out in right field, which has some racial overtones when you're talking about a black ballplayer playing below the Mason-Dixon Line. Who would let fans do something like that today? No way. It was tasteless, beyond anything that was called for.

The fans didn't get to hear that I offered to stay in Baltimore for about half the money the Yankees offered me. You know, I had played there all of five months. It wasn't like I came up through their system and played for the Orioles for years and now they were heartbroken I was gone. They acquired me knowing I could be a free agent, knowing they could lose me. But somehow, I had done something wrong to them.

I was a black man, but I didn't do what or go where I was told. I included my own desires in what I wanted to do. I went against the grain at the time and wound up the highest-paid player in the game. That was unacceptable.

I hadn't gone to New York for the money. I turned down a bigger offer from Montreal, from San Diego. I never even had a conversation with the Dodgers about their offer. The Orioles turned down *my* offer. It's a little like LeBron James today. He turned down *more* money to play with his friends. What was wrong with that?

LeBron has been a model citizen who has done nothing but enhance the brand of the NBA. He just moved on from the attacks.

I think Tiger Woods was unfairly attacked. No doubt, he was 100 percent wrong. But the level of criticism he got was beyond all proportion. His beat down, to me, was partially okay—but I think the continuance of it, and the unrelenting nature of it, had to do with the color of his skin.

I think Tiger does have the chance to become as loved and admired as he's ever been. That is one thing about this country: It can be very forgiving. The perfect example is Magic Johnson, who has become a noble presence, almost regal. I think the person I have the most respect for as a minority is Rachel Robinson, with the presence and the immense dignity with which she carries herself—for America.

It's possible for people like her, like Jackie Robinson, like Muhammad Ali, who were once looked down on, to become models of dignity for our country. Ali's become someone all of America is proud of; he's transcended color. He's become a part of American folklore.

The tragic part is that leading African American athletes, leading African Americans of all kinds, have to run these gauntlets of criticism. You see it with President Obama. Whenever it's convenient for his critics, he has to endure unfair attacks. When you look at the shape the economy and the financial system were in, he inherited a waste pit. But as soon as he got in, it was all his fault: "Well, I told you. You give 'em something, and they don't know what to do with it." This is who we are.

Meanwhile, Billy kept trying to show me up any way he could. He benched me against Milwaukee in one game when he told the press my arm was hurting too bad for me to play. He could've pinch-hit me on two at-bats in that game. We were down three runs, we got men on first and second in the eighth and ninth innings, but no pinch-hit appearance for me.

Instead, he hit Jimmy Wynn, who was in a terrible slump, and then Fran Healy, who was the third-string catcher behind Thurman and Elrod Hendricks—and who, by the way, had a neck injury. They both made out, and we lost the game. Billy never even asked if I thought I could hit. Later, he told the press he was protecting me, because he was afraid I'd say I could hit even if I couldn't. "Billy just didn't want me to hurt myself." What he really wanted was just to win without me!

I didn't say anything. I just told the media, "No comment." I told them I accepted what Martin had to say.

But it *never stopped*. A little later, we were up a run or two in the ninth, and he had Mickey Rivers try to steal third and get thrown out when I was at the plate. You don't run somebody from second in that situation. But everything had to be a little demonstration that Billy was in charge, that he was going to play his kind of ball—and that he couldn't count on me to come through.

There were some teammates I had trouble with, too. Graig Nettles had a very witty sense of humor, but it often had a very negative slant to it. He always thought I said too much, was too full of myself. He was always saying things like, "With Reggie here, we don't have to do interviews." He liked to say, "The best thing about playing for the Yankees is you get to see Reggie Jackson play every day. The worst thing about playing for the Yankees is you get to see Reggie Jackson play every day."

You had to give it to him, though. He was witty. I didn't like the quote, but it was a good one!

There were some guys who just followed the manager's lead in disliking me. I was disappointed that they didn't think enough for themselves.

Then there was a group of guys who were close to Thurman. He had a faction that supported him because he was a very likable guy, he was their leader and our captain, and he was the guy who had been there and done it all. At the same time, I think Thurman was very angry about his contract situation. I think he felt violated. I think he felt that George went back on his word not keeping him the highest-paid player on the team. I don't think he got bitter, exactly, but I think he was hurt because he didn't get the deferred money I got and because he thought George had given me a $63,000 Rolls-Royce.

Most people thought I had too big an ego. Thought I wasn't a team guy, thought I was a self-promoter.

Nobody—*nobody*—really wanted to locker next to me. And I don't mean just the group of guys who were close to Thurman. We must've had at least six, seven other guys who were black, and they didn't want to locker near me, either.

I had this little corner to myself, which was weird. The craziest thing, I found out later from Pete Sheehy, the clubhouse man who had been with the Yankees since 1927, was that the locker had been Lou Gehrig's.

I was honored by that—by chance, I later became the honorary chairman for the Amyotrophic Lateral Sclerosis Association, the group leading the fight against Lou Gehrig's disease. But honored or not, I was on my own. The locker on one side of me was empty, and the locker on the other side was supposed to go to Ron Blomberg, but he tore up his knee and was out all year. After that, the next locker was Elrod Hendricks, but he was really more a coach than a player, and he wasn't there most of the time. I was really alone.

The one exception was Willie Randolph, who was at the very end of the row of lockers where I was. Thank goodness he was very friendly, or I would've been all alone there.

The rest of them? They wanted me on the team, but I wasn't a teammate.

By the end of May, I was doing a little better with the guys, getting along with Thurman better. When you're winning, a lot of things, including animosity, disappear in a clubhouse. If we could've just got a little streak going, I think it could've been all right. I thought it was maybe about to be all right.

Then that *Sport* magazine piece came out. Oh, my goodness!

9

The Article

I never wanted to talk to Robert Ward. Absolutely not!

I had enough going on in spring training as it was. I remember that I didn't want to do the interview with him, but he hung around and hung around until I talked to him. He was a young guy, trying to do a piece for *Sport* magazine. I had compassion for him. He had a job to do, and I wanted to help. Oh, boy.

I don't know if he caught me on a good day or a bad day, an up day or a down day. But my whole time in New York really turned on that one interview, that one piece.

And it never happened. At least not like he said it did.

Later, he turned it into part of a book: *Reggie Jackson Wanted to Kill Me.* I never read it. Last I heard it was remaindered at Walmart. Well, I never wanted to kill him. But I can't say I feel bad his book got remaindered at Walmart.

The way I remember it was Robert Ward finally got to interview me at a bar called the Banana Boat Lounge, in Fort Lauderdale, after a game that day. At the time, we still needed a shortstop. Our shortstop just then was Fred Stanley, and the team wanted to trade for another, so we were talking about that.

I remember he kept trying to goad me into a quote. He kept saying, "Well, what do you like about this team?" Just seemed the conversation we were having wasn't what he was after. Just regular conversation about the team, our chances, other teams in the division, and how we compared. What was different this year, our competition—Boston, Baltimore. Our change of a few players. "We got there last year, what is different this year . . ."

That wasn't his interest.

And I said, "The team is all there. They got to the World Series, but they lost four in a row there, and so there was something missing. It looks like I could be one of the last ingredients. We still need a short-stop." Or maybe, "I'll have the chance to be the last ingredient that's necessary for the mix."

At the time, I was sitting there stirring around a mai tai, or iced tea. And he comes up with the quote, he said something like "You would be the straw that stirs this drink," or "You mean, you'd be like the straw that stirs the drink."

And I said, "Not really, more like the last ingredient." And he said, "Well, it just seems like you're here to stir it up and get things going, and help them, you know."

And I said, "Well, if that's the way you want to say it. But I would think I'm hopefully going to be the final piece that's necessary to win the championship. The '76 Yanks have a couple more big pieces, Don Gullett and me."

The whole time, he was trying to feed me that quote, but I know I never said it. However, somehow when his piece came out in *Sport*, there it was, along with a whole lot of other crap. Page after page of it that he attributed to me: "You know, this team, it all flows from me . . . I've got to keep it all going. I'm the straw that stirs the drink. It all comes back to me. Maybe I should say me and Munson . . . but really, he doesn't enter into it. He's being so damned insecure about the whole thing."

And then later: "Munson thinks he can be the straw that stirs the drink, but he can only stir it bad."

No way.

There's no way I'd be that dumb, to knock the captain of the team—and, by the way, the guy who told George Steinbrenner to go get me on the free-agent market. I was Thurman's recommendation, when Billy wanted Joe Rudi or Grich. It was Thurman who said, "Go get Reggie Jackson." George told me that, and so had Thurman himself.

Why would I knock him in an article for a major sports publication?

To this day, I don't know how Robert Ward got that out of what I said. I'd be interested to know if he had a tape recorder, or just a pad. I would love to hear that tape if he has one. Because I know I didn't say anything like that.

I've tried to get Ward to sit down with me and talk about it, but he won't do it. I've heard he's afraid of how I would react. I'd love to hear his version of that whole day at the Banana Boat.

I didn't think he had any malicious intent. But why would he put that out there? I don't think he was there to hurt me. I wish I knew what he was doing. It came out so bad. It came off as negative, egotistical, because he wanted something to sound sensational. Obviously, it came off as a disparagement of the captain, Thurman Munson.

It came out with a whole story around it, too. One that got repeated and repeated until everyone thought it was true. All about how while Robert Ward was interviewing me, Billy Martin came in with Mickey Mantle and Whitey Ford, and they started playing backgammon and having a few.

Ward wrote that I sent a round of drinks over to them, and he said that Whitey told the waitress he'd rather have the *Superstars* T-shirt I was wearing—from that TV show. According to what Ward wrote, I took it off and went over and gave it to Whitey right there, running bare-chested across the bar. And then Whitey laughed and gave me this sweater he was wearing in exchange, and I acted thrilled to have it. Ward had me "looking down lovingly" at a pink cashmere sweater.

The way he wrote it, I went over and watched the three of them play backgammon and drink for a while, and they were supposedly laughing at me and kind of ignoring me. And then I went back to talk to Ward and started saying bad things about Thurman Munson, because I was that insecure or felt that insulted.

It never happened. I don't remember any of that happening, I don't know where that came from. I draw a complete blank to that. Taking off my shirt and giving it to a superstar like Whitey Ford?

I was never in there with Billy Martin.

I was in that bar with Mickey Mantle and Whitey Ford maybe a few times. They liked to go there for casual drinks in the afternoon, and I did as well. They sat in their usual place, I sat in my place with my friends, and we did our own thing. They never said anything embarrassing to anybody, not just me. It just wasn't in their makeup. Mickey and Whitey were about a good time, enjoying their friendship with each other. If I was a fellow Yankee, they rooted for me. No matter who I was, or what color I was, or how good or bad I was.

They were a welcoming presence, all the time, to any- and everybody. Mickey and I became good friends. He was always friendly, and he came to my Hall of Fame party in New York in January 1993 at McMullen's restaurant. Whitey to this day is always friendly and respectful and playful. True Yankee class.

I was never in the Banana Boat with Billy Martin in there. There were rules. It's one of the oldest rules: You don't drink in the same place the manager drinks. If I'd seen Billy come in there, I would've left.

In those days, I was a young kid who was half-crazy. I wasn't hanging out with Billy Martin. Just wouldn't do it. Whether we liked each other or not, he was still the manager.

I traveled alone then. Almost all the time. I still enjoy traveling alone today.

No, I don't think of Robert Ward as a bad guy. But I sure would love to see what he thought about the article and how he heard our conversations.

Things do happen with writers. So I can tell one and tell all: If you're ever talking to a writer, make sure you're reading what you're saying as you're saying it. Most writers will take the liberty of using *their* variation of what you're saying. They only need to change one word . . .

I think what Robert Ward did was to take the opportunity to make things sound the way he wanted them to sound, not as I said them. For me to say, "Thurman Munson can only stir it bad"? Anyone who knows me, knows I *might* say, "I'm the straw that stirs the drink"—which *I did not say*. But with all the ego I've got, or whatever I had then, I'm not going to come out and say, "Munson can only stir it bad."

I'm not that dumb. This guy just came off an MVP year. That's not a statement that would make sense. If you look at my history to that time, I might say something flamboyant, I might say something egotistical, I might say something self-promoting. But I'm not going to say something stupid.

I just don't think Robert Ward knew that much about baseball or that much about me. One of the other things he wrote in that article was that I was envying the kind of relationship Billy and Mickey and Whitey had.

Ward wrote, "Mantle, Ford, and Martin have a kind of loyalty and street-gang friendship that today's transient players don't have time to develop."

I don't think he knew what he was talking about. Because players weren't any more or less *transient* in my day than they were before. I played for years with all those guys on the A's. We were close as family. If you want to describe any team as close as a street gang, that's what the Oakland A's were in the '70s.

That wasn't these New York Yankees.

I had thought I was alone before that article came out. I found out what alone meant.

I remember when that issue of *Sport* went on sale. The June 1977 issue: "Reggie Jackson in No-Man's Land." Came out in late May.

The night it did, my teammates already had a few copies going around the locker room. They were just waiting for me to come into the clubhouse, to see what I was going to do or say.

There I was at my locker, all by myself, and there were these little groups of players huddled around the magazine, staring over at me and muttering imprecations. I didn't know what was going on. I hadn't read the article. I didn't pay any attention to it. It wasn't until Fran Healy came over and said, "Read this."

And I started reading it, and I said to Healy, who was the go-between by then with me and the rest of the team, "Oh, my God. This is sickening. All of it. What am I going to do?"

Fran said, "Reggie, I don't know." I told him I was misquoted. So he went to Thurman, because he was friends with both of us, and he told him, "Well, Reggie says he was misquoted."

And I have to say Thurman had the best quote I've ever heard. He said, "For three thousand f—in' words?"

I just laughed when I heard that. Bad as I felt, I had no comeback for that. That was a pretty good line.

That night, I got dressed and got out on the field as quick as I could. I heard later that a few guys went by my locker first and made sure to give my shoes and my equipment bag a good kick. I don't know, I didn't see it. It couldn't have happened with me there. But if it did happen, because I was lockering by myself in one corner of the clubhouse, they would have had to go out of their way to kick anything belonging to me.

Nobody knew if I'd said what Ward had me saying in the article or not. Nobody asked me for *my* side of it. Nobody came over and asked me about it, except for Fran Healy. Thurman never came over.

It was a situation where somebody needed to come in and say something. I felt just then like I couldn't say anything; I was too angry and resentful. Thurman was the captain, but he couldn't say anything. I think we were both in shock. And by then the writers were all over it, trying to make more of it.

I do remember that a couple days after the article came out, I was in the sauna with Fran and Thurman. And I remember that I told Thurman, "I didn't say this. I didn't say that." But there were so many things that I said I didn't say, Thurman just looked at me and said, "Reggie, how could you be misquoted that badly?"

It was just hard for him to look past it, with so many players on the team wondering what he was going to do about it. He was in as awkward a position as I was. If there was any hope for him and me fixing it, there were too many other negative things, too many other "people in the room" who were receiving it negatively—which was easy to understand. So it was hard for Thurman to take the lead and say, "Hey, I understand, let's forget about it." Something just between him and me would have been different. But I really think with everybody being involved, the media and everybody else, it was just hard to get past it.

It was a place where we needed someone in leadership to step up and say something. Get us together and have a talk with us both and try to fix things for the clubhouse atmosphere. Billy, our manager, wasn't about to do that. For Martin, this was like proving he was right.

Instead, Billy just let the bad blood fester between us. He wasn't going to help you out. I didn't even look there for help. I didn't talk to my brother about that. I didn't talk to my dad about that. I didn't know what to do. I just felt worse. I was embarrassed.

Looking back on it now, I think that this problem that I created was an opportunity for Billy Martin to prove that I was not a good fit. This gave him an opportunity to try to impress upon the team that he was in charge, rather than fix the situation. That he would embarrass me to get even. Billy was determined, regardless of the effect on the team, to prove I was a bad apple. He was so hell-bent to prove that I "wasn't a Yankee."

So I just went out there that night and played against the Red Sox. Bill Lee was pitching, and he was running his mouth, like he always was. Always going on about how we were fascists, or Nazis, or some nonsense.

I went out and had a line-drive double off Lee, and I hit another ball hard that got turned into a double play, and then I hit a long home run off a sinker that didn't sink. That tied the game in the seventh, though we lost in the end. After I hit the home run, I came back to the dugout, where the team was waiting to shake my hand.

I wouldn't shake hands. I was just fed up with all the nonsense of the last couple weeks. I kept my hands to myself, walked to the end of the bench, and sat down.

I just wanted to be alone. My thought was, "You guys are going to be that way? Okay. I'll deal with it. Let's just move on and be open about it."

You don't like me, I don't like you. Why hide it?

Of course the media made out like it was all my fault. Like I was just not going to shake their hands all of a sudden for no reason. Thinking about it later, I realized I shouldn't have given them that opportunity. I should have been the one trying to rise above it and get us back to being a team, playing for each other. Which is what I did, eventually.

But I took this opportunity to make a stand and sulk. It wasn't the thing to do. Not in the dugout.

Knowing myself at this point, I felt that it was time. Nobody was going to talk about it, and there was all this undercurrent going on . . . there needed to be a discussion. This had happened before at times, and it was why during my time in baseball I got the tag of being controversial. I wasn't willing to let things ride. There needed to be a discussion. And if you're not going to do it, then I'm going to do something and *make* you talk about it. We're going to get it out on the table now.

We're having a bumping of heads philosophically? You don't want to talk? I'm going to make you talk. I'm not going to grab you. We're not going to *physically* have a confrontation. But we are going to have a confrontation—and we're going to sit down and talk about it.

It's not that I want a pat on the back for being brutally honest. But you get to a point sometimes where there has to be a confrontation, an airing of issues and clutter. A clearing of the air. And whatever it brings, it brings.

You get to a point in time where it's gotta come out. You want to control yourself physically—and let the chips fall where they may. I was in those situations with George Steinbrenner on more than one occasion. I was in that situation with Billy Martin.

With George, it was a situation where our relationship needed work. I was not going to disrespect him, because of the changes he had made in my life and for my family and my future. But I wanted to be heard as a man.

With George, it really wasn't until I retired as a player and started to work with him. We had an issue in 1996 on the bus going to the plane to go to Texas for the playoffs. I went to talk to Joe Torre about where we were going to have dinner. I was very close to Joe, and I went up to him, and George pulled on my sleeve jacket and said, "Where do you think you're going?"

It was just that he was in a mood, and he wanted to ruffle my feathers and get on me in front of people. He sure wanted a piece of me. It was just a building up of issues and discomfort that he had with me, and I had with him. George could agitate you over a long period of time. You had to stand up to him, or he would steamroll you. He would Jim Brown you. He would Earl Campbell you. He would Joe Greene you.

We cleared the air with words, but it was very tense on the bus. We were going to Teterboro, and it was a long way. It was very tense on the plane, all the way to Texas. We didn't talk until the next morning, and it was suggested by him that I go home. When I went home, I didn't want to go *back*.

I wanted to talk about it, and he didn't. He said we would talk about it when I got back to New York, and I wasn't having any of it. I didn't want to come, but I came. We sat down and talked and started getting past it. We had another situation a few years later, but it really started a great bond between us.

George was the Boss, and he was going to let you know he was the Boss. He would start on you for some reason . . . I don't know if it was for practice or for an appetizer. He didn't smoke and he didn't drink. But he could chew you up and turn you into a salad, anytime he wanted.

I had been through that. Like George, my father was an agitator. Quick-witted, could heap a *load* of sarcasm on you. I felt that I had to stand up for myself. I had to establish myself.

I was about sixteen or seventeen the first time I stood up to my father. I had pretty good size; I was maybe 190 pounds. It was in the kitchen. We had those old aluminum chairs with the vinyl on them and the claw legs. I stood up and picked up my chair and bent it in half. I screamed, "Leave me alone!" and walked out of the room.

He was startled. Stunned. We didn't talk for a day, and then it was over. He was disciplining me, riding me for something. He could ride you until you bled. And always in front of an audience. If he had a crowd, you had a chance to be in trouble.

My father didn't drink or smoke, either. This was his recreation, gettin' on your ass.

My dad was tough. Raised as an orphan. He barely knew what date he was born. He used to tell us, "How do I know when I was born? They just wrote the date on a wall. So it's either 1903, 1907, or 1910."

He was just making us tough. He knew that the world was tough. He knew that we would be raised as colored children, that's what we were. You were going to be tough, or you could leave home, he didn't give a dang. My older sister left home; my oldest brother went into the service, to get some peace of mind. I went to college—my dad went to prison. Went to jail for six months for driving without a license—a third offense or something.

When he was younger, my dad ran numbers for some of the Italian and Jewish bookmakers in Philadelphia. It was an extra "hustle." He was a tailor and a dry cleaner, but he would do that on the side. I remembered big bags of change being around—five-, ten-pound potato bags, filled with nickels and dimes for betting the numbers.

My dad's favorite number was 010. He hit the numbers once in a while, made $100 here and there. Not bad for a nickel bet.

So by the time I came to know the Boss, I was used to a guy who could beat up on you, use you as a punching bag. During my confrontations with George, though, the comments would never broach something that you couldn't take back. You could say you're a pain in the ass; you could say you don't know what you're talking about. But we would stay away from something that would scar and could leave a mark. I swore in arguing with George, but I never swore *at* George.

With Billy, the ridicule and the embarrassment got to the point where I couldn't take it. Whether I wasn't humble enough, whether I didn't understand my role, or whatever it was—it was bumpy, it got ugly, and I couldn't handle it anymore. So I just had to let it go.

Now, that's been my past. I certainly changed that. When I got out of the game, I was able to be a lot more diplomatic about it. The reason why was, when I got out of the game at forty-something years old, a lot of the tension was gone. The demand for excellence, the demand for success, the demand for production, is no longer there on a daily basis. So you're able to relax, even in business. There's no longer the everyday demand to produce the way there is being a cleanup hitter in baseball—especially in New York, where it's just different than anyplace else.

But when you're back in the office every day, I would be in a situation where I felt it was necessary to talk. I'm going to clam up, walk by you enough times that you're going to reach out and say, "Hey, man, what the hell's wrong with you? You're too important a figure to walk around like nothing's happening." So eventually we would have some kind of conversation.

I'm not here to say my way was the right way. But this is what I did to try to get it out.

That's how I saw it at the time. Me against them: "We don't need to go to dinner; we don't need to be buddies. I'm good with it. I don't even need to come into the locker room. I'll dress down in the street. I can go dress around the corner."

So I told the writers afterward I had a bad hand, that's why I didn't shake hands after that home run off Lee. I knew they wouldn't buy it. I didn't expect them to. I was just saying stupid stuff because I thought what was going on was stupid.

Of course they went and asked the other players if they believed me. They asked Thurman for a quote. He said, "He's a f—in' liar. How's that for a quote?"

I didn't care. Except for Fran Healy, and maybe a couple of other guys, most everybody on that team was against me anyway. I wasn't going to let them get away with everything they did in the clubhouse, stare at me, curse me from across the room, kick my equipment bag. Refuse to locker next to me, not even ask for my side of the story. I wasn't going to let them do that and then have them act like it was all okay out on the field. That they were above it all. I wasn't going to pretend that that wasn't going on.

We get back in the clubhouse. Billy Martin tells the writers about me, "Ask him about the ball that got away from him at the start of the eighth. He probably forgets about those things."

Here's a manager, his team's in crisis, and all he can think to do is taunt one of his best players about a fielding play. He was right that I forgot about things like that. That's what you have to do as a major-league ballplayer: forget about the mistakes you make and move on.

But Billy wasn't going to let anything go. Have you ever heard of anything like that? You ever hear any manager saying anything like that today?

Things just kept deteriorating from there. A day or so later, someone put a note in my uniform pants that I found when I put them on. It said, "Get your f—in' ass out of here."

I saved that note for a long time. I never did find out for sure who put it there. Whoever did it, the whole situation was getting out of control fast. Finally, the next day or the day after, I went into Billy's office and had a meeting with him and the coaches. I told him I thought we should have a team meeting so I could apologize. By then, I was just trying to do the right thing.

Billy told the press he didn't think we should have a meeting. I don't know why. I just thought, "Wow, why would he say it was a bad idea?"

So instead, over the next couple days, I went around and apologized to everybody in the clubhouse myself. I said, "I just want to tell the guys I'm sorry for not shaking their hands after I hit the home run."

A lot of them, including Thurman, didn't say anything. Some of them had been out in the bullpen, and a couple of them told me, "What are you apologizing to me for? I wasn't there!"

One of them told the writers, "Can you believe this? This is becoming a f—ing circus." Another one said, "It's like *Mary Hartman, Mary Hartman*," the soap opera send-up of the time. Both said it anonymously, of course.

I didn't see why it kept going. I mean, we got into it, and I apologized. That kind of thing happens on a team over the long season, especially when you have a lot of high-spirited guys trying to win. For me, it was over.

A couple days later, I hit another home run, and when I came in the dugout, I shook every hand I could find. I would've shaken the peanut vendor's hand if he'd come down there. Thurman made sure to go and walk to the other end of the dugout. Nice . . .

A little later, Thurman tripled and scored. I tried to shake his hand. He ignored me. The next day, he scored a run, and I stuck out my hand to him on the on-deck circle. He ran right past me. I felt like a traffic cop.

When the writers asked me about why he didn't take my hand, I told them, "I don't think he saw it." When they asked him, Thurman said, "I saw it."

I thought that was funny, but I had no one to share a laugh with—only Fran, and he was in the bullpen.

I told the press, "I'm just trying to be a good guy." And I was.

Next game, Thurman shook my hand again.

"Peace, it's wonderful!" It seemed like things were starting to get right again. By now Billy had started taking me out of right field in the late innings because he said he couldn't trust my fielding. This was his way of showing me up and maintaining control, showing George and me.

I just ignored that. I just kept coming to the park, trying to play my game.

By mid-June, we were in first place again, and I thought we might finally be ready to turn everything around and play like I knew we could.

Then we went to Boston.

BOSTON

I KNOW I'VE had worse days in baseball than that series up in Boston. I just can't remember when.

The Red Sox that year were a great team, with a great lineup. Tremendous. Jim Rice, George Scott, Freddie Lynn. Yaz. Dwight Evans, Carlton Fisk. They had Butch Hobson batting ninth, where he hit thirty home runs and drove in 112 runs.

That's how good they were, their number nine guy driving in 112 runs. And we caught them just when they were getting hot.

Second pitch of the first inning in the first game there, Rick Burleson hit a ball off Catfish Hunter into the screen over the Green Monster in left. Next batter, Freddie Lynn, homers to right-center. Before the first inning was over, they had hit four home runs. Four of their first six batters.

We actually came back in that game and tied the score, but later Dick Tidrow gave up a couple more home runs, and we lost, 9–4.

You thought, "Wow! These guys are just killing us!"

You know, you never like to get beat like that. And I was very concerned about Catfish, because it was obvious that his arm wasn't right, not being able to get out of the first inning. I'd never seen that from him before. But sometimes you just run into a team that's hot, and there's nothing you can do. I mean, it was just *June*, and that was just one game. It was a drubbing—but after it was over, we were still just a half game out of first place.

The next afternoon, I was still feeling pretty good. I was feeling like, they got us yesterday, let's go get 'em today.

But what I heard much later from Fran Healy was that Billy Martin was already thinking before the game of what he could do to embarrass me. I only found this out in 2012.

Why, I don't know. Before the game, I was sitting on the bench with Bucky Dent. Billy didn't have any confidence in Bucky's bat; he kept making him bunt all the time and pinch-hitting for him. The day before, he put on a squeeze play with Bucky at the plate and Lou Piniella on third and me on second. It was just the third inning, with one out, and the score was tied. But Billy had Dent try to lay one down, and he missed the pitch and Lou was tagged out at the plate, and there went the rally.

Billy comes over to us before the game, and he tells Bucky not to worry about missing that bunt. Then he says to me, "I thought it was a good play. What did you think?"

Now, all of a sudden, he wants to know what I think. He wants me to back him up in front of Bucky.

I thought, "Whoa, here's the enemy, at my locker. Now we're buddies? Huh? I was born at night, but I wasn't born last night."

So I told him, "If you really want my opinion, I think Bucky feels like you take the bat out of his hand, making him squeeze in the second and third inning."

What was I going to say? "You don't trust your hitter enough to see if he can hit a single in the third inning of a tie game in June?" If he wanted to put on a squeeze, fine. But if he wanted to ask my opinion, I was going to tell him the truth.

I think in the end Bucky Dent proved he could hit the ball all right in Fenway Park.

Who knows, maybe that was another test, I don't know. Maybe I was supposed to prove my loyalty to Billy by going along with whatever he said.

Whatever the case, come the seventh inning, they're hitting Mike Torrez hard this time. The Sox are up 7–4, and they get a runner on, and then Jim Rice takes a full swing—and hits a pop fly out toward right. I was playing Rice deep because . . . he was Jim Rice, a great slugger who'd hit thirty to forty home runs a year.

Right field is a sun field in Fenway Park. Rice took a big cut, but he hit the ball off the handle of his bat and flared a short pop into shallow right. I took a step back at first, and only then did I see it was flared. Then I honestly thought Willie Randolph had it, so I held up. But the ball kept going over his head, it fell for a hit. I ran in and fielded it, but with the big swing, the sun, and the step back, the ball fell in. Rice was running all the way, and by the time I could get to the ball, he had a hustle double.

Billy goes out to make a pitching change then. But that wasn't all. When he got the ball from Mike Torrez on the mound, Mike said later, Billy told him, "Watch this."

Thurman told Fran Healy the same thing later. When Billy got out there, Munson said, "How'd that ball drop in?" Then, while they were out on the mound waiting for Sparky Lyle to come in from the bullpen, Martin told them, "I'm going to go get that son of a bitch," looking out at me. Mike said, "Billy, don't do it." But he was already getting Paul Blair to go out to right field and replace me.

The crowd saw Blair coming before I did. I was talking with some of the players over the railing in the bullpen in right, like I usually did during a pitching change. I heard this roar from the crowd, and I looked around, and there was Paul Blair, coming out to take my place.

I was in total amazement. Completely surprised. I asked him when he got out there, "You coming after *me*?" And he said yeah, and I asked him why. And Blair said, "You got to take that up with Billy"— though I felt Blair was enjoying it.

I ran back to the dugout, and Billy was waiting for me on the top step. He was ready for it. It was like he was onstage, and he was dying to show me up.

I put my arms out and I asked him, "What's going on?" I asked him, "What did I do?" because I genuinely didn't understand.

He said, "What do you mean, what did you do? You know what you did!"

I responded, "No, I don't!"

I just didn't know what was going on. I said, "What are you talking about?" and I started to walk away. And he goes off again. He started cussing, and he was so mad he was incoherent. I couldn't understand him very much.

I took my glasses off when I came into the dugout, and people took that to mean I was getting ready to fight. But I came in there with complete control. I was disappointed, I was confused, it was hot and muggy, and I was sweating. You sweat, your glasses fog up. And I was a little concerned, because he had a reputation as somebody who would sucker punch you, so I wanted to be prepared for that.

But I knew enough not to fight Billy Martin. I knew at that time, 1977, here I was the highest-paid player in the game, black, and my thoughts were then—and still are today—that people were going to say, "I told you *they*"—blacks—"can't handle the money. I told you that they don't know what they're doing when they're on top. Look at how they act." Regardless, I was representing minorities at this time and on this stage.

There was no way I was going to embarrass my community, or my family, or George Steinbrenner. No way I was going to embarrass *myself* by getting in a fight with this guy and scar my career.

Martin was older, a little guy, and he liked the sauce. And regardless, he was still my manager. He was the acting authority. I'm a black man. I would lose every way you could add it up in that situation if I had responded physically.

So I basically turned away. I said, "Billy, I don't know what the *freak* you want . . ." I told him, "You are not a man." And I walked away.

And he's yelling behind me, "I'll show you whether I'm a man or not!" He was yelling that he was going to kick my butt and all this kind of stuff.

Billy was almost fifty years old by then, and he must've weighed 155 pounds soaking wet. All that alcohol was going to his brain if he thought he was going to whup me.

I just said, "If you think you're going to kick my butt, you must be crazy." And I walked out of the dugout and down to the clubhouse.

Afterward, they said how Dick Howser had to grab him, and Ellie Howard and Yogi Berra had to grab him. But you have to look at how close Billy Martin was to me in those pictures of the dugout. Now, Howard was a great catcher; Yogi was a great catcher. Those guys had great reflexes.

But neither one of them would've been able to stop Billy Martin if he really wanted to fight me. Nobody could have got between us if he wanted to go.

He knew he was acting. He didn't want to take me on. It would've been like ordering an ice cream cone and getting a whole gallon.

I just walked back into the clubhouse. I had the first locker as you come out of the tunnel there in Fenway Park, and I just sat there in my uniform. Spikes, pants, shirt top, tape on my wrist, hat. I just sat in the chair there. Fully clothed. My glove over my knee. I didn't know what to make of what had just happened.

I remember Bucky Dent was in the clubhouse then, and he was seething because Billy had just pinch-hit for him again in the sixth inning. He was on the phone to his wife, wanting her to come pick him up. He was about to jump the team because he couldn't take it anymore.

And I told him, "I'm going to confront Martin when he comes in." I said, "I'm going to ask him, 'Where were you going with your comments? What were you talking about?' "

The more I thought about it, the more I felt misused. I was going to wait for Billy. I was ready to talk to him.

Then Fran Healy rushes in from the bullpen. You know, one of the writers, Ed Linn, wrote later, "Healy has the kind of competence that allows him to move very easily in any situation." I think that says it all. He looked at me, and he looked at Bucky, and he took care of everything.

Fran told me, "Reggie, whatever you do, get out of here. 'Cause this guy"—Billy—"will start a fight with you."

All I wanted to do was talk. But I told Fran, "That's all right. If he does, I'm gonna kick his ass."

And Bucky Dent was standing over there just across the clubhouse going, "Kick his ass! Kick his ass!" I think Bucky would've sold tickets, the way he felt about Billy just then.

But as always, Fran was a voice of reason. He told me, "He will start a fight with you, and you won't be able to win it. If it happens that you lay this guy out, it'll kill your reputation, you'll be suspended. And if this guy sucker punches you or hits you with something"—the way he supposedly sucker punched Dave Boswell in Minnesota—"you'll be ridiculed throughout the nation."

That's what he told me, and after a few minutes I could see that he was right. They used to call Fran "Henry Kissinger" in the clubhouse, and now I could clearly understand why. Around the top of the ninth inning, I changed into my street clothes and just left. I never did take a shower, just changed into street clothes and walked back to the hotel.

When I got back there, Henry Hecht from the *New York Post* was there. That's really all I remember. And I did an honest interview with him, and he wrote probably the most negative article I've ever had written about me. Just about how I'm an egomaniac who thinks he's an intellectual. Just a sick mess.

Later, more writers came in to talk with me—Phil Pepe, Paul Montgomery, Steve Jacobson, others. I had Mike Torrez, who was a friend, come over. I trusted him; we had the same agent, Gary Walker. I wanted him there because I didn't want to go too far. I didn't want to say too much while I knew I was still angry about what happened.

Meanwhile, in the postgame interviews, Billy's telling everybody how he pulled me because I didn't hustle. He's telling them he's thinking about hitting me with a big fine. The press is writing about how the whole team's behind him, 100 percent. How that could be, I don't know. I know Fran Healy wasn't behind him. I know Mike Torrez wasn't behind him; he was back in the clubhouse. I know Bucky Dent wasn't behind him; he was about to jump the team.

But there were a lot of guys giving the press quotes. Again, all off the record, nobody wanted to put their name to it. Saying I wasn't hustling, saying Billy was right. Without any of them even asking me about it. Without any of them getting my side of the story.

So there I was, back in the hotel, trying not to say too much, trying to restrain myself. And there was Billy bad-mouthing me to the media; there are my teammates bad-mouthing me without finding out what I had to say.

That's how the press wrote it, mostly negative about me. I had some enemies in the press box. Joe Donnelly, Moss Klein. But others, I never understood it. Henry Hecht—much as he burned me down a couple of times, he had his own issues with Billy Martin. They knew what he was like, the anti-Semitism, all the rest of it. But all they would write about was me and how I was the problem.

I had let the writers into my hotel room that night. Today, there is no way on earth I would let a writer into my room. But I did then, and to me the story is, "Here's a guy who was nice enough to have us into his room, who was open enough to have us into his room for a press conference."

Instead, I came to understand later that they wrote about it like it was this wild scene. They wrote about all these insignificant things, like how I was walking around with my shirt off. I honestly don't remember how I was dressed, but I was in *my* room. What's the big deal if I'm in my room with my shirt off? Why would they bother to describe how I was dressed in my room?

Some people even wrote that there was a blonde in my shower while the writers were there. That wasn't true. If I had someone there, why would I tell the girl to hang out in the shower for half an hour? If I had a woman in my room, I would not invite the media in. I would not do it. But if there *was* a blonde in the shower—lucky me. Why would you write about that?

There were some accounts of how I was walking around with an open Bible. I got through it, I got through that whole year with the help of my friends and by the grace of God. But anytime that I mentioned the Bible or God back then, there were some people who did their best to ridicule it. I was told they made mention of how I had my shirt off and I was wearing a cross, a gold cross I bought in Oakland in 1969 and wore most of the time, and some other gold chain . . .

That made me crazy. It made me sound like I had a Mr. T starter kit around my neck.

I did not see *The Bronx Is Burning*. I saw enough of it advertised on TV to turn my stomach. I've been in ten movies, and I've never seen one I've been in from start to finish. I've been in probably thirty or forty sitcom episodes, and I've never seen one from the first minute to the last. I've seen the *Yankeeography* on me, but I've never watched it from beginning to end. But the portrayal of the person I was in *The Bronx Is Burning* really hurt me.

I barely remember the scene in my room that night. I don't even remember who *was* there. I know that Fran Healy came by, Mike Torrez. What I remember was only talking to Henry Hecht and Murray Chass. I had a close relationship with Steve Jacobson, so I probably talked to him as well. I might have talked to some other reporters just because they were there.

I did have support from some people. I heard from George. He was supportive in general, though he didn't quite understand what was going on. I remember I got a call from Jesse Jackson, a "stick with it" call that was helpful. My father called, asked me how I was doing. My oldest brother, Joe, called to support me.

I don't know if I handled it well or if I should have been more diplomatic. Color stood out back then. It was a lot of what people saw in 1977. And if you spoke, you were arrogant, you were self-centered, a clubhouse lawyer. Try to express yourself with honesty—it didn't work. The media weren't used to it.

I remember around that time I said, "I'll take it, but I won't eat it."

I wasn't going to internalize it. But it was a galling situation I was in. I had my pride—sometimes that's not a good thing. Later in life, I realized that pride gets in the way sometimes. To be a good Christian, sometimes you have to lose the pride.

What I was really trying to protect, I think, was my integrity and dignity. With your integrity, sometimes you have to walk a fine line of honesty. Sometimes I would think, or say, "They're screwing with me again. They think, 'Why isn't he just glad to be here? Why doesn't he just shut up and pretend?' "

But that's an angered response. You have to be careful not to let your anger run away with you, because when you do, you lose time to learn.

That's what I was starting to figure out. I knew you really couldn't touch a manager. You couldn't physically fight back. You had to stand at home plate and fight with your bat. You can speak in your own defense at times, but you must realize there is no one who is going to come to help you. You realize you're one against all the rest (Fran, Dent, Catfish, and a few others excepted).

I was learning. But it would still take more time.

Fran knew so much that went on. He knew all the people who were instigating and who were into their childish plans and plots. He knew what was going on between the manager and the players, between the players and other players; he knew what was going on between the owner and the manager. He knew it all. It was strange: They knew we were friends during this time.

He told me later, "I wouldn't tell you half the stuff that went on." He said if he had, "it would just have made you crazy." He felt I would've torn Billy Martin apart. (No.)

What nobody told me at the time—what not even Mike Torrez, who was on the mound, told me—was Billy saying, "Watch this," before pulling me out of that game. I have no idea why they didn't tell me, and I really don't care.

But if it was out of worry about what I was going to do with a physical confrontation, I just wish that people would have more respect for me than that.

Was I going to fight Billy? That's stupid. What would that do? How would that help?

I understood the situation I was in, being African American, the highest-paid athlete in the country at the time. To have created dissent at the time, with the social mores the way they were?

You can't rebel physically in front of a nation. You have to get back to trying to level the field with patience and great play. With performance, so that you're trying to prove what you say by doing things. That takes time. You can't just go into the guy's office and create a confrontation. It's not what you do no matter who you are and what color you are.

When you're in a situation where the authority has most of the power, you can't just run and rewrite what goes on socially. What is respected in the world. You got to take your time and try to traipse through it. And my time would come.

Fran is a really nice guy and got along with everybody. He served as the peacemaker. He came into that clubhouse in Boston, saw what was going on, and sorted it out. He got me to leave; he helped get Bucky to calm down.

You know, he not only helped me, but he probably helped save Billy Martin's job with what he did. I mean, if Bucky Dent leaves, then the story is not just about me and Billy Martin. Then it's about another discontented player, a *white* player walking out, too. Then the story becomes "Billy Martin has lost control of his team." And that's probably the end of him.

Instead, the next morning, I had a meeting with Billy and Gabe Paul at the Boston Sheraton. I always liked Gabe. I don't think he was ever against me in any way. I know he had trouble with Billy as well.

Later that year, he had an incident, a small stroke, I think. And Billy and some of the players used to make fun of that, used to make fun of how he spoke after that. I liked him. It was easy to see he cared.

The meeting was at eight o'clock in the morning. I got there at eight.

Billy got there about eight thirty. Still with alcohol on his breath.

I don't know if he was drunk at our breakfast or if he'd been up all night. Gabe started talking about everybody getting along and how the Boss had called to see what needed to be done. He asked us to say something, and I just told him what happened. I said I was hustling. I was just playing deep on Rice, and I thought Randolph had a chance at the ball. I told him how Rice took a big swing, and right away I took a step back. I couldn't get in after the step back, and it fell in.

Right away, Billy's furious. He stood up and looked at me, and he said, "Get up, boy! I'm gonna kick the s—t out of you!"

I looked at him. I couldn't believe what was going on. I turned to Gabe, and I said, "You heard it. You heard him call me 'boy.' "

I said to Gabe, "You're Jewish. You understand the comment! How do you think I feel when he says that to me?"

And Gabe told Billy he was out of line. He said, "Sit down, Billy. Sit down or get out."

Billy sat down then, and he started trying to defend himself. Started trying to make out there was nothing racial about what he said.

There really wasn't a meeting. The writers all called it a meeting when they heard about it later. But there was no meeting. There was no attempt to have a meeting. Billy was too far gone, thanks to alcohol or whatever. Pretty soon Gabe said, "You need to leave now." I then sat down and had breakfast with Gabe, and he basically tried to soothe me.

He said, "I'm sorry. I'm sorry for that." But then the next thing he said was, "You gotta get along with him."

I said, "Gabe, you know I wanted to be traded. Why wouldn't you let me go away from here? Why wouldn't you let me go? Be human, let me go. It's too painful here for me. Please."

But there was no conceding from Gabe. They wouldn't let me go. I guess I was needed. They couldn't just turn loose their free-agent signing and admit a mistake was made. They weren't going to fire Billy.

I always thought about society at the time. In the 1970s, referencing my color with the word "boy" was no big deal to people. Today, he'd be fired. The mores of the world were what they were. Things hadn't caught up. It was the way of the world. He could call me "boy," but if I spoke out, as a black man, I was the troublemaker. I was supposed to feel lucky that I was in the league. I should have been glad to have been there.

People knew what happened in that meeting. I mentioned it to people. I told Fran, and I told some of the writers. It came out in the media that he called me "boy." But nobody called on the Yankees to fire Martin. Instead, it was my problem.

People forget, but I went back out and played that Sunday afternoon. I remember I hit three balls hard off Fergie Jenkins, but all right at somebody. That's the way that whole series went up there.

They clobbered Ed Figueroa, hit another five home runs. They had sixteen home runs in three games, which was some kind of record. They outscored us by 30–9.

But somehow it was all my fault for letting Jim Rice take that extra base. In an inning when the Red Sox didn't even score.

Afterward, Figueroa called out the whole team. He accused everybody of drinking too much, playing cards all the time in the clubhouse. He was really accusing Martin of not running a tight locker room. Figueroa was mad; you had Dent thinking of jumping the team—it was starting to get through that maybe it wasn't all me. Maybe the trouble with the team had to do with somebody else as well.

We went to Detroit after Boston, and by that time the Boss had had enough. The way I heard it—through Fran—was that George came to Detroit planning to fire Billy right then and there. He was going to give his job to Dick Howser, who a little later became a terrific manager with the Yankees and the Royals. Billy would've been gone, but Dick wouldn't take the manager's job out of loyalty to Billy, who had hired him as a third-base coach.

After that, they managed to piece it together again. Gabe talked to Billy, and he talked to George. Fran Healy was talking to everybody, soothing everyone's feelings. He was used, really, as the person to communicate with me, from management on down.

What I was told was that they didn't think they could fire Billy because then it would look like I was running the team. They were afraid of what the fans might think if they fired Billy. Hmm-hmm. Nineteen seventy-seven. Think that would happen today?

You think about it now, it's crazy. You're managing a team, you show up looped for a meeting with the GM, half an hour late, then you challenge your star player to a fight and direct a racial slur toward him . . . you're going to end up in rehab. At best. Chances are you're going to be fired. Today, people try to clamp down on that sort of behavior.

But in 1977, with the Yankees, Billy Martin just went on managing.

Eye Exam

SOME OF THIS, when I look back now, I just have to laugh. I got through it, and I lie down at night now and I think, "Boy, I have had a great life." Some of these experiences that I've had were extremely interesting. I'm glad for all of the people I've had to share them with. Even the difficult times, they were special, when I think about them now.

But at the time, it was tough to get through. Those weeks right after what happened in Boston were the worst part of the season for me. It was the worst time I'd had in baseball. I don't know how I would've gotten through without my dad, my brother Joe, Gary Walker, Fran, and a local friend in town, Tony Rolfe. I could not have done it alone. Gary Walker called every day and kept talking about building character. I told him I had enough character, I didn't want any more!

It became very clear that almost everybody—not only in New York, but all around the country—was on Billy's side. The day after the Boston series, we arrived in Detroit for a nationally televised game against Mark "the Bird" Fidrych, who had been their rookie sensation the year before, famous for talking to the baseball out on the mound. There must've been nearly fifty thousand people there, and when Billy went out to give the umps the lineup, he got a standing ovation. Another trump card.

I knew what that meant. I knew Billy was still popular from when he managed the Tigers. But it was a message as well. He was going to be the hero, I the goat. (What was it, racial, social, me? Who knew? It didn't make sense.)

And from then on, it was like that everywhere. Boos for me, cheers for him. Didn't matter where we went. Billy was the hero. Whenever he put his head out of the dugout, they would cheer him.

Whenever I went out to right field, they would boo. I got booed all around the league.

It was heartbreaking at times. Every stadium in the league, it was "Reggie sucks." And that was the polite version. Whole ballparks chanting that. I got booed at home as well. Any little article that came out and was negative, they would boo me more.

I felt alone so much. The fans just beat me down. And the media did their best to pile on. It was brutal. Papers all over the country joined in.

Billy knew it, too. After the game in Detroit, he was going around telling the press about the hand he got: "Wasn't that super? I'll bet George just loved to hear that." Rubbing it in. George and Gabe Paul were having problems with him as well. They'd lost control of Billy. George had flown up to Detroit intending to fire him, but he didn't when Howser refused to take the job.

So Billy stayed and I prayed. And George ended up staying to give us one of his football pep talks before the game. He came into the locker room and told us, "You guys are a finger snapping away from firing your manager."

That was the first we knew for sure Billy *wasn't* fired. I wasn't really paying attention. I was in a whirlwind with what was going on from day to day, with being the why and the what for, and the reason why he was going to be fired, and then he's not. I was in an emotional knot. It was too big of a deal for me while I was just trying to play. At that time of year, I was just starting to get a little better.

George came right out and said, "I think this ball club is prejudiced against certain individuals on the ball club." He didn't come right out and say it was a black-white thing, but it was implied that he meant me. I was impressed and felt good about his awareness and sensitivity. It showed compassion that I didn't know he had.

The great thing about George Steinbrenner was he really didn't care who you were. If he didn't like you, it didn't matter what you looked like. He just wanted the Yankees to win.

He told us that everybody in every other city was gunning for us, and they wanted to see us fall apart. We had to pull together. Then we went out and lost, on *Monday Night Baseball*. I drove in the only run we got off the Bird. But then in the seventh I tried to dive for a ball Mickey Stanley hit, and I lost it in the glare from the Tiger Stadium lights. He got a double out of it, and they scored what stood up as the winning run soon after.

At the end of the inning, I was so upset with myself I ran right through the dugout and into the clubhouse. I looked so bad even Billy and Dirt Tidrow, who never much liked me either, came back to see if I was okay. A rare moment of consolation. I said after the game, "Man, that's the worst I've ever felt on a ball field. I ought to quit. Give up."

I didn't give up. I never really thought about giving up. But that's how bad I was feeling. That's how much Billy and the whole situation were starting to affect me.

Instead, I went out there the next day, got two hits, and drove in a run, though we lost again. The day after that, we were leading, 7–2, got down, 10–7, but I had two more hits and drove in the winning runs with a double to help break our slide.

That's the way you have to play the game of baseball. You have to answer the bell every day. I watch the players we have on the Yankees today and try to explain to people the admiration I have for guys like Jeter, and Cano, and Teixeira. For Andy Pettitte, and Sabathia, and the great Rivera. They answer the bell every day. Tired or not. Can't get sick, don't get toothaches. Upset stomachs. No days off.

A couple years ago, the Yankees played thirty-six games in thirty-seven days, I think. They'd leave New York and go to Toronto. Then they'd leave Toronto and go to Chicago. After Chicago, they went to Texas. They flew home, got in at five in the morning, got up at two or three in the afternoon. Which means your "off day" is really four in the afternoon until ten at night, because you have to play the next day.

It's a degree of difficulty that's not understood by the public or the fans. It is understood by the players, how hard it is. Guys who think baseball and play baseball from February to November. Every day, all day.

You know, you're supposed to pray every day, all day. You have choices. In baseball, you play every day, all day. And you don't have choices.

You develop a different bond, a different relationship with the people and the players you hang with. You're with these guys for 162 games, thirty-five days in the spring, the postseason. For more than two hundred days a year, you're in this environment that becomes an extension of family. Relationships become strong. Look at Jeter, Rivera, Pettitte, Posada. They will be lifetime friends. Same with me, Bando, Holtzman, Rudi. Same with Randolph, Guidry, Piniella, Goose. Regardless of how far the friendship goes, you still develop great respect for players like Munson, Nettles, Lyle, and others, when you play with them. Over the years, you learn to respect great talent.

With Billy Martin, he was something else. He was something I hadn't encountered yet in my career. I'd always had managers who were master psychologists or at least able to go with the flow of a team. To make sure it kept running smooth, to keep out distractions.

Billy *was* a distraction on his own. If nothing else, he was always trying to get into your head, all the time. To play some kind of game, to prove something, I don't know. I didn't want to pay attention to all the nonsense that was going on out there, to what the fans thought, or the writers. To play baseball at this level, and to do it as well as you can every day, you *have* to tune the negatives out. But Billy made it almost impossible.

To give you an example, after we pulled out the last game of the Detroit series, we came back home to play Boston again, and I had to go out to get my eyes examined. This came from the front office and from Billy, after I lost that ball in the lights. It befuddled me, but I went and got a full exam anyway.

We were five games down to Boston by then, and we couldn't afford to get down much more, even that early, against a team like the Red Sox. They were threatening to run away and hide. They'd just smoked

Baltimore, four straight. They were getting great pitching, and you couldn't keep them in the park. Coming into Yankee Stadium, they'd hit thirty-three home runs in their last ten games, which was another record.

I guess their success was based on more than just me playing Jim Rice too deep.

They were starting Bill Lee again in the first game, and I couldn't wait to get out there. I was five for nine against Lee that year, with two home runs. Despite everything, I'd been slowly working my way into a groove at the plate, driving in runs almost every game. I was psyched.

Then, an hour before the game, Billy takes my name off the lineup and writes in Roy White's. He told the press that he was worried my eyes were still dilated. From the eye exam he and the front office wanted me to get. The eye exam I had the day before.

The joke was on me. He'd set me up real nice. Of course, he never asked me if my eyes were dilated. He didn't have time to do that. He didn't even have time to tell me, man-to-man, that I was out of the lineup for the biggest game of the year so far, just let me read it off the lineup card there in the dugout.

I'd heard, however, that he had time to sneak a dead mackerel into Bill Lee's locker.

I was so mad when I saw the lineup change I just threw my bat down and walked out into the outfield so I wouldn't say anything to the writers. I even forgot my glove. But that was all right, I was learning. I was just going to keep my mouth shut and take whatever that man had to give out.

I know Gabe Paul and George were not happy with it. In the second inning, Gabe sent the club doctor down to examine my eyes. He confirmed that, somehow, after thirty-six hours, they were no longer dilated. Gabe then had to call down to Billy in the dugout and tell him explicitly that I was available.

That's how crazy things could get on a ball team run by Billy Martin. The general manager has to send the team physician down to examine a star on the team during the biggest game of the year so far and confirm he's all right . . . so the manager won't lie about not playing him to the press. I've never heard of anything else like that happening in the whole history of the game.

But I didn't say anything. I didn't say anything, even though Billy insisted on starting Catfish that night and I knew his arm was killing him. Martin knew it, too, but he put him out there anyway. Catfish was a great, great pitcher, and Billy was treating him like that. That would come back later, too, because nothing ever did go away for good on the Yankees. But for the time being, I just sat on the bench and kept my mouth shut.

The game was entertaining. That was when I first understood how Boston–New York games were like a war. There was nothing else like that then, and there still isn't today. I'd seen it in Boston. I heard the stuff they yelled at me out in right. In center, Mickey Rivers had to put on a batting helmet; they were throwing so many metal objects at his head. Somebody threw a smoke bomb in the outfield.

It was like that in Yankee Stadium as well. All sorts of stuff being thrown on the field, fans from the two teams getting into fights. It was wild, like some kind of soccer match down in South America more than a baseball game.

Catfish was a gamer. He pitched about as gutsy a ball game as I've ever seen that night. He went all the way to two outs in the ninth before they had to pull him, and he only gave up five hits. Trouble was three of them were homers, and we were down, 5–3. Bill Lee *wasn't* hurting, but—what a surprise—he came up short in a big game and didn't make it out of the fourth inning.

Bill Campbell came on in the sixth, though, and he was trouble. The Red Sox worked him like an old horse that year. He was their closer, but they brought him in in the sixth inning, as if they were playing a World Series game. He'd pitched a lot of innings the year before in Minnesota, and it seemed like he could take it. He'd been saving or winning the game almost every night for them during their win streak.

Most managers then didn't have a set system for working relievers the way they do today. They didn't designate them for certain innings, the way Tony LaRussa came up with—a man for the seventh inning, a setup man in the eighth, and your shutdown guy in the ninth. Dick Williams was much more fluid about how he worked his bullpen. He'd throw in guys at all different times, particularly in the playoffs—though he never overworked them.

It didn't look like you *could* overwork Bill Campbell. He came in with men on second and third, nobody out, and got three straight pop flies, just like that. He breezed through the seventh, the eighth, into the ninth, throwing that big screwball of his, and all you could do was hit it straight up in the air.

Billy finally put me up to pinch-hit in the ninth, with one out and nobody on. He sent me up to hit for Bucky, which was perfect for him, a chance to show up two guys he hated with just one at-bat. The crowd booed me, of course. They'd given Billy a standing ovation when he brought the lineup card out before the game.

I just had to ignore it and stay within myself. Campbell didn't throw me screwballs, because you don't throw screwballs to a left-hander. (Don't ask me why, 'cause I don't know.) Instead, he threw me everything but the kitchen sink, fastball, changeup, curve. I hung in there, but Campbell got me to ground to first, and I thought that was it for us.

Everybody booed again, and I know Billy must've been pleased. It seemed to me it was almost a death wish he had by then. I wonder if everything would've exploded again if he'd lost that game without starting me. We would've been six games back then, and George would've been . . . well, you tell me! I wonder if Billy would've finally got himself fired.

I wonder if he cared. Or if winning whatever game he was playing with me took first priority. I didn't know what he was doing. It seemed crazy to me.

But instead of us going down to a loss that night, Willie Randolph sliced a triple into left-center that got past Yaz. Next pitch, Campbell left a screwball up, and Roy White, who was a great clutch player, turned on it and just buried it in the upper deck.

Two pitches, two big hits, just like that. The game was tied, and Billy was off the hook.

I stayed in the game. Sparky pitched a couple great innings of relief and outlasted Bill Campbell. They finally pulled him for the eleventh.

Remember, this guy was their closer! He came in in the sixth inning, and he stayed till the *eleventh.*

I came up against Ramón Hernández with guys on first and second. Besides my eyes, the reason Billy said he didn't start me was that we were facing a lefty, Bill Lee, who I was five for nine against. Hernández is a lefty. I pounded a ball down the right-field line, and the game was over. We won.

Afterward, the press was all around, but I wasn't going to bite. I told them I was just lucky to get the hit. They asked me what my emotions were like, and I said, "I try to forget my emotions these days." They asked me how my eyes were, and I just said they were fine. When they asked me about being taken out of the lineup, I had no comment.

They asked me how I felt before the game, and I told them, "I forget how I felt. I forget a lot of things lately. I can't say anything. If you were in my water for a week, you'd understand why. It's cold over here."

That was as much as they were going to get from me. At least on this day.

Calling My Dad

The next afternoon, Mike Torrez came out, and he wasn't taking any nonsense. He shut the Sox down, beat 'em, 5–1, and we beat them again in the ninth inning the following day. All of a sudden we were only two games down, and everything was right with the world again. The Yankees win, the Yankees win.

But of course it wasn't over. It never really was with Billy. We played a little better for a while, got back into first place in early July. But then we started to struggle again. We just couldn't seem to sustain anything.

Thurman was in a bad mood. He was a typical catcher; catchers are always nicked up. I got to say, most of your catchers are underpaid—it's the toughest position on the field. Try putting an extra fifteen to twenty pounds of equipment on before you sit down at your desk in the morning. He kept getting hurt: He got cut over his eyes; he needed seven stitches in his hand. He kept playing, because that's who Thurman was. But he wasn't happy. He was still fuming about his contract. He started ripping Steinbrenner for interfering with Billy and dictating the lineup.

When we fell behind the Orioles in the standings, George started ripping Billy, saying Earl Weaver should be manager of the year, telling the press he'd got Billy everything he wanted and he still couldn't win. Billy started telling the writers he just ignored all the notes George sent down.

And then, of course, Billy brought the whole merry-go-round back to me, telling the reporters that what the players were thinking is that "the whole club lineup has been changed since we got Reggie."

Now, here we go again. This was about Thurman's contract, Billy, and George. Now Billy has me back in the mix. Uh-oh, maybe I *am* the straw stirring the drink again!

Yes, the lineup changed. I was playing right field and hitting fifth or sixth. Instead of Carlos May, who hit .227 for us with two home runs, before Gabe sold him to the Angels. That was one terrible change. I could see why that would upset everything.

It went on and on like that, all the pettiness and the silliness. It wasn't just me, either. I would get down to first base sometimes in a game, and guys would say to me, "Man, I don't see how you can be here." As in, "I don't see how you can put up with all that crap." Billy. Everybody talking to the press but never putting their names on it. I didn't operate like that. Everything I said, I put my name on. People knew right where to come and find me.

The worst was a series we had out in Kansas City in mid-July, just before the All-Star Game. It was the tail end of a long road trip for us. We were playing bad and had fallen a couple games out of first place.

Everybody was tired and on edge, and of course there was another big controversy going on over nothing. Mr. Steinbrenner called a meeting while we were in Milwaukee and gave all of us who were going to the All-Star Game $300 so we could bring our wives and girlfriends and families. He gave everybody else $300, too, so they could get out of town for a couple days.

I thought it was a very generous thing to do, and I told people so. I told some of the writers, "I mean, how nice can you be?"

Wrong thing to say. Believe it or not, I even got in trouble for that. It seemed there might or might not have been some rule about giving guys money like that, so the league announced it was going to look into it. Some of the guys started worrying they were going to lose their money, so they blamed it on me, of course.

Why not? It's like throwing dirt on a guy's grave. Other players going around ripping everybody anonymously—that was okay. Me thanking the owner for giving us all a bonus he didn't have to give us . . . that was a crime.

When we got to Kansas City for our next series against the Royals, everybody was mad at me for not keeping my mouth shut about their $300. I had another bad series in the field. In the second game, Hal McRae hit a ball deep to right-center. I ran into Mickey Rivers going after it, and it rolled all the way to the wall. I tried to pick it up there, but I dropped it.

Picked it up again. Dropped it again. Before I could get it in, McRae had gone all the way around the bases for an inside-the-park home run.

I would take the blame for that, because I'm the right fielder. Mickey's the center fielder; he's in charge of everything out there. He was calling for the ball, but I just didn't hear him. I accept the blame, no question.

But then it just turned out to be an excuse to get on me.

The end of that inning, I came back to the dugout, and Sparky Lyle, who was pitching, was standing on the top step. He looked right at me and said, "Get your head out of your ass and play the game right!" And I looked back at him like, "What are you talking about?"

I really didn't understand. I was still a little dazed from running into Mickey. It wasn't like I had dropped the ball or made some bonehead play on purpose. I was embarrassed by what happened—though it also didn't make a damned bit of difference in the game. We were already behind by 4–1 in the seventh, and it only meant that we lost 5–1.

Sparky, I felt, was making a grandstand play and putting on a show, talking down to me like that: "Get your head out of your ass!"

I just looked at him, and I didn't know what to say. I went in and sat down. I felt like, "I just ran into a guy, and screwed up a ball, don't tell me that." I wondered where his reaction came from. You're supposed to pick up a teammate. I wouldn't run in to the mound right after Sparky gave up a dinger and say, "Get your head out of your ass!"

I thought, "Why would you say that to me?" It pierced me. It hurt. I felt bad. I wasn't prepared for a player to almost challenge me with fighting words like that. And nobody said a thing; nobody came to my defense. It was a lonely feeling.

Things just kept getting worse. Billy would sit me whenever he could, come up with some new way to insult me. That July alone, I was booed, benched, and sued.

The suit came after the All-Star Game, which was in Yankee Stadium that year. After the game I was going to the parking lot with George Scott, who was an old friend and was staying at my place while he was in town. Along the way to the lot, I was signing autographs for a bunch of the kids out there, but finally I said all right, I had to go.

One of these kids—no more than maybe ten, twelve years old—he calls me one of the vilest names I've ever heard. I started toward him, just to chase him away, and he takes off running and falls down. The next day, his family files suit against me. Nice, huh?

The kid wasn't hurt, and the suit got dismissed. But nothing else seemed like it was ever going to change. That was when Phil Pepe called to ask me about the whole incident with the kid. I just told him, "I don't want to play in New York. I don't want to be here anymore."

That's how bad it really felt. I don't know what I would've done, I don't know what I could've done, if it hadn't been for faith and family and the friends I had.

I usually had good support from George Steinbrenner. I said it at the time, "I love that man. He treats me like I'm somebody. The rest of them, they treat me like I'm dirt." It was true, too. I could go into his office at any time, he'd listen to me, and I'd cry on his shoulder a bit. I had support from my agent, Gary Walker. He would read the Bible to me over the phone from Arizona on a daily basis, whenever I'd listen. He didn't travel, but he would get on the phone with me and read me passages, things of support. He would stress, "Get personal desires out of the way." He would say, "Stop thinking of yourself."

He would tell me, "Always remember, when God reaches out and grabs your right hand, He never lets go." He used to say, "Reggie, behold. That is, 'be whole.' You know that God made all of those things around you. Enjoy them. Put your manly thoughts out of your mind, and do not create clutter. Appreciate. Be grateful. Be humble. Ask God to help you clear your mind." That's all I was asking God: "Help me stay with it. Stay with me now. Stay with me."

Once I did that with Gary, I was good to go. I was good to compete with whatever the world was bringing me. But I needed that every day.

Fran Healy was a tremendous help, as always. There was a guy here in New York, Tony Rolfe, he was very supportive. He was one of George's very close friends who became my friend. Also the Fisher brothers, Larry and Zach, who've both passed. A guy named Ralph Destino, who was chairman of Cartier, the elegant jewelry company, he was always there for me. And of course my dear friend and agent, Matt Merola.

These were solid businessmen who understood what was going on in the city socially and appreciated what I was going through. They were staid businessmen in their late forties or early fifties, but they knew how things worked in New York, what the press was like, and you could talk to them about it, I could share things.

They'd just say, "Reggie, you're playing ball, the city loves you. Don't worry about small-minded people, worry about your job. Listen to your father. You're going to be all right. Keep playing hard." Things like that.

So I did. So I tried to.

My father was the key. He pounded it into me that I had to keep one thing in the foreground, and that was hitting baseballs. When I was going bad, or when George Steinbrenner thought I was letting Billy Martin bother me too much, he would call my dad.

That he did. He would call up my father and say, "Mr. Jackson, Reggie is letting Billy Martin bother him now. And the press as well. I can tell these things are bothering him, because he's not hitting. I need you to come up and see me on Monday."

This would be on a Friday. My father would call me and say, "I need you to meet me at your brother Joe's house," which was near McGuire Air Force Base in New Jersey. He was stationed there in the air force at the time.

My father would call and say, "I don't have time to go see George Steinbrenner. I've got to be at work on Monday at eight in the morning." He would say, "I'll give you an hour and a half to get down there after the game on Sunday, and we can have supper together. I need to straighten you out so you can start pounding on that ball again and just get Billy Martin out of your mind."

So he'd have me down there with Joe, and sometimes with my other siblings, and he'd talk. I had tremendous support from Dad. He would tell me, "Billy Martin is nothing to you. Don't worry about him. The money Mr. Steinbrenner is paying you should be your focus. Do your job. You don't want to come out here in the real world and get a job with me, working in my shop at $60 a week."

My dad was still a tailor, still owned a laundry and dry cleaning business. That was who he was. He'd say, "You've got a good job, you're getting paid well, take care of your family. Go on and do what you're supposed to do. Beat on the baseball."

For my dad, you just went on, and did what you needed to do, and appreciated that you had the opportunity. You appreciated God for having blessed you with the skills and the ability you have—for the opportunity you had to put good meals on the table and get a good home for your family. If you had the other essentials—a roof over your head, a pillow to lay your head on, heat in the house—you were blessed and lucky.

My dad liked to say, "I'm not concerned about you being happy. You be grateful and thankful. And go on and do what you need to do."

My oldest brother, Joe, was the same way. He was a chief master sergeant in the air force then. He's a wonderful guy, very understanding of the necessities of life. He had that same attitude: "Go and do your job, Reg. Forget that Martin guy. Don't worry about him. He is not your family."

But my father really knew what playing baseball every day was like. He'd played ball with the Bacharach Giants, down in Atlantic City, and with the Newark Eagles in the old Negro Leagues, and he knew what it was like. I'm sure he could have been a major-league player if the color line hadn't been in place.

It was harder in his day. He also had to work as the traveling secretary and drive the team bus, which was typical back in the Negro Leagues. But he knew what it meant to keep your mind on what's most important, to keep concentrating on the task in front of you. He would tell me, "You get back out there and beat on that ball, son."

It may seem strange to some people, I know, to have Mr. Steinbrenner, the team owner, calling up my dad. I thought it was cool.

I wasn't a grown man. I was thirty-one. At that age, even when you have two, three kids, you're not grown yet. At least I wasn't, being on my own, in this big town. I needed help—and it was nice to know somebody cared. Thanks, George.

I can't tell you how much it brought me back into myself, going down there to southern New Jersey on a Sunday. Having most of the family there. Not everybody. My mother was ill at the time; she had a bad heart. But she was still supportive, still let me know she was behind me. Having the rest of the family around the table there, knowing that they cared, that they wanted to help and see me do well in the world—that was everything.

We all know the importance of family. Everybody cooked and helped out, then we'd sit down and eat home-cooked food. It was extremely important, getting to be around your brothers and sisters, having your dad talk to the family at the time. Give everybody support, correction, comfort. You'd go in with need and come out armed for the world.

That was tremendous. That's one key to the whole conflict between Billy and me, too.

You know, I had a dad. Growing up, he could be hard on me when he thought I needed it, but he was always there. He was always proud of me. When he was older, he even had cards made up that read, "Marty the Tailor, Father of the Famous Reggie Jackson."

George Steinbrenner, he had a dad who was important in his life. He sounds like he was always hard on him as well, always pushing him. But he was there.

Billy didn't grow up with a dad. I understood he was always looking for one. The story has it that Billy was always hoping Casey Stengel would be a father to him, when he was playing for the Yankees back in the 1950s.

I remember hearing that Billy always complained, "I'm sitting in my hotel room, and George is wining and dining Reggie all around town. Why doesn't he ask me, too? Why doesn't he invite me to lunch, why doesn't he take me to dinner?"

I think Billy was looking for George to be a friend, and he saw me as competition. That's what Fran Healy thought as well, that Billy saw me as soaking up all the love from George.

There never were that many owners who really hung around with their players. I know Horace Stoneham used to like to hang out with Willie Mays, but other than that . . .

George really liked it. I know he thought of Thurman like a son. I'm sure he thought of Piniella that way, as well as Mariano Rivera or Derek Jeter. I know George felt very close to Derek. I remember when he was telling me that he was going to go to Cincinnati and make him the captain. It was a big deal for him.

I'm sure that he felt that way about me as well. The number of George's suite in the new Stadium could have been anything he wanted, and he made it number 44. I was aware of how Billy felt. I stopped hanging out with George because it bothered Billy so much. I know George was even complaining to his friends, guys like Tony Rolfe and Larry Fisher, "Reggie doesn't hang out with me anymore. I don't know what's wrong. He doesn't talk to me."

I don't know, maybe if George had invited Billy along things would've gone differently. But you know, Billy had trouble letting people know what he wanted. He had trouble letting people in, letting them see what was going on with him.

I did know that he had a habit of coming to the ballpark late. He would show up ten to thirty minutes before the first pitch sometimes and have alcohol on his breath. He'd have his sunglasses on, his hat pulled all the way down over his glasses. He would go in his office and fall asleep on the couch, while Dick Howser got the team prepared to play, wrote the lineup, and so on, sometimes. Dick really ran the team until it was time for Billy to wake up, just before the game. You'd see Billy wandering down the hall to the dugout. It was strange, obviously.

Sometimes Dick would take the lineup out to the umpires on his own. Billy wouldn't like it, he'd get mad at him, but Dick would tell him, "I gotta give 'em something! You weren't here. You weren't in the dugout. What was I to do? We're playing in five minutes! The umpires are standing at home plate. Should I just tell 'em to hold on?"

There was always plenty of drinking in baseball. There is less today, without a doubt. Back in the old days, guys *drank*—and drank and drank. It was like the pictures you'd see of old movie stars: They always had a drink in one hand and a cigarette in the other. That was accepted; that was then. But even for that time, Billy drank a lot. Billy drank too much. It impacted him and those around him.

You just couldn't drink like he did. It wouldn't have been tolerated by George if he'd known about it—if he'd known the full extent of it. George didn't drink himself; he was a Diet Coke guy. But obviously, everybody would cover for Billy. Writers would cover for him, players would cover for him, staff would cover for him. It never got in the papers. Except in the winter.

Now that I think back about it, it's amazing that word never got out of the clubhouse, nobody ever said anything, and as a team we just . . . went by it. We didn't walk by it. You just went by—without attention being called to anyone upstairs. I think it went back to the old locker-room placard:

What you do here
What you see here
What you hear here
What you say here
Let it stay here
When you leave here.

I understood the coaches. They were loyal to their manager, and Billy was lucky to have them to back him up. That was maybe the best coaching staff that I was ever associated with—Yogi, Ellie Howard, Bobby Cox, Gene Michael. Dick Howser, who really was the manager. Hall of Fame, anybody? Guys who played on championship teams, or managed them, or built them. There was a lot of baseball knowledge there. They had all been with the Yankees for years, even decades.

George made sure to keep past Yankees with the organization. It was the same thing with the great coaching staff that Joe Torre had. I think if George were still around, there would be more former Yankees players still associated with the team. George kept people around; he paid 'em—even if they didn't do anything, he still paid 'em. George had great understanding of the Yankees brand.

You really didn't expect them to say anything. The players didn't say anything. Nothing wrong with that. To this day, there is a baseball rule where you just don't talk about so many negatives. You just ignored it. You were true to the code of the locker room. To this day, nobody really talks about Billy's battles with the bottle. It's laughable, it's tragic—and it's like it never existed. It's an amazing story. It was so blatant.

Somehow the writers could put in everything that I said and did and what everybody thought about me. But they couldn't write about Billy sleeping on his office couch ten minutes before game time. That's just not kosher.

Certainly, I was there to do a job, and so was Billy, but his act was just off the wall. The way he did things after a while that summer, there was no rhyme or reason. If he liked you, he treated you one way. If he didn't, he treated you another (good luck figuring out why he did or didn't like you).

I felt he always wanted to make it about him, about his strategic decisions. I guess because I've never been a manager, but have always been an important part of a team, I never much paid attention to all the strategy things Billy was trying to do. The bottom line is, you can't win without great players.

All the great head coaches and managers in history had great players. Casey Stengel, Miller Huggins, Joe McCarthy, Joe Torre, Walter Alston, Sparky Anderson, Tom Landry, Chuck Noll, Vince Lombardi, Don Shula, Phil Jackson, Gregg Popovich—no doubt these guys have great value and are important. But without the horse, there is no jockey. Put the feed bag two feet in front of the horse, he wins the race.

Billy always thought he could win it alone, just like he thought he could do everything alone. And that was the sad thing about Billy. On the ball field or off, he was always more alone than he needed to be. Sometimes, we all are. Sometimes, when we get too big for our britches, we wind up alone.

Being around my family always got my mind right. My dad just had a plain way of saying things. My brother Joe was just a great, plain Joe. My dad and Joe would say, don't get into a contest with Billy or try to outwit the media. They told me to tell the truth and let the chips fall where they may. Sometimes it will hurt you and others, but just say it like it is. Dad would say, "If you tell the truth, you don't have to worry about remembering anything."

My family was key, and friends were key. Praying every day with Gary Walker, I really thought that kept me insulated from a lot of the strife.

You know, Fran Healy was rooming with me while I lived in New York, at Seventy-ninth and Fifth Avenue. He spent a lot of time there with me, and he'd try to warn me sometimes in the mornings. He'd tell me, "Man, did you see what they said about you in the newspaper?"— just so I'd have a heads-up.

But by then, I knew enough to just say, "Not really. Let's go eat!" I might glance at it, look at the headlines, and put it down. Then I'd say, "Hey, man, let's eat." We'd go over to the Nectar Café. Get some eggs and bacon from George, the owner. I don't think it seats more than fifteen, but it's still there, and I still patronize it. We knew we had to get ready to leave for the ballpark by 2:30 if it was a night game, so I'd just have breakfast, or lunch, and be on my way. I loved getting to the ballpark early. Sometimes I'd go as early as 11:30 in the morning, to have time alone and to make sure my head was right for the game that night.

There was a kid there named Ray Negron. He would go out and get me soul food from Harlem. Love the smothered chicken, black-eyed peas, greens, and rice—corn bread on the side. I was addicted to it.

I could put everything else in the background. My dad told me what I needed to have in the foreground.

Hiding in the Bathroom

THE THING THAT bothered me most, that just seemed to stick in my head, was how Billy kept moving me all over the lineup. Hitting me fifth, or sixth, or benching me all of a sudden. Even batting me second sometimes.

However, I knew enough to stay focused on the game, to put the other stuff behind me. I stopped thinking about how he was trying to screw me or what his next plan was going to be. I got past it affecting my game on the *field*.

I had always hit fourth. I was a natural number four hitter, a power hitter, and the four spot was the natural place for me on the Yankees. My teammates understood that as well.

That was one of the great things about those Yankees, 1977–78. They were consummate pros in the end. Some of them might not have liked me. They were all about going out and trying to win, every day. They knew if they were going to win, I was an important part of the lineup. Hence the phrase about me, "Love him or hate him, you can't ignore him." I think that came from Ken Singleton, my old teammate on the Orioles.

We were in Milwaukee, in the middle of a long road trip. We'd just dropped three out of four in Baltimore, and we weren't feeling too good about ourselves. We were 49–39. In baseball, ten games over .500 is a start toward where you eventually want to be. We were in third place but still only a game and a half out. That night, we'd got down 9–3, then almost came back, fell just short, and lost by a run, 9–8.

Nobody felt good. We felt like we weren't living up to what we could do; we were just dropping a couple, winning a couple. That night, after midnight, Thurman and Lou decided they'd had enough, and they went up to Mr. Steinbrenner's suite—he was in town. They banged on his door, and when he let them in, they told him he had to take charge of his team.

The stories that abound around that incident are amazing. I don't know them all, and I wasn't there. Everybody has his own rendition—but here's the story that was told to me, by people involved in this comedy.

They told George, "You run your businesses. Why not do the same with your team?"

That whole night sounds pretty hilarious, right from the beginning. I mean, telling George Steinbrenner to get more involved running the Yankees? That's like telling a lion to eat more red meat.

They went on telling him that he should just let Billy manage, George was putting too much pressure on him. George and Gabe had worked out a whole list of standards Billy had to live up to. They told him he should fire Billy or let him manage. They also wanted Lou to DH more . . . and me to bat fourth.

I had no idea this was going on. I understood later that Graig Nettles, who didn't like me at all, was behind this, too. I wouldn't be surprised. That's one thing I'll say about Nettles: On the field, he was a consummate pro and cared most about winning. Overriding it all, everyone wanted to win, and we felt we had the best team. Baltimore was great, so were the Red Sox, but we thought we could beat them.

Then, while this convention is going on in George's room, Billy gets suspicious. He's got the next room over. When he hears people talking in George's room, he figures they must be plotting against him. Because Billy always thought people were plotting against him, period. Billy was being Billy. He knocks on Steinbrenner's door and wants to know what's going on.

George tells him, "Nothing, Billy. I'm just getting ready to go to bed." He'd told those guys, Lou and Thurman, to go hide in the bathroom so Billy wouldn't see them and get the wrong idea. But Billy comes barging in anyway, and he catches them, and now he really wants to know what the hell is going on. He's yelling that George is lying to him again.

George tells him, "We were just talking about what's wrong with the club." Billy tells him right to his face, "You're what's wrong! You're what's wrong with the club!"

Then, finally, Billy settled down, and the four of them had a long talk about the team. What they decided was, or so I heard anyway, that Lou would DH more, George would stop hanging over Billy's shoulder and having all these meetings with him—and I would bat fourth.

They told Billy about me, "Why don't you just leave the guy alone? He's a good ballplayer. The guy wants to hit fourth; he feels more comfortable hitting fourth. He'll be a better player for it 'cause that's what he wants to do, and more important, we'll be better for it."

Later, Lou said that Martin didn't seem happy. He was pretty pissed off that they were up there. But he finally told them, after all he put me through, he told them okay, he was going to put me in the four spot. And the next night, Billy comes out to the ballpark and bats me . . . sixth.

It's funny how much you get wrapped up in the game when you're playing. Particularly that season, on that team. That night, the night of the bathroom plot, was July 13, when they had the blackout and the terrible riot back in New York. All those stores looted. That same summer, the "Son of Sam" case was still going on, with people living in fear.

It was a terrible summer, a wild summer in New York—but we were barely aware of it.

I was caught up in my drama. That's how you have to live when you're playing. Like you're in a bubble, a cocoon. Guys were aware of the killings. The really crude and insensitive way it was said around the clubhouse was, and I'm paraphrasing, "Don't have sex in a car."

That's awful. That's an awful thing to say when people are actually being killed and maimed, which they were. But it wasn't meant to be as bad as it sounds. That's just the hard logic of the locker room talking.

The game requires so much concentration you have to be brutal sometimes about tuning things out. It was like, "It's too bad about that nut running around shooting all the brunettes. Now, can I go to the ballpark and get a couple of hits?" I'm sure we saw the riot in all the papers and on TV. But I can't say it affected us much. We weren't there.

There was so much nonsense and craziness that I was personally at the center of—between the players and the manager, and myself and Billy and Thurman, and the media. The cliques and the factions, and how this writer hated me, and that guy hated me . . . You know, all I wanted to say after a while was, "Can I go and hit, please? Can I get in the batter's box and get some peace?"

There wasn't room for anything else, no matter how bad it was. I had to block it out to survive.

Sometimes I'd go to hang out. Usually in Manhattan, where I knew people wouldn't bother me. It was quite a scene then.

I would go out to a restaurant called Oren & Aretsky, up on Third Avenue and Eighty-fourth. All they had was a little, nineteen-inch black-and-white TV over the bar with the sound off. Nothing to bother you. I would go to McMullen's, at Seventy-sixth and Third, where they'd always hold a table for me. It was a classy place, a steak house. I wouldn't stay out late, didn't drink much—maybe a beer. Just went there to unwind, eat, and look at all the models who would come in.

Sometimes I'd go to Studio 54. I could just walk in there, see all the celebrities. Richard Pryor would hang out there, Diana Ross hung out there, Liza Minnelli. Lots of Elite and Ford supermodels. It was a great watering hole. All the stallions and the fillies went there.

I could park my Rolls in the street out in front of Studio, and a policeman would watch it for me. I could park it anywhere, park it and leave the keys in. Inside, they had movie seats up top. You could sit and watch the whole scene and not be bothered. Liza and Diana would often wind up singing. Good time.

More and more, though, it was the game that took up all the time, all the concentration, I had. The game makes you commit to it like that.

All the aches and pains of the long season. I had a badly bruised knee by then, and my arm was killing me. I took another cortisone shot for the elbow. I must've taken three that year. Now they wouldn't let you take more than one or two. But that's all right; that's what it's like playing the long season.

Trouble was Billy still wouldn't bat me fourth, and we still couldn't jell as the team we should have been—and would be. We went out to the West Coast for another road trip, and you could see we didn't have our game together. We swept Oakland three straight, but Billy North, my old friend, came right out and said what the difference was between the A's teams we had been on and the Yankees. He said about us, "You see all the talent they have, and they're caught up in all that bull." He called us a bunch of hens and said we should be ten games out in front. He talked about how the A's used to play: "Players bitch and moan, we all do it over a drink after the game, cut up the whole team. But on the field, show me some heart."

In other words, you can complain and criticize each other all you want, but get it together on the field! He had a good point. He had an even better one when he said, "For that money, they *conscripted* to every bit of scrutiny."

He was right. Taking that money, we couldn't object to anything. By then, I was speaking out. Back in Oakland, with the press guys I knew, I said right out, "Right now, they all think of us as a zoo." I told the Oakland media, "Ninety percent of what the New York press has written about this team isn't true."

The New York writers confronted me about that comment after they heard it, but that's how I felt. I didn't care who was hurt by anything or who said what anymore. I was through with that. I was just going to say what I wanted.

And what I wanted was for all the nonsense to stop. I wanted us to stop making excuses, even when it came to Billy or George.

There were all these rumors still circulating that Billy was going to be fired—because nothing ever totally dies in New York, I had learned that by now. But I told the press, "The manager, he's a fine man. He doesn't try to discipline anybody. He tries to let everybody be their own man. We don't have to like the guy. You don't have to be his friend, but we should stand by him for nine innings a day. The manager doesn't strike out, he don't make errors and he don't throw up [pitch badly] on the mound."

I told them, also, "You can't ask for a better owner."

I just wanted to put it all behind us. By then, it really was becoming farce. August was looking like it was going to be as awful as July. We went to L.A. to play the Angels, and I visited Dr. Frank Jobe, from the renowned orthopedic group Kerlan-Jobe, still a significant medical group today, to have my elbow looked at. Some woman rear-ended me on the freeway. Then, when she saw who it was, she asked for my autograph.

Half the team was in revolt by then. Munson and Don Gullett were starting to grow beards, in defiance of one of George's strictest rules, against unruly facial hair. Mickey Rivers was pouting over something, probably about not getting an advance to play the ponies. Gullett's horse farm back in Kentucky got raided by the state police because they found pot growing there.

Really, it was something new every day. The only trouble was we weren't getting anywhere.

By August 6, we were 59–49—still just ten games over. We'd just spent twenty games treading water, going 10–10, after losing two games in Seattle to a truly horrible expansion team they had. We were still in third place—only now it was a lot worse. We were two and a half back of Earl Weaver's Orioles, who obviously weren't going away. We were now *five* back of the Red Sox. They had turned hot again, winning nine in a row and sixteen out of seventeen.

We had fifty-four games—exactly one-third of the season—left. If we didn't start to make a move soon, we were going to get left behind.

By then, I didn't even know if I cared anymore. I was talking openly to the press about trying to get out of my contract, going to play somewhere else. Going to play somewhere sane.

Billy had started benching me again against left-handers, saying it was because my elbow was hurting. That was a lie and he knew it, and I was beginning to think this stuff would never end. There was a rumor going around that Billy was going to be fired at last, and Frank Robinson, who had been fired from managing the Indians, was going to be brought in to take over. When one of the writers asked me about that, I told him, "Just say that Reggie Jackson smiled for the first time all year."

This time it was Gabe Paul who took care of things. We took the last game in Seattle, then flew back east and went up to Syracuse to play an exhibition game against our top farm club—about the last thing we wanted to do right then. Gabe used the occasion to corner Billy and get him to promise to hit me fourth.

The next day, back in New York, he followed through by having Billy meet with George, too. George got on him to bat me fourth, every day, the way he had promised in that Milwaukee hotel room drama, and Billy agreed. The way I heard it was, to save face, he made out he was thinking of doing it anyway because I was swinging the bat well, and Chambliss was in a bad slump.

Whatever. What he asked in return was that George let him keep Art Fowler, his pitching coach and drinking buddy, who loved being hammered more than anyone I knew. Gabe thought that Art wasn't a good influence on Billy—really?—but by then he'd try anything. It was me for Fowler.

Wow, how far I had slipped!

So Billy makes another trade to save his drinking pal. Nothing for the good of the team! Just to save his buddy to go to the watering hole. The Yankees that year were not your usual baseball team.

But from then on, there was no stopping us. Everything just came together. August 10, we come back to New York, the Son of Sam gets arrested—thank goodness—and we took off. Including that last game in Seattle, we won forty out of fifty games, and twenty-four out of twenty-seven. Even though the Red Sox kept winning, we went from third to first, from five back to four and a half on top, in a little over three weeks.

I've never seen a team play that well. I don't think many have, save for maybe the 1951 Giants on their run, the Yankees of 1998 all year long—or us, in our stretch drive in 1978.

Certainly, it wasn't all me. I was playing great, and I'm sure it made a difference. But everybody seemed to get hot together, everything jelled. Ron Guidry had pitched well all year, but now he really came into his own. He ran off eight straight wins, including three shutouts. Mike Torrez became the ace of the staff, the workhorse. He won seven straight complete-game victories. Seven straight complete games! Can you conceive of anyone doing that today?

Playing all the time now, Piniella got hot. Nettles was blistering; he was doing everything. Making every play in the field. He was Player of the Month for August, with ten homers and twenty-five ribbies. Chambliss revived and hit .386 over a two-week stretch.

Mickey Rivers brought his game up to an unreal level. He hit .405 for August and drove in twenty-one runs from the leadoff spot. That was his best season. He seemed to be driving in the winning run or tying run every night for us, hitting home runs into the porch out in right, bunting his way on to start rallies. He never looked very imposing, but I think that put the other teams to sleep. There was nobody better in the clutch. Steinbrenner announced after the season that Mick hit .452 with men in scoring position. Today, they'd be all over that stat; he'd be the MVP.

Everything was working for us, everything that Billy did, or Gabe did in the front office, worked. Catfish was still hurting, and by then Don Gullett had hurt his back and missed all of August. Billy inserted Dick Tidrow into the rotation, and Dirt went 4–0 for the month, ended up 11–4 on the year. Tidrow was always underrated. He did everything—starter, long man, short man, middle relief, and even closer at times.

Gabe brought in Cliff Johnson from Houston, part-time catcher, part-time first baseman, and a premier pinch hitter. Cliff was a big man and hit monster home runs all over the Stadium, left, right, and center. He didn't want to play every day, and he'd tell you such. He did a good job catching when he filled in for Thurman from time to time, throwing runners out. Later, in mid-September, Gabe picked up Dave Kingman in a waiver deal, and he hit four homers for us in just twenty-four at-bats. I mean, can you imagine, deep as we already were, having a guy like Kingman who would lead the National League in home runs a couple of times? Coming off the bench for us as our maybe second-, third-, fourth-string designated hitter? We were tough and getting tougher.

I told the press we were playing "connoisseur's baseball." That's what it was.

We were winning games in all sorts of ways. We threw seven shutouts down the stretch, or one almost every seven games. We crushed teams with hits and home runs, beat them 10–1, 10–0, 11–1, 15–3, 15–0. We won close games, too.

We beat Texas 1–0 when Guidry pitched a two-hitter and I singled in Nettles with the only run, off Dock Ellis. We beat the White Sox, after we blew a 9–4 lead in the ninth inning, and got down, 10–9. I was already out of the game with an injured knee, but Piniella took over in right and made a leaping catch over the wall in right off Richie Zisk. Then, in the bottom of the ninth, Thurman worked a walk, and Chris Chambliss hit the ball into the second deck in right. Just like that, we won after all, 11–10.

When Seattle came into the Stadium, Sparky Lyle bailed out Figueroa as he was blowing a 5–2 lead in the eighth, struck out Larry Milbourne with men on first and third. Then Sparky pitched all the way through the eleventh. Talk about a closer, dude! If Sparky could have spent his career pitching just the ninth inning the way closers do today, he might still be pitching. Mickey Rivers hit another home run to win that one for him. That same home stand, we came back from down 5–1 in the sixth to Texas, when Nettles drove Rivers in with a triple for the winner.

It didn't matter who we played or who pitched against us. We went 16–5 against teams with winning records. We went 19–3 against left-handers, who we weren't supposed to be able to hit, winning fourteen in a row. We had so many left-handers in the lineup it seemed like teams would go down to the Bowery, and if a guy was drinking a beer left-handed, he'd pitch against us that night.

Of course, with that, out the door went Billy's theory about how he had to sit me against lefties. Not that he would admit it. He even used the occasion to take another shot at me, when the reporters asked him about it.

"I can bat Chris [Chambliss] any spot in the lineup, and he won't complain," Billy told them. "I wasn't getting the best out of Reggie."

So it wasn't his mistake, benching me all the time and batting me in the wrong spot. It was my problem, for complaining.

You know what? I didn't care. I was so pleased to be able to come to the ballpark and know where I was hitting and that I was playing every day. One of the writers asked me if I was having fun now. I told him I felt more *relieved* than like I was having fun—but I'd take it.

Like I say, it wasn't just me. It was the whole team turning it around. But if I was that one piece—that one last, missing ingredient like I'd been trying to tell Robert Ward back in spring training—that piece was finally in its right place. And I really think that made everyone better.

A good lineup's like a finely tuned machine—like a great car. It works best if everything's in its proper place. Because I was batting fourth, everybody was where they should be.

Mickey leading off. Willie Randolph, or maybe Roy White, second. Thurman, who was a great, productive hitter, in the third slot. Lou Piniella or Chambliss fifth or sixth, Nettles sixth or seventh, where he would absolutely kill you. All the way down to Bucky in the nine slot.

And me. I was ready to play. I had gotten my game together—I don't think I'd really had it together most of the year. I started really swinging the bat, being productive. Down the stretch run, I had an on-base percentage of almost .400, a slugging percentage over .500. I had twelve or thirteen home runs, almost fifty runs batted in, in as many games—and I just thought, "Thank goodness."

I was picking up the ball well; I was getting big hits. Against the Angels in mid-August, I had a double and a triple, drove in Thurman twice, and broke open a close game. Next day I led off the sixth with a home run against California, broke a 3–3 tie, and we coasted, 9–3. Couple days later I tripled with the bases loaded and finished them off. Same week, I had a homer and two singles and drove in three runs to beat the Rangers.

We didn't lose two games in a row for almost a month. When we finally did, I helped get us going again out in Cleveland, hit a run-scoring double and a three-run homer. A few days after *that*, I really got going on a good home run tear, best one I had all year. I hit eight in the space of sixteen games. Hit two in one game in Detroit.

Hit a three-run shot in the first when we crushed Toronto, then came back home and hit a slam in the first inning against the Indians.

But even as well as we were playing, we still had to shake off the Red Sox. They couldn't quite pitch with us, not with the staff we had. But they were capable of so much offense; they had such a great lineup they stuck with us almost all the way. Rice, Carlton Fisk, Yaz, Dewey Evans, Hobson who hit ninth. They started to come back on us, even after we got so hot. Mid-September, they came into town just a game and a half back, with 18 to go. We were 144 games into the season, playing great, and we couldn't shake 'em. Even with all we'd won, we still hadn't won nothin' yet.

It was wild, those three games in the Stadium. It was the middle of the week, up in the Bronx, but we drew fifty-five thousand every game. The park was shaking. This was all I'd dreamed about, playing baseball as a ten-year-old in my backyard. I was Mickey Mantle against the Dodgers . . .

First game, Ron Guidry was a little unsteady. He gave up a triple to Yaz, let him score on a wild pitch, and we got down, 2–0. Then it was like he just shut the door. He struck out Rick Burleson with men on first and third, and that was that. He used to *dominate* the Red Sox, and this was no exception. He pitched a complete game, nine strikeouts.

Mike Paxton was starting for them, and he was a gutsy pitcher. But we knew we could beat him, and we chipped away at him. Not trying to do too much, just getting our at-bats.

First Lou drove in Chambliss with a single. Then Bucky got a hit to lead off the fifth, and Mickey Rivers dropped another one in the right-field bleachers. Chambliss scored me with a double, and we were up, 4–2.

In the ninth, Billy left Guidry in to pitch to the heart of their order, even though we had Sparky rested, and this was the biggest game of the year. Neither Billy nor Art Fowler, his pitching coach, liked to play young players. They had to go with Guidry, who was young, but they called many of his pitches for him. That almost led to disaster for us in that last frame. Jim Rice hit a single off him, and then Fisk took him all the way to the wall in left-center, almost 430 feet. Mickey *just* pulled it in there.

Billy was always yelling at Guidry not to throw his slider, not to risk grooving one. Ronnie had this very fast, very deceptive slider that looked more like a fastball. The next year, when he was allowed to throw it when he wanted, he used it to just overwhelm the league. But you couldn't tell Billy anything, as usual. He just had Guidry keep throwing fastball, fastball, fastball that ninth inning. Guidry threw ninety-five and above, but even when you're throwing that hard, someone has a chance to catch it for a feast. He kept going behind the mound, shrugging those skinny little shoulders, and it seemed like he always came back throwing a mile or two harder. Fortunately for us, he had enough left to strike out George Scott and Butch Hobson, who drove in more than two hundred runs between them for the Sox that year.

Another key to the game—a big piece in our whole stretch run— was Thurman. Typically, he had an important night. Got two key singles that started one rally and kept another one going. By then, he was playing with all sorts of hurts, big and small, the way big-league catchers do by the end of a season, but he didn't complain.

That September, he was unbelievable. He hit .380 for the month, four homers, eighteen ribbies. Got back over .300 and a hundred RBIs *again*. He really showed me something. He was a paragon of professionalism.

I had a lot of admiration for him, watching him play like that. By then, we were getting along better. I respected the fact that he was one of the guys who went out of his way to get Billy to hit me in the cleanup spot—to get Billy to leave me alone. He was largely responsible for getting me there and for getting Billy to put me in the four spot. Thurman was a big enough man to do that. He and Lou got Billy to take his foot off the back of my neck.

It wasn't always easy to know what to make of Thurman. He was a very quiet guy. Silent at times. But I think more and more, the longer I was on the Yankees, the more we came to respect each other. I remember Fran Healy, of course, and Ray Negron, who was another peacemaker. Negron was a clubhouse man who Steinbrenner caught as a kid trying to graffiti the Stadium. George got him by the arm, pulled him aside, and gave him a wagging-finger-in-the-face conversation. He then hired Ray to work for the Yankees, and he's still working with the team. George changed his life.

Fran and Ray got Thurman and me together to have a burger when we were in Detroit, and that went very well. We talked about different things, from baseball to family—Thurman always had a big soft spot for his family. That conversation started us on having more respect for each other. He had a sneaky sense of humor. I remember at one point, he snuck up on me and asked me if Steinbrenner actually gave me a Rolls-Royce. He didn't, but I told him he did. (He didn't really give me the Rolls, but he did give me the money for it.) We both got a chuckle out of that, and after that it got better, and after our problem with the article we got along great.

The second game against Boston was going to be the big game of the series. We had Ed Figueroa going, who was a terrific pitcher, but he'd been up and down all year, trying to adjust to Billy Martin's constant changes in the rotation. Eddie liked his arm to be a little heavy so his ball would sink. He liked to pitch out of a four-man rotation, going every fourth day, and when Billy wouldn't do that, it bothered him. Plus, I think he was hurting a little by then.

Meanwhile, they were starting Reggie Cleveland against us. He was a righty, just a little better than a .500 pitcher that year, but he used to give us fits.

When the game started, they were hitting Figgy hard. Rice hit a triple in the second, and they got men on first and third, but he got out of it by striking out Butch Hobson. The next inning, they got two more men on, but he got Freddie Lynn to ground out and Yaz to fly out. Fourth inning, they got a guy to second. Fifth inning, they loaded the bases with nobody out.

But Eddie got Lynn to tap back to him for a home-to-first double play. Then Yaz hit a shot back at him, but he stopped it with his foot and threw him out.

Figgy was stumbling, putting men on base all the time, but he never broke. We couldn't do a thing with Cleveland. Fortunately, Mickey was running down everything in center, and I was finally playing right field like I knew I could. I still had a bruised knee that night, but I was running well. I don't know if it was the natural adrenaline, or what.

But in the fourth, Boomer—George Scott—hit a ball all the way back to the wall in right-center, and I ran back, leaped high, and pulled it away from the fans. I made an even better play in the seventh. They had Denny Doyle on second with one out, and Bernie Carbo hit a little flare, a dying quail, out to right—just the sort of liner that makes the most trouble. I got a good jump on the ball, came running in full tilt, and caught it just before it hit the ground, making a diving, tumbling catch.

After that play, you could feel the Stadium physically shake; you could feel the ground shake. If I wasn't excited enough already, I was then.

Bottom of the ninth, it was still 0–0. People forget, those Red Sox were also a terrific fielding team, and they were making great plays all over the field against us, pulling in long flies and line drives. It was a hell of a duel.

Leading off the ninth, Thurman gets another clutch hit, singles to center. I was up now . . . and Billy gives me the sign to bunt.

That would come back on me, too, because, like I said, on the Yankees—with Billy Martin—nothing ever really died. When he gave me the bunt sign there, Dick Howser had to call time and come down from the third-base coach's box to make sure I got it.

I struggled to believe it. I mean, I'm hitting cleanup to lay one down?

Dick asked me which side I was more likely to bunt to, which was ridiculous since it had been years since anybody last asked me to lay one down. You don't ask people to do things they can't do. I told him, "Third base, I guess," which was also a joke. He told me to bunt, but to look at him—Howser—with every pitch, in case the sign changed as the count changed.

This is what I mean about Billy Martin making a team all about him. This is what I mean about his big strategy always being something that turned the spotlight on him. "Billy-ball."

It sounds like a good, fundamental, by-the-book play, right? Get the winning run on with nobody out, bunt him over to second. But how well is that going to work with a guy who hasn't bunted in years? How does it make sense with a guy like me with power—and also good speed, so he can stay out of the double play?

That whole season, I grounded into exactly three double plays. Three of them. Chances were, I was either going to get a hit, get a walk, fly out, or strike out. A good manager doesn't treat his players like interchangeable pieces. He doesn't pretend one's the same as the other and they can all do the same things. All you're likely to do is distract your player, as well as do the wrong thing by asking him to do something he can't do.

Do you ask Babe Ruth to bunt—or Cookie Lavagetto? Willie McCovey—or Phil Rizzuto?

But I was learning. Billy Martin said bunt, I was prepared to bunt. Reggie Cleveland threw in on me, though, so I couldn't get the bat out and had to take it for a ball. I looked back down to Dick Howser—and now the bunt was off. Cleveland threw a fastball, and I fouled it off.

I looked back at Howser. The bunt sign was back on. Tell me, does this make any sense at all?

I got ready to try to bunt again, but Reggie Cleveland threw another ball in. It was like they were picking up the signs, which maybe they were. It was like they knew I was going to try to lay one down.

Personally, I thought they were making a mistake. If it was my team and Reggie Jackson wanted to bunt, let him bunt.

Instead, the count fell in my favor, the bunt was taken off, and Cleveland hung a slider. It was room service. The rest is history.

I hit that ball to right-center, over the 407-foot sign, probably fifteen to twenty rows deep in the stands. Ball game. The whole place was shaking again; the crowd was going nuts. They were chanting, "Reg-gie! Reg-gie!" again. I think that's when I finally won them over for good.

And at the plate, whattaya know, there was a whole mob of my teammates. Slapping my back, pounding away at me. Billy Martin, too. When we got back in the clubhouse, he even told me, "I'm sorry I gave you the bunt sign."

Getting Billy Martin to say he was sorry—getting him to say he made a mistake on the ball field . . . I wanted to know who that really was wearing his uniform. I just told him, "I understood the situation well." (Which I didn't.)

We'd won, that's what mattered. Some of the other players and Ray Negron pulled me back out to the dugout, and the fans were still there, still shouting for me. I took off my cap and waved it, I gave them a bow, they went wild.

That felt really good. That felt like what I came to New York for, what I imagined it could be. And afterward in the clubhouse, in the interviews, maybe I got a little carried away, but I didn't care.

I told the media, "If Reggie plays well, if we win, and if Billy and Reggie get along and George looks good, sociologically this city will be in better shape. I may be crazy, but that's what I believe."

What I meant by that was, I guess, that just then anything seemed possible. Despite everything we'd all been through, despite all the nonsense, we really could put it together and make it work. And I know it probably doesn't apply, but it seemed like it could be an example, maybe, for all of New York then. That if we could come together, anybody could.

With the Son of Sam murders, the economy in the tank, the riot that summer, it just seemed like the right thing to say at the time, to say that we could all come together as a city. That was what it felt like, especially in the excitement of that moment. That was what was so strange with my first two years with the Yankees.

There were all these moments when it just seemed, "Good, great, we won, everything's right with the world now. Let's hope it stays that way."

But it never did.

PINCH HITTER

TWO WEEKS AFTER the Reggie Cleveland game, I hit a grand-slam home run in the first inning against the Indians. We rolled from there, 10–0. It was my twentieth game-winning hit of the season—and with that win we clinched at least a tie for the division title, going four games up with four games to play. The race was over. Time for the playoffs. Ahhh!

In those days the league championship series was still best three out of five, you against the other division winner. Only two teams in the league playoffs, and not seven games, five. It was almost sudden death, a short series, and you were always playing a great team.

We would be playing Kansas City, which was a formidable organization. They were outstanding at the plate, outstanding in the field. They had a deep staff, led the league in pitching.

They had the great George Brett at third, Hal McRae, a tremendous offensive player, and Al Cowens, who had a terrific season in the outfield and at the plate. Amos Otis in center, great offensive and defensive player. Darrell Porter behind the plate. Big John Mayberry, left-handed power hitter at first, Frank White and Freddie Patek, a couple excellent gloves up the middle who were also good offensive players. Whitey Herzog was their manager; he was a good one, a Hall of Fame manager. Their general manager at the time was John Schuerholz, who of course went on to have a great career in Atlanta, too, and became one of the greatest general managers of all time.

We won 100 games; the Royals won 102. They had a season a lot like ours, but without the clubhouse drama. They had a tough race with two or three teams most of the way, then got hot down the stretch and just ran away and hid. They pulled off winning streaks of eight, ten, *sixteen* straight games. Won thirty-five out of thirty-nine and went from five and a half back at the start of August to ten and a half up by mid-September. They came close to beating the Yankees the year before, when I was with Baltimore, and they wanted this bad. The Royals thought they were the better team, and they wanted to prove it.

They always played us tough, regular season, postseason, whenever. We'd split the ten games in the regular season. They were especially tough at home, where they went 55–26 and beat us four out of five that summer. This year, they would have the extra game there. They were a team built for the AstroTurf they had at home, in Royals Stadium. When you play on turf, you need lots of speed on defense. The ball travels so much faster on carpet. They were a team that could steal bases, run down anything in the outfield. They were going to be hard enough to beat. It didn't help that our manager would play them with a handicap.

When we finally won the division title, it seemed like there was a kind of truce in the clubhouse. At least, I did my part to try to make it that. I'd make sure to stop in Billy's office, just talk with him a little. Not much, just a little—Fran thought that would be a great idea. For his part, Billy would come in and make sure the writers saw him come by my locker and say, "How you doin' today, Big Guy?" or "We need you today, Big Guy." Like we were all getting along.

Now, I knew from some of the writers that when they asked him how he really felt, Billy told them, "Off the record? He's a piece of s—t." But I went along with the act. I figured we didn't need any more distractions. I even went into his office after we clinched the division and offered him a drink from my champagne bottle. We drank together, and he told me, "You had a hell of a year, Big Guy. I love you." I guess he thought I had changed my name to Gullible.

Was it all a pretense? I don't know. I don't know if Billy Martin knew how he felt, either. Maybe he meant some of it. Maybe it was more that he was already trying to lobby for a new contract from Gabe Paul and George. He was in the papers trying to take credit for everything, saying about George, "He'll find out these guys aren't that easy to manage." So subtle.

George wasn't having any of it. "He's crazy if he tries to take credit for our success," he said. "I would just tell him that he's not indispensable. That this is just another example of his immaturity."

I couldn't argue with that. Even the best managers in the game, guys who were light-years ahead of Billy, didn't win when they didn't have the team. If you don't have the horses, you can't win. And that's something Billy never cared to understand.

I was past caring much about what Martin said about anything by then. And even though I thought I was getting along with Thurman better than ever, he was quoted as saying, "How could I ever like that blankety-blank after what he said about me?"

That really got me. I think we really became friends; I think we were in the process of becoming friends even then. But Thurman had his pride, and people were continuing to tell·me that he was still grumbling about the fact that he didn't get the bonus money he thought he was promised and that he was still bitter about the article in *Sport* magazine. He was a very prideful man, Thurman, but I respected him no matter what he thought. If I can't control something, if it's beyond my capabilities, then I try to move forward. That was all I could do.

So even though it seemed like we were going into the playoffs full of serenity, there were still a lot of resentments just under the surface. How much it distracted us, I don't know. I just knew you couldn't let up against the Royals, they were too good a team.

First game, they smoked us in New York, beat Don Gullett, 7–2, when his shoulder tightened up. We had pitching issues now. Catfish hadn't pitched in a month, with his bad arm. Figueroa pulled a muscle in his last start; he was out nine days. Billy had to pitch Dick Tidrow almost seven innings in relief of Gullett. We were running out of arms.

Ron Guidry came back and pitched a three-hitter against them the next day to even the series. Thurman got three hits; Cliff Johnson had a double and a home run. But now we had to go to Kansas City, and all the Royals had to do was to win two games out of three to beat us.

When the series moved out there, they beat Mike Torrez, 6–2. They beat him just chopping the ball into the turf, the way they liked to do. Now we're down, 2–1, in games, we had to win both games remaining in their park—and we didn't really have a pitcher for the fourth game.

We didn't have any off days in that series. Gullett's shoulder was still bothering him, and he'd just gone three days ago. Tidrow had pitched most of a game, Catfish was out, Torrez had just lost, Guidry had only two days of rest. We were in trouble. Suddenly we were down to a six-man staff, counting Sparky.

Billy decided to throw Figgy, even though he was still hurting from that muscle he pulled. He gave it his best, and we got him some runs early, got up, 4–0, but he couldn't get out of the fourth inning. Billy brought in Tidrow again, but he didn't have anything, either.

So Billy brings in Sparky with two outs in the third inning still, with our lead down to 5–4 by then. I think that shows the whole difference in relief pitching from now. You'd never bring a closer in that early now. And Sparky had pitched over two innings just the day before.

He'd had a tremendous year that year for us, one of the great years for a reliever. He pitched 137 innings, won thirteen games, saved another twenty-six, and earned the Cy Young Award. He was tough, and he had tremendous endurance. It was nothing for him to come in and pitch three innings.

As it happened, in that fourth game of the 1977 ALCS he went the whole rest of the way. Five and a third innings, two singles, no walks. That must be one of the all-time great relief performances in a postseason game. Thurman drove in an insurance run with another single . . . and we were still alive. The series was all even, 2–2.

And Billy Martin decided to bench me.

He told the press it was because I didn't hit Paul Splittorff, who was starting for the Royals. It was true I didn't have a great season against him. He was a good left-hander, a mainstay of their staff, great control. Counting the first game of the playoffs, that year I was 2–12 against him, although I hit a double and my first home run as a Yankee against him, in Kansas City. But he pitched all of us tough. That year he was 3–0 against us, going into that last game of the playoffs.

It was true, too, I'd been having a bad series. I was only 1–14 in the championship series, with just a lousy single. It was about the worst playoff series I ever had. I just stunk. But a lot of guys weren't hitting that well. Nettles hit .150 on the series; Bucky wasn't hitting. Chambliss went only 1–17. But all those guys were going to start; they were playing.

I honestly didn't know what Billy thought he was trying to do. I don't know if he was trying to make a statement, show he could win it all without me. I heard in 1981 that George Steinbrenner got into the same head when he was about to let me go. George did things at times with an advisory committee. He tried to listen to his advisers, and then he did the implementation. The loudest voice saying "Reggie Jackson's career is going to end quickly" belonged to our hitting coach, Charley Lau. That was the story I heard, anyway. George then tried to show that the Yankees could win the 1981 World Series without me and tried to sit me down.

That didn't work out so well.

What was Billy thinking? I don't know. At this point, I didn't know, and I didn't care why. It was an insult, and I was offended. Billy didn't even have the guts to come and tell me to my face. What I heard was that he told Stick Michael, who was one of our coaches then, to go tell me. Gene told him, "I ain't telling him. You tell him."

That was Billy. If he was pleasant, he would talk to me. If he had something negative to tell me, he wouldn't talk. Not to my face, anyway. He would say a lot of things behind my back.

When Gene Michael wouldn't do his job for him, he went to Ellie Howard to do it. Ellie told him to get lost. Finally, he found Fran Healy and asked *him* to tell me. Fran told Billy, "Why don't *you* tell him?" But Billy said, "No, you do it for me. You go tell Reggie."

That was an interesting choice, because before the playoffs started, Billy wanted to put Fran on the disabled list. He was hurting, and Billy didn't want to play him, so he was going to put him on the DL, and the Yankees were going to put him in the broadcasting booth, as a color commentator.

Fran would go on to make a great career for himself as a broadcaster. But if he goes up in that booth just then, he's not around to tell me. I wonder who Billy Martin gets to do what he was supposed to tell me as the manager—or if he ends up having to tell me himself.

That would've been interesting. Anyway, Fran comes into his office. Fran said he looked scared to death: "I need you to tell Reggie he isn't playing."

Fran was a little ticked off at how Billy was trying to get him off the team, too, and he told him, "You're the f—in' manager, you tell him."

"I don't wanna," he says.

"So tell the coaches to tell him."

"They don't wanna," he says.

Fran figured he better tell me, or I wouldn't know I wasn't playing. He told me he was thinking, "F—k, I'd better tell Reggie or he'll be in right field. We'll have two right fielders."

Fran ended up telling me. I was in shock when I heard it. I was like, "Wow, this is a different dude." I don't think I ever fully realized before, even after everything I'd been through that year, just how different this guy Billy was.

Supposedly, he even went around to Catfish and asked him in front of the writers if I could hit Splittorff. The way they wrote it up the next day, Catfish told them, "Not with a f—ing paddle." That's what they wrote. I would doubt Catfish said it that way. He might have said, "Well, I've seen Reggie struggle with him," or something like that, but he wouldn't say, "Can't hit him with a paddle." I mean, I played with Catfish almost his whole career, thirteen seasons, and we were friends. The comment attributed to him didn't fit the person.

But no matter what anybody else said, I wasn't starting. Billy made Cliff Johnson the designated hitter and put him in my number four spot, and he put Paul Blair out in right field.

Both fine players. But you know, Cliff Johnson had played fifty-six games for us that year. Paul Blair played eighty-three. Neither one of them had two hundred at-bats. Counting the playoffs, Cliff was something like 3–5 against Splittorff. Blair was 1–3. That was no kind of measure; that's not enough at-bats to make a decision like this one.

That season, even with all the distractions, I had thirty-two homers, 110 ribbies, thirty-nine doubles. I was fifth in the league in homers, sixth in RBIs, third in slugging, tenth in on-base percentage, second in doubles. Anyway you sliced it, I was one of the premier hitters in the league, the premier hitter on the Yanks. It was crazy to play your biggest game of the year without your cleanup hitter being part of it.

It was an attempt to put me down, I felt. Billy had this opportunity, he had his reasons, and he wanted to show the world that he was in charge, that he could win the pennant without me.

The only good thing to be said about it all was that Fran did end up telling me I was benched for the game. Because he didn't just come over and say, "You're not starting." He also said, "Make sure you don't say anything negative. You've gotta be a team guy here. Watch what you do in the dugout. Whatever you do, make sure the camera doesn't catch you emoting or doing anything they can tag a comment to. That camera will be on you. It will be looking for you to make some sort of scene or something. Just make sure you're out there rooting for the team."

Then he told me, "Stay ready. You never know, you could wind up winning the game for us. So make sure you stay in the game."

It was great advice. I didn't follow all of it. I didn't really stay in the game. At times, I just thought about anything but the game. I was broken and couldn't get past not playing.

I couldn't be mad for three hours, so I just kind of checked out. I just sat there kind of emotionless. Somewhat removed. Thinking about why Martin would bench me. I was just thinking, "What are you doing? What are you trying to prove? You're going to prove that you can manage me? Show people who you are?"

It was a crazy chance to take. If Billy had lost that game with me on the bench, he would've been fired immediately, or so I thought.

But I didn't let any of those feelings show. I took Fran's advice, made sure I looked like I was in the game all the way, for the TV cameras. Made sure it looked like I was leading the cheers.

When I went out to the dugout before the game, the press was all over the place, but Fran had told me what to say: "You've got to be down; your pride has got to be hurt. But if a man tells me I'm not playing, I don't play. I sit down and pull for the club. I'm not the boss; I'm the right fielder. Sometimes."

All of that was Healy. Except when I said "Sometimes." I had to have a little authenticity.

It was a crazy night. I might've appreciated what a game it was if I'd been allowed to play in it.

Billy was starting Guidry with just two days' rest, and he didn't have anything; it's lucky he didn't end a great career right there. But he had the guts to keep trying. We were scrapping. Nettles got into a ruckus with George Brett when he came in hard at third on a triple. Thurman singled in a run, but we were still down, 3–1, with just one out in the third.

Billy brought in Mike Torrez. It was a desperation move, just like his move with Lyle had been the day before. Mike had only lasted five and two-thirds innings in Game 3 of the series, but he just had one day's rest. Still, he was great; he mowed them down. Thurman threw out a couple guys trying to steal. But somehow we struggled to score off Splittorff, even with me on the bench. Ha!

Top of the eighth inning, we were still down, 3–1. Just six outs left. But Healy, who had caught Splittorff when Fran was in the Kansas City organization, was telling us, "Stay close. He's coming out of the game, he's gassed."

He could see it, he knew it—and sure enough, he was right. Willie Randolph led off with a single, and Whitey Herzog decided to pull Splittorff for Doug Bird. Bird struck out Munson, then Piniella singled, and we had men on first and third, one out.

Bird was a righty—so Billy has no excuse now *not* to bring me in. I think maybe George might've made him the first manager ever fired in the middle of an inning if he hadn't. I pinch-hit for Cliff Johnson. Over forty thousand fans in the seats, all of them booing me, of course.

I wanted to succeed more than at any time in my life. In all honesty, who wouldn't feel that way? I mean, I had been in the postseason many times before, with the A's. But this was different. This was unique. I think it would be normal to have that feeling, that need to succeed—and to say that would only make me normal.

It's hard to recall everything I was feeling at that moment. But I was also kind of stuck between "Should I give it my all? Or should I

At Arizona State, I loved playing for Frank Kush, who taught me so much. Could I have excelled in the pros? Take a look at the film of me getting off the field at Yankee Stadium after the last out of the 1977 World Series. Now that's some broken-field running! Collegiate Images/Getty Images

Charlie Finley and Dick Williams, before the star of the 1972 World Series. Playing for Dick, a terrifi manager, was a treat. Pla ing for Charlie was . . . w an adventure! Both of th look pretty glum—proba because I tore up my leg the ALCS and would not be playing. We won any which shows you how much depth we had. *Spo Illustrated* via Getty Images

Two in a row! That's me on the left, celebrating the A's victory over the New York Mets in the 19 World Series with Dick Williams (middle) and Catfish Hunter (right). was named the MVP of Series and the America League that year. Catfis won twenty-one games during the season and a critical Game 6 in the Series, to keep us alive. Mets should've drafted when they had the chan Ron Riesterer/*Oakland Trib*

"A team of gunslingers. That's me on the right with two of my best frie in baseball, Dave Dunc (left) and Ken Holtzma (middle). Ron Riesterer/ *Oakland Tribune*

art of a beautiful
nship. I was working
C in this picture,
ng the 1976 American
e playoffs. By the next
, George would be
his best to sign me
e Yankees. Please note
t beautiful hair I used
e! AP photo

g on the pinstripes!
ankees announce
ning, November
6. From left, that's
mortal Yogi Berra,
nan Munson, and
hite, who is placing
st Yankees cap on
ad. For some reason,
Martin is nowhere
t . . . AP photo/Marty
andler

ud moment for us all.
my mom and dad at
rsailles Terrace with
the day the Yankees
nced I would be
ng my skills to New
AP photo

Me with my dear, departed friend Catfish Hunter, who battled through so many injuries and illnesses to make a success of his time in New York. I'm told that only four players in major-league history have played on consecutive World Series champions for two different franchises. Two of them were Hall of Famers Babe Ruth and Herb Pennock—the other two you see in this picture. I think that's more than mere luck. MLB Photos via Getty Images

Somehow, we made it this far. From left: Billy Martin, Mickey Rivers, Willie Randolph, Thurman Munson, and me, announced as the starting lineup before Game 3 of the 1977 World Series. AP photo

Billy and I clowning in the outfield before Game 5 of the 1977 World Series. You would never guess that we were in the middle of yet another running feud. Life with Billy was always . . . complicated. AP photo

Game 6, 1977. Hitting the first one out off Burt Hooton. I was locked in that night like I never was before or after. *New York Daily News* via Getty Images

Circling the bases after the first of three home runs I would hit that night. My feet were already off the ground. They would stay that way for the rest of the evening. *New York Daily News* via Getty Images

The reception in the dugout after that first home run in Game 6. It was the closest the team had been—literally!—all year. For once, nobody's worrying about who's shaking whose hand. *New York Daily News* via Getty Images

ing to the fans in the Canyon of Heroes
ing our ticker-tape parade in 1977. It was
ific—though I couldn't wait to jump in
new Rolls and head for the Berkeley Hills.
York Daily News via Getty Images

Explaining myself after the Great Bunt
Controversy of 1978. I had knowingly brought
things to a head and had sparked a confrontation. As it turned out, this would stop the
bleeding on a Yankees team that was falling
into chaos and allow us to get back into the
race. AP photo/Requena

We'eeerrre baaaack!" Thurman and I, back in the World Series in 1978. It was our time of year.
ifetime, Thurman hit .373 in the Series; I hit .357. He was a tremendous clutch hitter and some-
ne who played through all sorts of injuries. *Sports Illustrated*/Getty Images

Ron Guidry, "Louisiana Lightning," in 1978, the year he won the Cy Young Award and should have won the MVP to boot. It was one of the greatest years any pitcher ever had, and he single-handedly kept us afloat for most of the season and then won the playoff game against Boston. Ron was always a real gentleman and one of my best friends on the Yankees. MLB Photos via Getty Images

When he came to the Yankees in 1978, Goos Gossage went through pretty much the sam hazing I got from Billy Martin, but he was tough enough to not let it keep him from h ing a great year, on his way to a Hall of Fam career. Here he is closing out the Dodgers, a he closed out the Red Sox in the playoff. In World Series that year, he pitched six innin allowed no runs, one hit, one walk, and str out four. *Sports Illustrated*/Getty Images

A few more pounds, a little less hair . . . but look at that smile! Acknowledging the fans at the annual Baseball Hall of Fame ceremonies in Cooperstown in 2011. On the left is Dennis Eckersley, who made the Hall in 2004. I made it in 1993. It was one of the proudest days of my life, and both my parents were there, something that put a smile around my heart. Getty Images

just say to Martin, 'Dude, you think I stink? Let me just stand there. Take three strikes and go back to the dugout.' "

I knew that didn't make sense. That would only make me look like a fool. And I thought, "We don't need two fools. We just need one." I wasn't going to prove Billy right by being wrong, by looking foolish.

I knew better than to get up there and go for the fences. We needed a run driven in. Needed to keep the rally going. Nothing would be going on if I struck out. You can't think home run there. A home run could happen, sure. But I needed to get that ball in play, get the run in.

If you're raised as a baseball player to win, that's what you do. It's what you're supposed to do, as a professional. If you want to say I did the right thing, and I had the right things in mind, great. But it's not a tribute. Any professional would do the same.

I was always able to set aside the negativity when I played. To strike when the game was on, say what I wanted to say that way, with a bat in my hand. My dad would always say, "As long as you have the bat in your hand, you have the last say."

The game itself was kind of my place to escape. People would say I was always so clutch in the big situations. No, I think it's just that I didn't let myself get distracted the way a lot of players do in those circumstances. I had the ability to focus and to keep it narrowed down to the need to hit the ball.

It all comes down to the nature of the person. Not everybody can be a shutdown closer. Not everybody can be a pinch hitter. Not everyone can hit cleanup. It's just not in their nature, not in their DNA.

There's a thousand reasons. Some guys can and some guys can't, and it's up to management to realize that. Look in a man's eyes; they are the windows to his heart. They will tell you if he can or he can't.

I remember when I was a kid, my father sent me to the grocery store one time to get a pint of Neapolitan ice cream. You remember that? The kind they used to sell, one-third chocolate, one-third vanilla, one-third strawberry? Called Neapolitan.

I had twenty-five cents—and there was no pint of Neapolitan ice cream. So I went to the corner gas station and borrowed a quarter from one of my dad's friends, Bob Bradshaw. I then went to the grocery store and borrowed a quarter from the grocery store owner, Bob Kelso. I then went to the store on the corner, Fleischer's Drug Store, and I bought a pint of chocolate, a pint of vanilla, and a pint of strawberry. I went home and my father said, "Good job, son."

You know, I wasn't going to bring an excuse home. Nobody wants to hear an excuse. That's the way it is with baseball and life in general.

Man on third base, and there's one out, and you're two runs down—you have to figure out how to get him in. I got to hit a ground ball to the second baseman if the infield's back. If the infield is in, I got to square the ball and punch it through. If the pitcher's a sinker-ball pitcher, I got to get the ball in the air. If the guy's a left-hander and has got a good breaking ball, I have to try to figure out how to get the barrel on the ball.

You got to figure it out. *How do I get this run in?* You got a lot of choices. But some guys look at that situation and they just go, "OMG"—"Oh, my goodness! What the hell do I do?"

There are certain guys everybody knows in the clubhouse you want up in those situations. Guys who are going to be able to stay calm and figure it out. On the Yankees, Jeter's the type of guy you'd want up there. There are some guys who aren't supposed to be clutch, but they are.

You can get on a bad streak. That happens even to great players—even to clutch players. It can happen to anybody.

It happened to me sometimes. Not much. Not in October. A lot of people used to say that was because of my ego.

I don't know. I don't know how the ego goes. I don't know the definition of ego.

But I think your ego helps you, if you want to be honest about it. I think knowing who you are helps. I don't have to say, "I'm going to get it done," because I'm Reggie Jackson. That's who I am. Whatever that is, good or bad.

I go to home plate in a clutch situation, I look at it as an opportunity to succeed. It's like my friend Gary Walker used to say, "Reggie, get your thoughts out of the way. Don't get in the way of the ability that God gave you. Don't create unnecessary clutter in your mind."

All I would say, at certain times before the game, was, "Dear God, guide me." Because a lot of the time you can put doubt in yourself by thinking too much.

But I always knew that I had God on my side. And that 1977 season, I was praying more than I had at any other time in my life.

I just stayed in there, when I finally got to bat in that last game against the Royals. I figured out what I had to do.

I was only told I was going to pinch-hit at the last minute. I think it was by Fran Healy, who came in from the bullpen and sat next to me for a while on the bench. Not by Billy. I remember leaving from the end of the dugout, walking to the on-deck circle, taking a couple swings, then walking right up to the plate. I remember being announced as the pinch hitter—but not before you looked around to see who was going to hit.

It wasn't like, a couple minutes before, "Reggie, you're going to be the hitter if we get this far along in the eighth inning. You're going to hit, go get ready." I remember being by the end of the dugout, sitting with my bat for most of the game. I never walked down toward the bat rack to get a bat, grab some pine tar and a helmet. I was down there with my helmet by my side. I put on my helmet and walked from the dugout, up the stairs, out on the field, and then down to the on-deck circle. Swung the bat a couple times, I didn't even pick up the leaded bat. Walked across home plate, not even around back, and got in the batter's box, ready to hit.

Didn't stretch, didn't do any knee bends. It didn't matter. I was locked in; I was somewhere between mad and disgusted. I just got in the batter's box and just locked down. I figured out what I had to do, I didn't let anything distract me, I stayed within myself even when I got behind, 1–2, in the count. Then Bird came in with a fastball, and I just took what he gave me and hit a line-drive single into center field. Not a lot, just what I could do. Just took what there was. It scored Willie and cut their lead to 3–2. Job done.

Whitey Herzog pulled Bird for Steve Mingori, and Mingori got Nettles and Chambliss then to get out of the inning. But we'd cut their lead to one run. In the bottom of the eighth, Mike finally got tired and walked a couple guys, but Billy brought Sparky in again, and he struck out Cookie Rojas to keep us in it.

We had just one more inning now; the whole season came down to this. Whitey replaced Mingori with Dennis Leonard, who was usually their best starter, to begin the ninth. We had a great inning, one that exemplified what a great clutch team we were, all working together to get it done.

First, Thurman coached Blair on how to hit Leonard, and Blair hung in there; he spoiled a couple sliders from Leonard, and then he fought off a tight fastball and plunked it into center. A professional piece of hitting. Next Roy White pinch-hit for Bucky, and he battled Leonard all the way, fouled off some more great pitches, and drew a walk. Another clutch at-bat.

Herzog brought in a lefty, Larry Gura, who was normally another starter, to pitch to the left-handed-hitting Mickey Rivers. It was great baseball, the crowd was going nuts, every at-bat going to four, five pitches or more. Everybody expected Mickey to bunt, but when he couldn't lay one down, he worked the count to 2–2, then lined a single into right to score Blair and tie the game.

Herzog went back to the pen again; he brought in Mark Littell, a closer. Same guy who gave up the home run to Chambliss that cost the Royals the pennant in 1976. This time, Willie Randolph hit a long sac fly off him to center to put us ahead, and then Brett, a future Hall of Famer, booted a ball by Piniella, and suddenly we were up, 5–3.

You should have heard how quiet their more than forty thousand fans got then. Bottom of the ninth, the Royals were still battling, and Sparky was tired. But he got Freddie Patek to hit into a double play to end it, and that was that. Somehow we'd won the pennant.

Afterward, a lot of people were saying that Whitey Herzog overmanaged those two innings, bringing in five pitchers, including three to face just four batters in the ninth. I know that's the way it can look.

Did he overmanage?

This is for all of us who manage when we're watching TV, or at the game, without background knowledge. First of all, if the players do their jobs, the manager never leaves the dugout. That makes him a great manager. If the players don't do their jobs, then the manager has to go to other players, to try to get the one player out of trouble. Whether it's a player who's struggling on the mound or a player who's struggling offensively. The great players Casey Stengel had made him a great manager with the Yankees in the 1950s. The great Cardinals' teams Red Schoendienst had in the 1960s made him a great manager. Frank Robinson, Brooks Robinson, Jim Palmer, Dave McNally—they all helped make Earl Weaver a great manager. Dick Williams was a great manager with the Oakland A's. The team had three future Hall of Famers on it. Derek Jeter, the great Mariano Rivera, and all those other great players the Yankees had in the 1990s helped make Joe Torre a great manager.

What people don't realize is that you need to understand people's makeup and what a guy is cut out for. Because a guy does not do well under pressure does not mean he's not a good player. It means that we as management need to not put that player in that situation.

So, when managers use a player in certain situations and not in others, it may be because that player is not suited for the situation. All of your great players—from Whitey Ford to Ruth, Gehrig, DiMaggio, Frank Robinson, Gibson, Marichal, Koufax, Aaron, Jeter, Rivera—they have a meanness to them that you would be shocked to discover that they have. They have a killer instinct in them that's a very controlled, very managed part of their character and ego that's almost anger. It makes them extremely difficult to beat in a one-on-one situation.

You see it in other sports. Guys like Bill Russell, Michael Jordan, Jack Nicklaus, others. They truly are special people, and your managers know who you can trust with the baby and who you can't. Guys like Munson, guys like Nettles—love 'em or hate 'em, they're great players, and you must respect 'em. You're in a dogfight, you want 'em on your side, because they're going to go down scratching.

You can beat them sometimes. You can whip those butts. But when you get over 'em, your comment is, "Gee whiz, if I ever run into that guy again, I'm sure gonna do my best to talk my way around it. Because even though I won the fight, my jaw hurt for a year. Every time I took a bite out of an apple, I thought of Thurman Munson." You know, when people in the other dugout look out in the bullpen and say, "Oh, Mariano's up," that manager, that coach, says, "Boys, you'd better score now." Because they don't have Mariano up for practice. "This is not a fire drill. That blankety-blank is coming in. He ain't down there playing catch."

All of which is to say about Whitey Herzog, like other managers, most of the time he's making moves, it's because the other guy can't handle it. Sometimes a guy overmanages, but usually it's when you force his hand. When he doesn't have one of those killers out there, he has to do what he can.

Now, I'm not saying who Whitey had out there in that ninth inning maybe couldn't handle it. I have no idea. But I know that we had plenty of guys with that killer instinct on our side. Munson, Nettles, Piniella, Mickey Rivers, Chambliss, Randolph, so many guys. They set their mind to square up that ball, and they're going to hit that ball off anybody. It doesn't matter to me who's on the mound when I set my mind to square that ball, hit it on the barrel of the bat.

There are exceptions. When you go out and a Koufax or a Bob Gibson is on the mound in the ninth, or when you're facing a Mays or a McCovey, some of the all-time greats—you're maybe going to get something you never saw before, which is why people pay to sit close. They can stop anyone, and that's how history is made.

But certain guys, like a Jeter or a Miguel Cabrera today, they can make you a bad manager. They can beat you no matter what you try to do. Sometimes you have to go strength to strength, and you can still get beat.

Postseason, sometimes you'll bring in your starters when you have to, the way Whitey Herzog did. Starters have their "throw day," when they throw thirty-five pitches or so to keep their arms loose between starts. In the playoffs, you'll have the starters down in the bullpen, ready to take their throw day on the mound, if you have to—particularly in a situation like the one we were in in 1977, where it came down to the fifth and final game. You have a few days before the World Series starts, so ELAIA—"every living a—h— is available."

Most of the time bringing in the starters works out. Or maybe you want to pull the starter, because you know he's done, or you don't think he's going to get the batter out. Doesn't mean it was the wrong move. Maybe the reliever isn't as strong as he usually is; maybe he's pitched too much. But he's your best lefty—and you're facing a great left-handed hitter. Especially near the end of the year, when it's win or go home. It's different in the playoffs, we all know that.

All you can do is put together the best-case scenario. The best you can say is, "Well, the reliever's arm was fresh. This was the best matchup at the time." There are so many variables, so many things that can go wrong, it's so easy to say the manager made a mistake. That's baseball most of the time. You're always being second-guessed, and you're always wondering what would have happened if you shoulda, woulda, coulda.

That playoff series against the Royals, our pitching staff was hurting. We were out of pitchers, and Billy, to his credit, took some big risks. He left Sparky Lyle out there a lot of innings in Game 4, and he brought him back again in a key situation in Game 5, the very next day. A tip of the cap to Sparky. Billy started Figgy when he was hurt, then he started Guidry on short rest, then he brought Mike Torrez on with short rest.

All risky calls. But we win! So the manager—great job. More important, great job by the players. No slight to the manager. He's in a no-win situation. If the players do their job, he's a great manager. If they don't, he's a bum. That's part of the deal.

Not all of that worked out. But almost all of it did. Taking *me* out of the lineup so he could prove something to somebody? That was a huge risk he didn't *have* to take. But he got away with it. Good for us.

Whitey Herzog, he thought, "Why mess around and take a chance on letting somebody who's not my best pitcher lose this game?" So he brought in his best arms, his best starters—the way managers have always done in the postseason. The way Casey Stengel used to do with Allie Reynolds, or the way Bob Brenly brought Randy Johnson out to face us in that seventh game in the 2001 World Series, when he pulled Curt Schilling.

It worked for those managers. It didn't work for Whitey Herzog.

As long as you're a manager, you're going to be second-guessed. It's fair and it's unfair. It is what it is. Start letting it bother you and get in your head, you need another job.

It bothered me some that I didn't get to be on the field when Sparky got the last out. But they wouldn't want to put me in for defense at that point.

We won. That was the one thing we all wanted. But afterward in the clubhouse, I became the big issue again.

George was supportive at least. He told the press about me, "When he came in, he delivered a hit instead of sulking. That shows everyone in New York he's a team man."

Most of my time in New York, George stayed in my corner. George and I never really had any problems until I had a bad year, an off year in 1981, and I was let go. That was George. He'd stand behind you as long as you produced. He later admitted publicly that was a mistake. He told me jokingly on the phone that he had listened to his advisers for the first time.

I was disappointed to see what still wasn't behind us. Paul Blair was giving Munson a lot of credit for advising him on how to hit Denny Leonard, and Thurman told the press, "Yeah, this beach ball can't stir the f—ing drink, but he can show you how to hit."

Okay, so he still wasn't over that. So what?

The press asked Billy why he couldn't be a man and come tell me himself that I wasn't going to be in the starting lineup. He told them, "How do you tell a guy he's been butchering the outfield and not hitting worth a damn? How do you do that diplomatically?"

S.O.B. Doing this book was the first time I learned some of this stuff. While I'm here in my sixties now, I have to tell you it's still unbelievable to hear it. Yeah, that was Billy. Always worrying about how he could do things diplomatically. I gotta say, the only word I can use is "crazy." I'm glad I didn't know all that went on.

I hadn't made any errors in the outfield for a while, and I hadn't been hitting for all of four games after having a great stretch run. You can run up a list of Hall of Famers long as your arm who have had bad postseasons, much worse and much longer than mine. It happens, because it's only a few games.

You don't bench one of your best players over it. You don't rub it in—especially not after he takes the benching with class, doesn't say a thing, and comes off the bench to get a big hit. You don't bring up fielding errors from months before to taunt him with as well.

Whatever. I knew somehow I'd be in the middle of everything again, getting it from all sides even when we won. Thurman was talking out loud about wanting to go to play in Cleveland the next year. Billy was taking the opportunity to mock me . . .

"All season I had to eat it in here," was what I told the writers. "Thank God. I can't explain it because I don't understand the magnitude of Reggie Jackson and the magnitude of the event. I am the situation."

Seriously, what I meant was how I couldn't understand how it kept coming back, even when I didn't do anything. It just seemed like a recurring nightmare. I'm getting away, and all of a sudden the guy starts to grab me—and I wake up. It never seemed to end.

You could say, all right, some of the trouble I got in my first year in New York was my fault. Some of it was me not understanding yet how to say nothing. I didn't understand how to measure and weigh my every word before speaking it. I didn't understand how the press thought of themselves in New York. I didn't understand what a different dude the manager was.

But here we go again. I had a great stretch run, didn't hit so well the first four games of the championship series . . . and we were tied. I got benched. Unlike everybody else who wasn't hitting so well. Then, when I got benched and I took it well, I got called out by my manager anyway and ridiculed in the press.

Whoever my manager was.

The next day, when we met the media the day before the World Series started, the press was fifteen-deep. All of them asking me, "Reggie, are you playing tomorrow?"

I said, "I don't know. Let me ask the manager." Then I called over, "Hey, Fran, am I playing tomorrow?"

15

"ANOTHER CHAPTER IN THE TUMULTUOUS LIFE OF THE 1977 YANKEES"

AS WE WENT into the World Series, the press attention died down a little bit. Thank you. Mostly because whenever anybody asked me anything, I replied, "I just work here."

Also because there was a big fuss after they screwed up Joe DiMaggio's tickets, and he refused to throw out the first ball of the Series. I was a little surprised they didn't blame that on me, too. I kind of expected Billy Martin to say the assistant ticket manager hadn't been the same since they signed me. Anyway . . . thank you, Joe.

We were facing the Dodgers, who were a tough, well-rounded team. Back in that stretch, they took four pennants in eight years, 1974–81. They had that infield that played together forever: Steve Garvey at first, who hit for average and power. Davey Lopes at second, who could do almost anything, hit home runs, steal bases, field great. Bill Russell at short, Ron Cey at third, "the Penguin," who could hit home runs and was a very good glove.

In the outfield they had Rick Monday, my fellow Arizona State alumnus. Dusty Baker, who was a terrific power hitter. Reggie Smith, a great all-around player, who used to pound us in the postseason. Veterans like Steve Yeager behind the plate.

They had a very deep pitching staff and a very diverse one. Guys who threw hard, guys who were crafty, all outstanding pitchers and competitors. Starters like Don Sutton, who's in the Hall of Fame. Tommy John, Rick Rhoden, Burt Hooton. Charlie Hough, who was a knuckleballer. Doug Rau. Elias Sosa out in the bullpen. They were an outstanding staff.

I couldn't help but wonder how good they'd be if I'd signed with them. Like us, they stood up to all comers in the season. They beat out a great Reds team that year, ended Cincinnati's streak at two straight world championships. They beat a very strong Phillies team in the National League Championship Series, one that had Luzinski, Schmidt, Carlton, Bowa, Maddox, Gary Matthews, Bake McBride, Bob Boone. They were playing great ball—and the way the media set it up, they were the good guys against us free-agent bad guys, the Earps against the Clantons. Tommy Lasorda always had them talking about team loyalty and "bleeding Dodger blue." Sometime during the Series, Lou Piniella said the biggest thing the Dodgers had to fear was that they might hug themselves to death.

We were still hurting for pitching. Remember, our playoff series went five games, so we had just one day off between the end of the ALCS and the start of the World Series. The Dodgers had only two days off, but that gave them enough time to get their rotation lined up. We were just lucky Don Gullett was able to get out there and pitch the first game, even though his shoulder and his back were hurting. He was wild, he walked six guys, hit a batter, allowed five hits, but he pitched well when it counted. Going right after guys, striking them out, and using our big ballpark to his advantage.

They were hitting him hard in the first inning, belting the ball all over the Stadium, but he got out of it with only two runs when Thurman threw out Reggie Smith trying to steal. Mickey Rivers cut down another run when he threw out Steve Garvey at home. I was back in the four spot, in right field, and I helped keep a rally going in the bottom of the first with a hit. We came right back, got a run, then tied it when Willie Randolph homered, took the lead when Willie walked and Munson drove him in with a double.

Billy brought on Sparky again with two on and one out in the ninth, and for once Sparky let up a run to tie it. But he was unhittable again after that, pitched all the way through the twelfth, and in the bottom of that inning Paul Blair—Billy got me out of there again, for defensive purposes—singled in Willie with the game winner.

That was a nice win—Billy Martin's first World Series win, ever—but we still needed a pitcher. I thought maybe Billy would throw Dick Tidrow, because he'd pitched so well as a starter down the stretch.

Instead, he put Catfish Hunter out there. Catfish hadn't pitched in more than a month, since he'd been bombed by the Blue Jays, an expansion team that year. It seems that he'd changed his arm slot, coming back after being hit by a batted ball on Opening Day. By October, his arm was killing him, he could barely come overhand when he pitched—and he had some sort of bladder inflammation that they thought was a hernia at first.

But Billy was going to put him out there. In the World Series.

It hurt me to see that. It hurt me to see what Catfish went through all year. It hurt me to see him humbled in front of a national TV audience.

Catfish was a great, great pitcher. Hall of Famer, Cy Young winner. Won more than twenty games five years in a row. He'd been a great big-game pitcher, a great postseason pitcher for us in Oakland as well, went 7–2 for us in October—4–0 with a save in the World Series. They worked him like a mule in New York. His first year for the Yankees, 1975—in part under Billy—he threw 328 innings and thirty complete games. For a team that finished third, twelve games out of first.

It seemed as though somebody didn't care; they just pitched his arm off. Threw him another three hundred innings the *next* year. Now he looked done, at the age of thirty-one.

The story they gave out in the World Series was that this was Billy's strategy to get his pitching set up. If Catfish could take up a day, he could pitch Torrez, Guidry, and maybe Gullett with sufficient rest.

But many felt this was the result of Billy not setting up his staff right, going back to early September. He could've started Ken Holtzman—if he hadn't decided he was useless for some reason. He could've started Ken Clay, who was a rookie but pitched very well for us at times. He could've pitched Tidrow, who'd been tough for us all year, was excellent down the stretch, and was well rested.

He should've at least pitched Catfish sometime before, instead of leaving him to rust for a whole month. I said it at the time: "They probably should've pitched him somewhere along the line, don't you think?"

But Martin just threw him out there anyway. First batter up, line drive. It was caught. So was the second one. Then Reggie Smith hits a double off the center-field wall. Ron Cey homered to left. Steve Yeager hit a homer the next inning to deep left. Reggie Smith hit a monster shot, into the bleachers in right-center. I was in right field, and I remember watching it and saying, "Wow, Reggie hit a bomb."

By then, even Billy had to come get him. It was 5–0; the game was over.

But guess what? *Then* he brings in Tidrow, who pitches almost three innings of shutout ball. *Then* he brings in Ken Clay, who throws another three shutout innings, doesn't even give up a hit. Then we're down 5–1 in the ninth . . . and Billy brings in Sparky, who's been pitching his arm off for us, to throw another inning. We lose, 6–1.

After that game, the big consensus among the writers was what a genius Billy Martin was for sacrificing Catfish to line up his pitching. All I saw was a manager who had put a guy out there who was injured, who couldn't pitch, and made him throw until the game was lost—and only then brought in two guys who were lights out. Either one of them could have started the game. Then Billy wasted his closer for a useless inning.

That's great managing? You managed your pitchers like that today, they would run you out of town. They would never stop talking about it on sports radio.

I was steaming. After that game, I was just slinging it back at Billy. I went into the locker room and told the writers, "Cat hasn't pitched for a month. In a World Series, how do you make a decision like that with a guy like Hunter? Cat did his best, but he hasn't pitched!"

I knew that was speaking out of turn, but I said what I said, and I meant it. In Oakland, if you'd said anything like that about Dick Williams using a pitcher, he'd've come back and said his piece, and we would move on.

I knew I was putting my hand back in the buzz saw by speaking out, but I didn't care anymore. I was fed up. Billy had told me he'd start me every game in the World Series, but he was already hinting he'd bench me in the next game because Tommy John, a left-hander, was going. When I challenged the idea, he cracked, "Splittorff isn't pitching, is he?"

Gosh, we were *so* close. He didn't like it so much when the press ran over and told him what I'd said about Catfish. When we got out to Dodger Stadium and had our workout there, he told them, "He can kiss my dago ass."

The writers were just about in ecstasy with that one. They ran back to me, and I told them, "I'd respond for you guys, but what difference would it make?"

Billy wasn't letting it go. He told the press, "If he's going to say things that hurt the club, and if he doesn't hit Tommy John, I may have to think about making a change. He has a little growing up to do."

Nice, huh? Another little threat, put on a little more pressure. How me criticizing him about humiliating Catfish hurt the club, I still don't know. Just how me saying anything would affect the club in the field, I don't know either.

Billy wouldn't stop, and the reporters just kept winding him up. He got in a few more digs, saying I wasn't hustling in the field. Oh, that again. He started going on about what "a true Yankee" does and doesn't do. That man *loved* to talk about being a true Yankee. He said, "A true Yankee player doesn't criticize another Yankee player or the manager."

I don't think a day went by that Billy didn't knock somebody on the club. I don't think a day went by that he didn't knock *me*. He was always saying, "If I'm going to back that prick, why doesn't he back me?" But he never backed me. Not for a minute. He was saying, "In Oakland, the players criticized the manager. The manager runs the club here, and he should've learned that this summer."

In Oakland, actually, we never criticized the manager much at all, because he was a man about things, he could take it if somebody looked sideways at him.

Of course, then it got out of hand. Billy trying to needle me, trying to get in my head, saying, "He's putting a lot of pressure on himself. Now he'd better get a couple of hits." I thought, "Billy, that's not going to work. You need to go down another road, bro. Not dealing with pressure? That's not on my menu."

He got Thurman to jump into it, which was hurtful to me. Talking about that *Sport* magazine article again. Thurman was quoted as saying, "We have a chance to win a Series ring and a guy is second-guessing the manager. If I was hitting .111, I wouldn't be second-guessing the manager."

After that, Fran came and talked to me, and George came and talked to me as well. George told me to apologize, and he gave me a statement to read out on the field. I didn't really much care anymore. I realized by then, if we lost, I was going to get the blame. And as long as it looked like I was responsible, they were never going to fire Billy.

So I went and read this statement. I mean, you can probably tell from it how serious I was about it all. It reads like a television script: "In the emotion of wanting to win the World Series, maybe I said something I shouldn't have said and it was taken the wrong way. I have no desire to comment on anything Billy Martin does in handling the ball club because he has won the pennant two years in a row, and I'm pleased to be a member of this club. I've had a good year because of the way he handled me."

It was nonsense. The way he handled me? Right. And he never apologized to me, not about that, not about anything.

He was the genius because he threw away a ball game in the World Series and humiliated a great pitcher. And I was the bad guy because I objected.

By then, I was just doing whatever it took for me to stay in the lineup. It took Gabe Paul to defuse the whole situation. He got out to L.A., and he made fun of it all, told the press, "This is another chapter in the tumultuous life of the 1977 Yankees."

He told them, "Controversial ballplayers are many times better ballplayers because they are not afraid of the consequences." He said, "We judge players by what they do on the field. If we want all nice boys, we'll go to the church steps and collect them."

Amen.

I just wanted to get back on that field. And that field was Dodger Stadium, where I had always played well. Tommy John was a very tough pitcher, tough lefty, ground-ball pitcher, but I plunked a single to left in the first, drove in Munson. Took second when Dusty Baker over-ran the ball, and scored on a hit by Piniella. I had a walk and scored another run later.

We got on top early, and Mike Torrez gutted it out, pitched another complete-game win, had nine strikeouts. What's more, I could feel I was starting to get on a roll again.

You can feel it when it starts to come. You start staying back on the ball longer, and you stay *through* the ball longer. The body is staying in the hitting zone longer; you're staying on the ball and driving it into left-center field more—for me, a lefty hitter. I was *seeing* the ball longer, and going with the pitches more where they were located, in or away.

When you're trying to do too much, you come *off* the ball. Your thoughts are to pull the ball to your power field even before it's thrown. You have the wrong picture in your mind. What you *need* to do is to use the whole field, not just your pull side.

If you stay over the ball, go through the ball longer, then you're staying on balance. You're keeping your body on balance and driving everything correctly.

Nowadays, they work a lot with film, with coaching. I don't even remember if we had a hitting coach in 1977. I don't remember one. You could go to Yogi. My hitting coaches were really Lou Piniella and Thurman, who was a great hitter. Both fundamentally very sound. You could go and talk to them.

Just why it comes and goes . . . it's in the mind. You got to have a little less going on. We all know that grooves come and go. In the mind, the body has a feel. It has a lot going on. You have to focus on the baseball and where it's coming from and take the barrel of your bat to the ball. You have to think only of squaring the baseball. You can't think about what you're going to do before you hit it. Stay back and use the entire field. You can't think big. You have to stay within yourself.

And I was there. I was settling into that groove.

Game 4 of the World Series, I led off the second inning and hit a low line drive to left for a double off Doug Rau. Just stayed with the ball, hit down the left-field foul line. Piniella drove me in with a single, Chambliss had a double, and Bucky hit a single. We were up 3–0 real quick again.

Ron Guidry pitched another beautiful game. He gave up a two-run homer to Davey Lopes, but he was never in trouble, struck out seven, gave up four hits, and pitched a complete game.

Sixth inning, I took Rick Rhoden, who was pitching by then, deep to left-center. A good sign. This meant I was staying behind the ball. Drove it out there for my first World Series home run as a Yankee. Top of the ninth, I hit another ball to the same area, almost as deep. It was caught, but I had it now. I had dynamite in the barrel.

It was around this time that Thurman Munson started calling me Mr. October. It was after the second game of the Series, and he was sticking up for Martin against me. He told the media, "Billy probably just doesn't realize Reggie is Mr. October."

Thurman had called me that back in Detroit. He meant it sarcastically. He was referring to the nickname I first got when Joe Garagiola called me "the autumn child, Reggie Jackson," during the 1973 postseason. Earl Weaver called me that down the stretch in 1976, but Earl meant it for real. He said I was a terror down the stretch. I'd already had some pretty good postseasons. But I was just getting warmed up.

Game 5 of the World Series, Billy pitched Gullett again, but this time his arm really was done. We were down 5–0 before Martin pulled him in the fifth inning.

Don tried to come back the next year, but he broke down early again and was out of baseball by the end of that season. Funny thing, of all the pitchers Billy and Art Fowler handled in those years, so many of them—Catfish, Kenny Holtzman, Don Gullett, Ed Figueroa—were done by the time they left; they never had another good year again. Guys like Mike Torrez, Sparky Lyle, Dick Tidrow, they were only shadows of their former selves. Hmm . . .

Just like with Dave Boswell, when he pitched for Billy in Minnesota. Or Joe Coleman when he pitched for Billy in Detroit, or Fergie Jenkins after he pitched for Billy in Texas, or all those young arms—Mike Norris, Matt Keough, Rick Langford, Steve McCatty, Brian Kingman—he ruined out in Oakland. They combined to throw the most complete games of any staff in almost thirty-five years—and then they were all done.

Maybe somebody should've said something to him a long time before. I said something—and got forced to read an apology for the cameras.

By the seventh inning, we were down 10–0, but I was just getting untracked in Dodger Stadium. I hit a single and scored that inning, then in the eighth I hit a long home run down the right-field line off Don Sutton. Matter of fact, Thurman and I hit back-to-back home runs that inning.

I remember Sutton was friends with Munson, and when Thurman hit his ball out, Don was joking with him all the way around the bases. He talked to the media about that—but of course Sutton also needed to get in that he didn't approve of my home run.

He said, "I didn't like it when Jackson followed with his home run. I object to guys who trot the bases like they had saved the world from utter chaos."

Thing was, Don Sutton didn't live in my world. My world *was* utter chaos.

I didn't know what to say to that. How was I supposed to run around the bases? With my head down? If Sutton had pitched the next Tuesday, he could've been part of history.

We had to fly back to New York for Game 6 of the Series, but that was all right. It gave the media another day to drum up more stuff.

First, *Time* magazine came out that Monday, our off day, with a big story. It was all about that episode with Lou and Thurman going up to Steinbrenner's suite and having to hide in the bathroom. Though, of course, it had to involve me, too—some quote from an unnamed source saying I wouldn't play another year for Martin.

I don't know who the heck said that. I really didn't care. But the idea of not playing another year for Billy was interesting. It would've been a great Christmas present.

It's amazing what people said and how important it seemed to say something about me. How I was always supposed to be the problem. You know, today with the Yankees I joke with guys. Jorge Posada always used to kid me about things I'd say, "the magnitude of me" and things like that. But always in good fun.

Then? I wanted to ask my teammates, "Where are you going with all this? Why all the conversation? Why don't you just do what you do and leave it alone?

"If you think I'm goofy and off base, then let me star in my own movie. I'll be the star, the supporting actor, the camera guy, the lighting guy. I can do it all. Just leave me dangle, dude."

I mean, like with Billy Martin, I used to look at him and think, "Who *is* that dude? What's the deal?"

But I got tired of making comments to the public about him. I never went out and said, "He's drinking so much that alcohol must be going to his brain." I never went to the writers and said, "He's out of control. He sleeps up to game time in his office."

You don't get me, and I don't get you. Okay. When the game starts and I'm in the lineup, root against me if you want. But just let me do my thing.

Part of it, I'm sure, was racial. This was 1977. Part of it, I'm sure, was *me*. Part of it was Billy. Part of it was the media's job in selling papers. The ingredients were perfect for constant drama, all of it happening in the Big Apple. George Steinbrenner had all the players for a Hollywood blockbuster, and I wouldn't let everything get by without a comment sometimes.

I don't know, it's funny. I wish I played today. In some ways, with ESPN and additional media, the controversy would be bigger. It would never stop. They'd have to bring back Walter Cronkite. They'd cover the things I said and supposedly said on the evening news. That would be such fun.

If I played today, I'd stay in trouble. I'd be in the commissioner's office all the time, I guess. I'd be everywhere—including where I wasn't supposed to be.

I remember asking Mickey Mantle, "Mickey, are all the stories that people tell about you true?" Mickey's response to me: "No, Reggie, if I'd have done everything everybody said I did, I'd have been three freaking guys."

On the other hand . . . you know, nothing I was saying or doing was that outlandish. I wasn't getting into fights in strip clubs. I wasn't getting arrested or doing drugs. I was never staggering around drunk, never made any stupid remarks.

I only wanted to play the game. I wanted to go out and play, be left alone and see what I could do.

And now that I was hitting, I was going to hold the deck.

16

"That's Three, Mom!"

My father always said, "As long as you have a bat in your hand, you can control the story."

Everybody was still yipping about this or that in the papers. I really didn't care. The Yankees held a press conference that Tuesday morning, the morning of the sixth game, and announced they were giving Billy a $50,000 bonus and a new Lincoln Mark V, and paying the rent on his apartment, as a reward for the brilliant job he'd done.

Good for him.

I didn't care. I had a bat in my hand.

Before the game, Joe DiMaggio came to the clubhouse. That was awesome. Joe DiMaggio was walking nobility. They finally worked it out where he was throwing out the first pitch, and we got him good seats up front.

Joe was royalty, he acted like royalty, and you were going to treat him like royalty, or he wasn't going to participate. Joe came to the clubhouse to see us before the game and talk to us, and that was a real treat.

Joe told me, "I know you've had some issues, but you've made the Yankees proud. Nice going"—something along those lines. I'd known him since Oakland in 1968, when he was a coach for the A's. He just hung out, got paid, and had some useful things to say about hitting. He was always nice, and I always got along with him. Everybody thought he was aloof, but I thought Joe was a regal guy.

Very private man, didn't let too many people in, but I got along with Joe very well. He'd always sign balls for me when I asked him. I remember one time, though, I asked him to sign a ball for Buck

Showalter, the manager then, and he told me, "I already signed one for Buck, a couple years ago." (He was keeping track.)

My father, my brother Joe in the air force, Fran Healy—they were all there, and I was in a good frame of mind. My sister Beverly, her family came up for the game, which I was glad to see. I was ready to go. I had an unbelievable batting practice that evening. *Unbelievable.*

I always hit for the last five minutes of batting practice. At that time, the starting lineup would hit for forty-five minutes, and the last five minutes were mine. I always hit last. I enjoyed it. You usually let your bomber hit last.

The teams are changing the field. Everyone's getting ready to go in, everyone's outside. The Dodgers are about to take the field for their batting practice, so they're waiting. All the Dodgers are there, all the Yankees are on the field, the media are five-, six-deep for the World Series. I mean, there are so many media there you can't even move.

During that batting practice, I probably had fifty swings in five minutes. In the span of those five minutes, I must have hit thirty-five balls in the right-field bleachers, within the space of a fifty-foot circle. Deep, high, majestic drives.

I remember Dave Anderson, Dick Young, Ira Berkow—I remember all those guys from the press there watching. Ross Greenburg, who later ran HBO for the longest time, was there as a runner for ABC, and he told me the story more than once: "Reggie, I'll never forget the batting practice you had that night."

I think it was a fun time for the people at the game. I don't think I ever had another batting practice like that. Either Mike Ferraro or Dick Howser was pitching; they threw batting practice to me all the time. The Dodgers were there on the foul line, watching it. Everybody was really enjoying it. People were oohing and aahing while I was hitting them out. It was crazy. The crowd kept getting louder and louder. And by the time I stepped out of the batting cage, they gave me a standing ovation—fifty-seven thousand people. It was fun, man.

People liked to say, "Reggie played well in big games because of his ego, he loved the spotlight." That wasn't true. There are a lot of guys who like attention, a lot of guys who have big egos—and they ain't worth a crap in that situation.

Did I like having an opportunity to show what I could do? Did I like having the chance to show my skill set? Yes.

After the game, I'd have no problem saying, "Did you enjoy that as much as I did?" And people would laugh at that and go, "What the heck's wrong with this guy?" Nothin' wrong with me, dude. I'm enjoying what I'm doing.

Did Koufax get called out because he enjoyed the spotlight? No, he was just great—no matter where he played, or when he played, back alley or the stage of the World Series.

I was just ready to play. As they write about the warhorse in the book of Job, "When the trumpet sounds, he says, 'Aha!' He smells the battle from afar."

I was ready for the battle. I had a bat in my hand, and I knew how to use it.

Mike Torrez was going for us that night, and this time he had three days' rest. That's not much nowadays; back then, it was the norm. He was a tough pitcher for us that year. Earlier, he'd already become the first Mexican American ever to win a World Series game. That's a nice chit to have on your sleeve. I remember when he pitched those five innings of shutout ball to keep us in Game 5 of the ALCS. When he finally came out, Munson was quoted as having paid him a huge compliment: "You are an *outstanding* Mexican!"—in a positive way.

That was how we all felt about him. We were confident. We were ready. Mike was the guy we wanted on the mound.

Sometimes, when you're up for a game, you can be a little *too* ready, a little too fired up. I know that I would get fired up when I was in the playoffs and the World Series in Oakland. In order to combat that, during the postseason I would manage to stay up late, one, two in the morning watching TV, and get up at six, seven. Slow myself down. I had found myself at times getting very antsy along the foul line before the game, during the introductions. So I thought I would make myself tired the night before and just stay up. It worked for me. When the Series was over, I could sleep for two days—stay in bed, eighteen hours. I don't know if other athletes do that. But it always worked for me.

I had stayed up late the night before the sixth game of the Series in 1977. I don't know if the other guys were too excited, but in the first inning Bucky made a rare error for him with two outs, and Thurman gave up a passed ball. Then Mike walked a batter and gave up a two-run triple to deep left by Garvey. We were already down, 2–0.

That's all right. We felt good, and we were confident. Bottom of the second, I got up for the first time, ready to go—and Burt Hooton walked me on four pitches. I don't know if he was being cautious after watching me in batting practice, but he was there. Chris Chambliss took him deep to center-right a couple pitches later, and we got it tied, 2–2.

Top of the third, Reggie Smith, who was a tremendous player and always played well in the postseason (at least he did against us), homered to almost the same place as Chambliss did and took back the lead. That was his third home run against us. As I look back now, he was having a great Series against us and was probably on his way to the MVP.

Right idea. Wrong Reggie.

I was back up the next inning with us still down, 3–2. "Old Reliable" Thurman on first with a single. I was ready; I was in a groove. But I had something else, too.

Back in those days, the technology we had was different than it is today, but very reliable. Sometimes we looked at video, but to be honest, I never really watched video that much. Things happened too fast for me on video, and sometimes it was archaic compared with today. We used to go out and shoot it, then take what we had and put it on a fifteen-inch screen. Stop it. Dissect it. Play it back. And that was just video of batting practice. There was no video of the game, not in the clubhouse like it is today. Today there are video people and a couple rooms of equipment set up.

Players now . . . sometimes they come in the clubhouse after an at-bat during the game and go and dissect their actions right away.

Not a fan of that. I think the focus should be on the game, on the bench. And then there's the preparation that the pitching coach, the catcher, and the pitcher have before the game as well—the preparation that the hitting coach and the hitters have, going over the game beforehand in great detail. It is of great value to today's player—going over the performance and the basic tendencies of the opposing pitcher, his history against your ball club, as well as the history of his last few starts.

It's become a science: what he throws first pitch; how many strikes, first pitch. How many curveballs during the game. How many curveballs to left-handers. How many curveballs on different counts. All good information. But sometimes too much creates clutter. I think it's awesome that it's available, but knowing how to apply it is also a challenge. So much information can be too much for players.

Some of the great players don't want too much information. Some want to get out of the way of all that and let their skill sets perform. Some players like all the information; some players don't.

I enjoyed it at times, but at others I didn't want it. As an example, I was not a player who did well if I knew what was coming. If a pitcher tipped his hand and had a different action when he threw a curveball or when he threw a fastball and you could pick it up . . . I did not want to know it. I got too anxious if I knew what was coming. Hard as that is for players today to believe, I did not want to know what was coming. It's rare, but there are players who do better just relying on their instinct. I was one of those guys. I believe Jeter is as well.

There are guys who analyze everything. The time the pitcher takes to release the baseball, how long it takes for it to get to home plate. They have it down to a tenth of a second—the amount of time it takes the catcher to receive the ball and then to throw it to second base. From that they will tell you precisely how long the leads are that you need to take if you're going to steal. They'll figure out that it will take a pitcher 1.7, 1.8 seconds from the start of his motion to the time the ball arrives in the catcher's mitt. They will also time how long it takes the catcher to receive the ball and how long it takes to get to second base on the throw, maybe 1.8 seconds as well. The combined total will be 3.6 seconds. If a fast runner can get enough of a lead and arrive at second base in under 3.6, then he will have an opportunity to steal.

This is how the game is played today. Valuable information, plotted down to that much of a microsecond.

Teams nowadays go over where the fielders should play against everybody, depending on who's pitching and what he's throwing. The length of the grass—is it longer on one side of the infield or the other?—and how much it slows the ball down. How much range the infielders have, whether we should cut the grass that day or not . . . the game is that detailed.

We didn't have any meetings with Billy like that. We barely talked. The pitchers and catchers went over things, but there really weren't meetings for the offense in those days. The bench coach was unheard of when I played. Some teams didn't even have batting coaches.

I think nowadays having specific coaches helps teams be more aware of tendencies, because there are some great baseball minds available to you. But my first couple years on the Yankees, we didn't have hitting coaches. Later, we had Charley Lau, but before that I don't think there was anyone specifically for hitting. You did it yourself.

You worked with other players like Lou Piniella and Roy White, who were knowledgeable about hitting. Guys like Munson and Bobby Murcer a couple years later, when he came back to the team—he was an outstanding baseball man. Chris Chambliss had knowledge. You might talk among yourselves with guys who knew how someone would pitch against you.

But before the World Series, we had reports from our experienced advance scouts. We had a guy named Jerry Walker, who had twenty-plus years in the game, but most of all we had the great Birdie Tebbetts. Birdie was in his mid-sixties, a former major-league catcher. I had worked with him when we were in Oakland. Both he and Jerry Walker were there as advance scouts, because the A's were usually in the postseason.

Gene Michael, who was a coach at this time for the Yankees, also had a tremendous baseball mind. He still does today. Many people give him some credit for the collection of great players who came through the Yankees' organization in the 1990s. You know, I learned a lot from Gene Michael about using scouting reports.

These guys all went out and scouted National League teams we were likely to see in the World Series. From them, you could learn the "tendencies" that their pitchers had, as well as hitters and defenders, who had a good arm and who was accurate. They gathered a wealth of info.

You had to have that, because in the days before interleague play you didn't really see the National League guys. Maybe at the All-Star Game, or a little bit in spring training. But not much. And in the spring, you wouldn't see as much. They'd be working on things, getting ready for the season. You never saw what they were like at the top of their game, giving it everything they had.

I leaned on Michael and Tebbetts most of all. I had my own meetings with them after they talked to the whole team before each World Series game. I would huddle with them for a good twenty to thirty minutes. I used our scouts in my own special way, to try to get a little more specific, more detailed knowledge. I'd asked them when they went out on the road to scout, "When you go watch the Dodgers, would you find out the pitch sequences for me? Find out what pitches they like to throw in different pitch counts. The counts I am most concerned about are 1–0, 2–0, 2–1, 3–1—when I have a free wheel. Take note of what they throw in those counts to guys like myself: Willie McCovey, Willie Stargell, Billy Williams, Al Oliver." Any left-handed hitter with sock. Boom in the barrel.

They were the guys I thought I was most like—the guys I *hoped* I was like. Left-hand hitters with power. Like me, they had the dynamite in the barrel. The danger level was the same. I thought if the scouts could see twenty at-bats with hitters like that by a certain pitcher, I could find out some tendencies.

And I thought if I had seven or eight of those situations, I could pick out which ones were the free passes—I could look for a pitch to hit. Eight out of nine times, or six out of eight—if they threw the same thing that often on a 2–1 count or a 2–0 count . . . I had a free look. I could take a shot for a banger. For a bridge piece. You know—a chance to collect a toll.

There were always fans—there were *writers*—who didn't understand the game. Who insisted on looking at me as just a big, unthinking guy who went up there and swung for the fences. They thought I struck out too much. Sometimes I did. They didn't think of me as a complete player.

They had it wrong, I thought. What I understood was what my role was. I understood that I had four chances a game to put a number on the board. One, two, three, four. That was my role.

That wasn't the role for everybody. Great as players like Derek Jeter and Pete Rose are, you can't ask them to go up there and try to hit it out. They have their roles; there's a lot of things players like that do. Their role is to get on base, move the runners along, keep the rally going. Jeter is a great clutch player, probably the best in the game in his era—it's either him or Mo! (When you add Mo to the mix, I guess, we all become second. Even Ali.) Jeter is a guy you always want there to drive in a big run. The greatest.

Roles change sometimes. You can expand your role. Jeter's hit some big home runs. I remember he hit a home run on the first pitch against the Mets in the World Series, leading off the fourth game after we'd lost the night before. Had a home run the game after that, to tie the score. Great players can expand their roles at times.

But I knew what my role was. It was to be a banger. Put a number on the board, and drive in runs.

In the sixth game of the World Series against the Dodgers, I remember calling upstairs to Gene Michael in the box in Yankee Stadium. Checking how he thought they would pitch me. I got a lot of insight from Stick and trusted him; I trusted our scouts. They had so much time in the game.

We were in agreement that they would try to come in on me. It's the most common approach with most players with power. Once a player gets his arms extended, he's able to hit the ball a long way. Better keep that player crowded, keep the ball in and make him hurry, keep the ball in on him so that he doesn't get a chance to extend his arms. If he does, it's a loud sound: boom!

After I got a walk my first at-bat, Stick said, "Hooton's gonna pitch you fastball in." That's what I expected. Nice to have him co-sign my thought.

What I did was, I stepped back in the batter's box about four inches—four inches farther away from the plate. From the tips of my shoes to the balls of my feet, that's how I measured it.

I always cleaned the batter's box before I got in. Did a little gardening. I didn't want to see another guy's mark and think it was mine. I always went in, swept everything away with my feet—and that gave me the chance to measure where I wanted to stand. Four inches farther away from the plate than where I would normally stand. Then I *leaned* forward, toward home plate, to make it look as if I wasn't in a different spot.

Soon as Hooton threw the ball, I was spinning.

I hit it hard, a low bullet—a nice four-iron—that went deep into the crowd in right field. It got out in a hurry, and it scored Munson ahead of me and put us up again. I came back into the dugout, saw the camera right there in front of me with the red light on, and just held up one finger.

I knew I was going to do well. The ball seemed big, and I was very comfortable and confident. The crowd was very much on my side, screaming on their feet, full of support. I could look in George's box and see he was standing up. I could see friends and family sitting close by. Nice feeling.

I got up again in the next inning. We'd scored another run in the fourth. We were up, 5–3, and the Dodgers had pulled Hooton for Elias Sosa. They knew they had to stop us there.

Sosa was an outstanding relief pitcher. Threw hard. Harder than Hooton, ninety-five miles an hour or so. Seems the Dodgers always had guys who threw in the high nineties.

This time Willie Randolph was on first when I came to bat. I knew Sosa was still going to keep the ball inside. I watched him warming up when he came in; I saw what he threw. I thought of Stick and Birdie Tebbetts again and what we had talked about. That was enough. I knew Sosa would try to pitch inside as well.

I was just hoping he'd hurry up and throw a strike early. Sure enough, he threw it in. I turned on it. Smashed it. I was worried it wasn't going to stay up because I thought I'd got on top of it a little. It was hit so hard I didn't think it had a chance to get up high enough to get out. I was afraid I smothered it a bit. I remember running down to first base saying, "Stay up, stay up, stay up, stay up, stay up."

It did.

It seemed like I hit it harder than the last one. Too fast for anybody to snare it. Went just four or five rows into the seats, but it was enough. I think it might have gone through the wall if it had been a little lower. I noticed that the moment it went out, Tommy Lasorda came running out to the mound to pull his pitcher. Too late.

I was just excited that I had put us ahead by 7–3. I knew we had a good chance to win then. And I could hear the fans. They were yelling, "Reg-gie! Reg-gie! Reg-gie!" The whole Stadium.

That was nice to hear. It helped, hearing that. It helped me to focus.

You focus on the moment. Just the pitcher and me. If I got anything to hit, I was going to be on it.

I'm just focused on the ball coming out of the pitcher's hand. And I was going to put a swing on it, and I was going to be on time. You want to have the barrel of the bat there, right on the ball. Oh, boy, did I!

In the dugout, I turned to the camera, held up two fingers this time, and dropped a big "Hi, Mom!" She couldn't be at the game, she wasn't feeling well, but I was the one who started that whole "Hi, Mom!" thing. This was October 18, 1977—so I want the copyright on "Hi, Mom!" LOL.

The crowd was yelling so much Ray Negron was trying to push me out to take a bow. I remember him telling me, "Go back out there for the fans."

Guys do that all the time now, even in the middle of a regular-season game. It didn't happen so much back then. You did that then, you were liable to get a fastball in your ear next time up.

I wasn't about to take a curtain call. Not in the sixth inning of a World Series game. I told Ray, "All I want to do right now is win this thing"—which is how I felt.

Ray was still elbowing me, saying, "Maybe you're gonna hit three." I kind of pushed that off. I told him, "I don't know about that."

I didn't need that kind of distraction. I'd already hit two. That's enough. Whoever heard of anybody hitting three? Babe Ruth. That's who did that—though I didn't know it at the time.

I was more excited because we were in the lead. Everybody was excited. We felt that we were going to win. Mike Torrez had got into a groove; he was pretty much in control on the mound. We had Sparky Lyle in the bullpen, who was rested, and he was the best.

For once, there was no envy, no jealousy. Billy was genuinely excited. He was happy for me and the team. We had a chance to win as the Yankees. We were a team at that point—a team at last.

When I came up again, it was leading off the bottom of the eighth. We were still up, 7–3, and the Dodgers brought in Charlie Hough, who led them in saves that year with twenty-two. Another outstanding pitcher, later had a whole new career as a starter for the Rangers, pitched twenty-five years in the big leagues.

He could do that because he was a knuckleball pitcher, a whole different kind of cat. A lot of guys had trouble hitting knuckleballers, especially after seeing a couple of hard throwers in the same game.

But I got to say, I was a little surprised to see him running in from the bullpen to face me, because I had a great history against knuckleballers. Hoyt Wilhelm, Wilbur Wood, Steve Hargan—I always banged them on the nose. I looked around, and I thought, "They must not know that I hit knuckleballers, they're bringing him in." I was really happy that they did because I knew I was going to get a couple of home run cuts, always did against knuckleballers.

The key to hitting a knuckleball is timing. I got this from Sal Bando, who was a great knuckleball hitter with the A's. He taught me about how to hit it: "Just stand there, Reggie. Don't even get into your stance. Just face forward, and take a nice full cut."

I sat the bat on my shoulder, just kind of stood there. When Hough wound up, I got ready, but I didn't sit there in my stance. I kind of stood there nice and loose, because the ball came so slow. Then when he winds up, get ready to time it.

You're never supposed to admit that you hit a monster shot. You're never supposed to admit that you got it all. You're always supposed to say, "I didn't quite get it." Oh, well.

But I got all of Charlie Hough's knuckleball, and a little more.

I must have hit it 475 feet or more, into the black in center field—the black background they had for hitters in the old Stadium, where no one sat. I was the only person to do that in the Stadium up to then except for Jimmy Wynn, back on Opening Day.

I hit the ball high and far. I just had to stand and watch it a little. The ball bounced once out there, and then all these kids were scrambling out of the bleachers to fight for it. People were throwing confetti on the field; they were throwing anything they could rip up.

It was like a movie, that whole scene. It was like the movie that I felt I experienced in New York when I first came to talk to George Steinbrenner and people were stopping us on the street, saying, "You got to come play in New York, Reg." On this night, it was the movie I had always thought New York could be.

Running around the bases, I almost couldn't believe my experience. I felt like I was running on clouds. Certainly, it was one of my greatest moments. The only moment that compared with it was when my parents were there together to see me inducted into the Hall of Fame. They were divorced for so many years, but they were there together. It put a smile on my heart to see them there, one that's still there today.

I remember seeing a picture of me running out that third home run the next day, I think in the *Daily News*. One they took of me when I was between second and third and both my feet were off the ground. That was exactly how I felt, just like I was off the ground, the whole way around the bases. I remember seeing the players on the Dodgers as I circled—Garvey, Lopes, Russell, and Cey. Seeing Yeager when I crossed the plate. I remember them looking at me in admiration. It was just a nice feeling of respect from player to player.

After I got across the plate, the first player there was Chambliss, who was excited. Everybody was excited back in the dugout. They were all looking to shake my hand—and I was looking to shake theirs. My teammates.

I was looking especially for Willie Randolph, who had always been supportive of me that year. Lockering over in the corner with me the whole season. I sought him out, and when I found him, he gave me a big smile, and then we had a big hug.

I looked over at the dugout camera, and this time I held up three fingers and said, "That's three, Mom!"

I was looking around for Ray Negron, who they'd sent down to the clubhouse for something. We hugged, and then he started on me again: "You ought to go out. You ought to go out. You owe them that much." Ray, always the director!

So I went. I went up to the top of the dugout steps, and I took off my helmet and held it out to them. The Stadium was rocking. I tried to turn around and wave to everybody. You could feel it shaking, like it was going to come down. Some 56,407 fans out there, and they were shouting, "Reg-gie! Reg-gie! REG-GIE!" like I'd never heard before.

SITTING IN THE ROCKING CHAIR

I WENT OUT to right field in the top of the ninth. I know Billy must've wanted to make a defensive replacement, put Paul Blair out there or something. But to his credit, he didn't. He let me go out there and take another big hand from the fans.

It was wild in the Stadium by then, like everything had been that whole summer. All the crazy stuff that went on—the Son of Sam, the blackout and the riot, the heat, the bad economic times. For me, I missed a lot of it. I was too caught up in my own crazy, jamma-ramma, soap opera episode, or whatever you want to call it. I had been stuck in my own little corner of the world for four or five months. On this night, stormy clouds were starting to clear. I was truly excited and happy.

The fans were throwing down everything. Not at me, not aimed at any of the Yankees, of course, but they were throwing out anything that wasn't nailed down. They were excited. I remember there were bits of paper coming down continuously. It was a little scary—I even went back in and got a batting helmet to wear. They were going nuts out there. They started sitting on the edge of the wall in right field, sitting with their legs hanging over the wall. I don't know what I would've done if I'd had to go back for a ball there.

I remember Rick Monday, my old friend, did hit a ball pretty deep, but I was able to haul it in. They got a run when Vic Davalillo laid down a bunt, but that was desperation. There was no way they were going to score five runs off Mike Torrez with the world championship on the line.

Big Mike, still dealing. He got the last out, caught it himself, and then it was off to the races. I knew what to expect. I'd seen the end of the game in the playoffs at Yankee Stadium the year before, after Chambliss's home run, when I was working in the broadcast booth. The moment Torrez caught that ball, fans were jumping down on the field by the hundreds. The police were racing right out after them, tackling them, grabbing them, doing whatever they could to try to control them. In an instant, it was a crazy running of the bulls—this time in Yankee Stadium.

I was a little afraid, it was so out of control. I pulled my helmet off, tucked it under my arm, and took off for the dugout like a baseball version of Jim Brown. The whole way there, someone was trying to steal my helmet, steal my glove, pull them right off me. Grabbing at me the whole way.

I wasn't panicked, but I knew I needed to get out of there, and I had the ability to do so. I made the greatest broken-field run of my life. Dodging around guys, running into a couple of them, giving them the slip. I could run pretty fast, and I just made my way through whatever obstacles were in front of me. Somehow, it was a lot like the whole season.

Back in the clubhouse, the reporters and the cameras were all over me. I was the MVP of the World Series, and they told me I had broken all sorts of records.

Five home runs in one World Series. Nobody else had ever done that. Home runs in three straight World Series games. Nobody else had ever done that.

Three home runs in one World Series game. Babe Ruth did that, twice.

But I had hit three home runs on the first pitch—three consecutive swings of the bat. Since I walked on four pitches in my first at-bat—and since I had homered on my last swing against Sutton the game before—that made four home runs on four consecutive swings of the bat.

Four swings, four home runs. Nobody could think of when anyone ever did that. Not in the World Series. Not in major-league baseball history. Not in minor-league history. Not in the history of organized ball. At least not yet.

For the Series, I hit .450, with ten runs scored and eight driven in. I finished with a slugging average of 1.250, an on-base percentage of .542, and a combined on-base and slugging average of 1.792. I set a record with twenty-five total bases.

But I never thought about it that way, what I did that night. I think there's a reverence for those records, for that performance, I get from the people, the fans, wherever I go to this day, and I so appreciate it. I'm grateful for God's work. I remember being thankful to God that evening. I remember those last few months of the season, I talked to God more than I ever had in my life.

I was praying every day. I was a dependent son. Still am.

I felt truly humbled that night, in the clubhouse. I thanked everyone—Dad, brother Joe, Gary Walker. And a tip of the cap to the Boss, for sticking by me. I told the press and the TV people, "I'm not a superstar, but I can always say that on this one night, tonight, I *was* a superstar."

That was how I really felt. You know, I thought of superstars as the guys in the Hall of Fame, the all-time greats, like Aaron and Mays. Clemente, Gehrig, DiMaggio, Mantle, Koufax, Frank and Jackie Robinson. I felt truly humble to have been in their company for that one night.

It was a strange time in the city. I wasn't able to pay much attention to all that was going on around us. None of us were; we were too caught up in what we were doing, trying to survive. This was the World Series when they kept showing buildings burning in the Bronx, not far from where we were playing. Howard Cosell talking about it on the air. With everything that was going on, it seemed sometimes like the whole city could just come apart at the seams.

I remember responding to a question about how I got through that summer and saying, "I couldn't quit this summer because of all the kids and the blacks and the little people who are pulling for me. I represent both the underdog and the overdog in our society."

Taken out of context, it can sound crazy. But I meant it. What I think that says, right there, is something about what it means to be a black man and a black *star* in this society—both in 1977 and even today.

I was the overdog. I was at the top of my profession. I was making the biggest salary. I was playing for New York, the biggest city, which lots of people thought of as the bad guys.

At the same time, I was a man of color in this society—in the America of that time. As minorities, we were always having to prove ourselves. I was representing all people of color, all who came from whence I came. For a person of color nothing was ever given, nothing was ever assumed, nothing was ever *safe*. There were people who disliked me just because of what I looked like, without ever knowing me. They wanted me to fail. They wanted me to disgrace my community.

That's what successful black men and women have to battle against in our country, far too often. That's what even someone like President Obama has had to deal with. The higher you go, the *more* of a threat you become to some people.

We all contribute to our social problems as the people of this great country. The laws try to make the playing field even, but we have to make the laws work.

My dad and my sister Beverly came down to the clubhouse after the game. That was good. He was pretty excited. I was very lucky my father and I had such a great relationship. Not only were we father and son, but we were best friends. I kept saying "Hi, Mom!" to the cameras for my mother, who wasn't feeling well enough to attend the game. But I knew she was there in front of the television, watching every out—and every home run!

I was feeling so good after that game I even went into Billy Martin's office and started talking with the man about next season. I told the press, "Billy Martin, I love the man. I love Billy Martin. The man did a helluva job this year." I told them, "There's nobody else I'd rather play for." I said to him in front of all the media there, "Next year, we're going to be tougher, aren't we, Skip?"

Billy was feeling pretty good; he agreed we would be tougher. I told them, "Next year is going to be different. We'll win because we have a manager who's a tough bastard and I'm a tough bastard. If you mess with Billy, you're in trouble, and if you mess with Reggie Jackson, you're in trouble."

Somebody asked what if we messed with each other.

"Then *look out!*" I yelled, and I laughed and laughed.

That was honestly how I felt that night. I was in love with everything, and I thought everything was fine. I thought now that we'd won, now that I'd shown him what I could do, the foolishness between us would stop. We'd move forward together.

I gave Martin a lot of credit, right out in front of everybody. I even invited Billy to the award ceremony when I was getting the car for being the World Series MVP. It was given out by *Sport* magazine, if you can believe that. I was just sorry Robert Ward wasn't awarding it himself.

I told Billy, "They're giving me the car Thursday, Skip"—we won the Series on a Tuesday night—"and I'd appreciate it if you'd be there."

"I'll be there," Billy said—but then I realized how early the ceremony was, and I didn't want to make it seem like an obligation.

"No, that's all right, it's too early in the morning," I told him.

"Don't worry about it, Big Guy. I'll be there," he said.

"No, you don't have to come. It's ten o'clock in the morning," I told him. But he just kept insisting, "I'll be there. I want to be there. I'll be there, you can bet on it."

He wasn't there. We both lost the bet.

To be honest, I don't think I even noticed. That whole week, I was walking on air.

After the game, about 12:30 or 1:00 a.m., when I finally got out of the locker room, I went over to Seventy-sixth and Third, to McMullen's restaurant, my usual hangout. I was driving a blue Volkswagen Beetle they'd given me for doing a commercial for Volkswagen. Ended up giving it to my brother Joe, who just loved Beetles. During that summer, I could drive it back and forth to the ballpark and sort of sneak around town in it because nobody expected to see me in a Volkswagen Beetle.

However, the night of the sixth game, there were so many people out I had to pull it up on the sidewalk when I arrived at McMullen's. I remember seeing Matt Merola, who was my agent for everything outside my baseball contracts, and some of his friends there. After twenty, thirty minutes the place started to fill up. People kept coming by to say congratulations, and I finally had to leave. It was overwhelming. I went to Rusty Staub's. He was playing for Detroit then but had just opened his first restaurant on Seventy-third and Third, and I went there.

Hugh Carey, who was governor, was there, and he stayed as long as I could remember. He was wonderful, great to hang out with. I saw him there, then I left and went back to McMullen's. Then a message came from the governor at Rusty Staub's: "Have Reggie come spend some more time with us." I said, "No, no, have him come to *us*." Everybody got a big kick out of that. He did eventually come down, a couple hours later. I stayed at McMullen's until about five, five thirty in the morning. After that I went back home, to my apartment on Fifth Avenue, but didn't go to sleep that night. I was supposed to be on the *Today* show that morning with Tom Brokaw. They sent a car over, and it was there to pick me up when I got home. I went in, changed, and went right over to do the show.

After that, I went to my Nectar Café, at Seventy-ninth and Madison, where I usually had breakfast. All the local people were there who I used to eat with, and they came in to say congratulations.

After breakfast, I went over to Seventy-first and York, over by the East River, where a friend of mine, Michael Schudroff, owned a dealership, and he specialized in Rolls and Ferraris. I had been driving my yellow Jeep CJ-5 and my little Volkswagen Beetle.

During that summer of 1977, I'd been hanging around Schudroff's service department. I'd bought a Ferrari 275 GTB 4 Cam from him and two Rolls-Royces. (I bought that Ferrari for $15,000. Today, 2013, that same model has a value of $2 million plus. I sold mine after fifteen years. At one time, I had a collection of nine Ferraris.) When I went back there, the day after the three homers, Michael—he had this very thick Brooklyn accent—said, "Boy, do I have the cah fuh you!" He kept insisting, "Come ovah heer. I'm not sellin' this cah till you buy it!"

I looked at it—and it was to die for. A 1976 Corniche convertible. I couldn't turn it down. It had a Yankee-navy convertible top, with two-tone silver and blue colors. Navy leather inside. It just looked like a Yankee.

"You need to get this cah. It belongs to you. It's got yaw name on it," Schudroff was going on. "Fuhgeddaboutit! You're gonna make millions a dollars this wintah wit' all the appearances you gonna make. It's nothin' to you, fuhgeddaboutit!"

It was $64,250. A lot of money in 1977. A lot of money even in terms of what I was making. I hung around there most of the day. Got in and out of the car all day long. We called in lunch, had corned beef and Swiss on rye. And we talked and talked and talked. I called a friend of mine out in the country. I called my attorney, Steven Kay. He asked me when I was coming home, and I said I would be home in a couple of days. I was calling all my friends, who were telling me it was okay to buy the car. If I thought they'd say don't buy it, I didn't call them!

That was all it took. I hung around for the ticker-tape parade. Hung around for *Sport* magazine to give me that MVP car. It was a 1977 Thunderbird, Yankee blue. Nice car. I signed it over to my sister Tina, who'd come up from Baltimore with her husband, Tony.

I went out and bought a Samsonite suitcase. I went out and bought a CB radio and an antenna you could attach with a magnet to the back of the car. Didn't want to scar my "new girl."

I went back to see Michael. And I bought the Corniche.

I threw a couple of jeans in the suitcase. Couple pairs of tennis shoes, couple sweatshirts, underwear. Took off for California and drove straight across the country in about forty-eight hours.

I just kept driving. I used the CB to avoid the highway patrol most of the way. My handle was Mr. October. Everybody was so nice. The truckers were nice. You know, if you got between two trucks, the term was "You're in the rocking chair"—no police ahead, no police behind. That's where I'd stay a lot of the time, sitting in the rocking chair.

I was rolling, eighty, ninety miles an hour almost the whole way.

I remember I did get stopped four or five times, in Ohio, Indiana, Oklahoma. But each time, the police who stopped me said, "I heard you were on the highway. I just wanted to meet you." No tickets. They just said, "I wanted to stop you and say hello. Congratulations on the World Series. Now go ahead, you got a clear shot." I could hear them sometimes on the CB: "Is this the ballplayer? Where you at?"

I would say, "I'm coming up on you. I'm in a Rolls and sitting on ninety." And that was okay. I could just sit and have fun with them, with everyone. It was so nice to get all that love, all across the country, after all the grief I'd been dealing with all year.

I'd stop and eat sometimes, but I never did any sleeping. I didn't need any sleep. I was still high on the World Series. I just needed a Pepsi and a Snickers bar, and I was on my way. (They didn't have a Reggie! bar yet.)

I was young and full of vinegar. Going, going, gone. I just wanted to get home. Home to family, home to my girlfriend. Home to my buddies. Sharing good times. I went across on Highway 80. Came down through Reno and Tahoe, cut across the mountains. And then there I was, back at 22 Yankee Hill Road, in the Berkeley Hills, if you can believe it. Boy, was I glad to see that house! Still own it. Still own the Corniche convertible. It was a beautiful car. Still is.

And I have to say that, thinking about it on that whole ride cross-country, thinking about coming to New York, all of it . . . I had to say, I thought it was all worthwhile.

That feeling would last until spring training.

18

REGGIE! BAR

I LET MYSELF enjoy the off-season. It felt good just to be back in California, good to be hanging around Berkeley and Oakland, all my old stomping grounds.

I had a place I went to all the time when I played with the A's: Lois the Pie Queen, which is in Emeryville now, at Sixtieth and Adeline, but which in those days used to be just over the city line in Berkeley, on Sacramento Street. It was a legend then and still is for its soul food, ribs, biscuits, and homemade apple pie. All Mom's cooking, made by Lois! They already had a Reggie Jackson special on the menu. Two pork chops, two scrambled eggs, grits, side of bacon, biscuits and butter, glass of milk and orange juice.

I can smell it and taste it now. It's a lot of food. I tried to stop eating it a few years ago, except for times when I want a treat. But I had it again, last time I was there.

It was added motivation to work out. I would give myself a few weeks to unwind from the season, then start working out hard again right after Thanksgiving.

The winter was great. Lots of commercials, lots of appearances, and off-field revenue. Michael Schudroff was right: I made a lot of money, played with my cars, as I was in the process of starting a collection that I still have today.

I came into camp the next spring training in good shape, with a good mental attitude. My arm had stopped hurting.

I thought everything that had gone on the year before would have to be water under the bridge. We were the champions of the world. I was the World Series MVP.

I mean, what could go wrong?

It *was* quieter that spring. There was a little ruckus when we went 10–13 in our exhibition games. I didn't really pay a lot of attention to it. Your record doesn't matter in the spring. You just want to leave healthy, ready, and in good shape. The fact that we had a losing record wasn't a big deal to the players and the manager.

For the Boss, it *was* a big deal. By the end of April, he was already upset enough that he was telling Billy Martin it was time he started pulling this team together. Every time George was around, he was concerned that we weren't playing well enough.

For me, at least, I didn't have anything to prove. I proved it all—in the World Series. People weren't asking so many questions about whether I could get along with Thurman or Billy Martin. People weren't asking if I could play in New York. We'd been through all that—or so I thought.

I don't know if I was really *happy*. As I've said, you know, growing up, I learned that life was not necessarily about being "happy" all the time. Because I was poor and a minority (black and Latino American), the thought was, "The next meal, heat in the house, food in the fridge," as my dad said. The focus was on getting a good education, to be prepared for the life ahead. There wasn't much discussion about college, because we couldn't afford it, and the only way to get to college was on a scholarship. I knew in high school that an athletic scholarship was the only way to college for me.

But I felt good to be there in spring training. Glad to be playing, glad to be there working out. Between the injury to my arm, and the holding out, and getting traded, and when I first became a free agent, and all else that had gone on, it was the best I'd felt in the past three years.

What's more, this time the spotlight wasn't on me. Sparky Lyle had such a great year in 1977 he became the first relief pitcher to win the Cy Young Award in the American League. But having one great closer wasn't enough for the Boss. When Goose Gossage came on the free-agent market that off-season, George went right out and signed him. Then he went out and signed Rawly Eastwick, who'd been the closer for the Big Red Machine during the Reds' World Series years.

I don't know who was giving George direction, but he was picking up outstanding talent. Again, word was at that time that Gene Michael was very involved in the makeup and the talent of the Yankees. He helped build the organization, especially the major-league club. He's been reputed to be the loudest voice that George would listen to when building a team.

Bam, just like that, we had three star closers. They said Eastwick was getting more than $200,000 a year, which was more than Sparky was making at a reported $135,000. Goose got close to the money I got, over $2.7 million, but for seven years, which shows you how fast free agency was changing everything. At the same time, major-league attendance in 1978 would finish up over two million from what it had been the year before. Over ten million from the year before that, 1976. Ticket prices were up, concession prices were up, TV ratings were up.

Teams were starting to put their games on cable television, constantly looking for new revenue streams.

Why shouldn't the players share in it? Free agency was shaking things up, giving teams a chance to get better right away. Some fans loved it and some fans didn't, I'd say fifty-fifty.

The truth is that free agency helped bring the top players to the marquee teams, and when the marquee teams are doing well, they can help a whole region. They help the whole league, the whole major-league brand. When the Cubs had a chance to make the World Series back in 2003, people were interested. When the Red Sox are doing well, when certain teams in every sport are doing well—the Packers, the Cowboys, the Patriots, the Redskins, or the 49ers, Montreal in hockey, the Lakers or the Bulls, Celtics, and others—the fans watch.

It's not as important for Philadelphia or Arizona to be doing well. They don't have the same impact.

The Yankees have more of that legacy effect than anyone. When they're playing well, it changes the whole league, the television ratings.

The Yankees *are* ratings. The teams they had with all the great players, the big *names* in the late 1990s—they were always on Sunday night TV, they had a lot of getaway games late at night on the West Coast because of TV ratings, and it made it tough for the players to play like that, always going on short rest, after tough travel.

The name teams get those TV slots. You don't see non-marquee teams on Sunday night games too much.

The big teams are revenue sources for the whole league. They're it. Freakin' Elvis Presley, Michael Jackson. They make you want to turn on the television set, sell potato chips and beer, and Pepsi. Watch those Cadillac commercials. That's what it is, $.

It doesn't matter if you love or hate this or that team, or this or that player. Love him or hate him, you can't ignore someone like Alex Rodriguez. Guys will say, "Oh, I hate him," or "Oh, I love him." But either way, you're gonna turn on the TV.

It was sad for me to leave Oakland, it was sad to leave Baltimore—but I wound up in New York. Gossage leaves Pittsburgh, winds up in New York. Roger Clemens leaves Toronto, he winds up in New York. LeBron leaves Cleveland, which takes a hit every way you can, but he goes to Miami and wakes up a town. Nobody ever heard much of Roger Maris before he came to New York.

Like it or not like it, free agency increased revenue. The pool of revenue gets larger, and the players' associations in the different sports leagues argue and discuss and work out with the owners how the players can share the revenues—and everybody gets more.

I think the fan does suffer to a point because the ticket prices go up. Some fans did not like the changes going on in sports because of that, and some still don't. They don't like to see their favorite players move on. But if you draw two million, three million people over a base-ball season, if you draw sixty thousand a game for twenty games in football, you draw fifteen thousand a game in basketball—the ticket prices are going to go up. The talent demands to be paid.

I was a free agent at the beginning of these changes. It was an exciting era, there were all kinds of great players coming into the game, and that was only the beginning.

I don't know whether the Boss was lucky or had a vision of what would happen, but he surely added tremendous value to the Yankees brand and franchise. Probably more than any other owner, he saw the changes and the opportunities that free agency would bring. He loved the Yankees so much—and through his design, his will, and a lot of luck, he produced a new Yankees dynasty. But then, as Branch Rickey liked to say, luck is the residue of design!

It was said that George mortgaged the franchise to build a champion and didn't pay attention to the budget. You heard stories that he'd say, "We need to sign so-and-so," and the chief financial officer would say, "We don't have the money." George would say, "Find it. Or I'll get a new one of you!"

The reality, though, was that George understood what all great owners before him understood—you have to spend money to make money. George was willing to pay to keep the Yankees a marquee team, even if that meant acquiring three top closers. He wasn't wrong, particularly when it comes to pitching. Guys get hurt all the time. And if they didn't, what would be the problem? Theoretically, between Sparky and Goose, we'd have the best left-hand-right-hand closer combination in baseball history.

But the reality was that signing Goose was really tough on Sparky. No matter what you want to say about left-right combinations, it's usually one guy out of the bullpen who becomes your shutdown guy. And it was pretty clear that was now supposed to be Goose.

From Sparky's point of view, here he was, he'd been the best pitcher in the league the year before. He'd pitched his arm off, threw 137 innings in relief—about twice what a closer throws today. Did everything Martin and the Boss asked of him. Did it all brilliantly, saved the playoffs for us against Kansas City, got a big win in the World Series. And then not only do they bring in Goose to take his job, but he's being paid more than three times what Sparky was getting then.

Yes, Sparky had a signed contract, and yes, you need to respect and honor that. But that old evil, money, caused ill feelings. Even a year in, guys still hadn't adapted to free agency. It was still causing problems, particularly with guys who hadn't been able to take advantage of it and get their payday yet. It still causes an uncomfortable atmosphere now. New players come in with big new contracts, and other guys feel,

"Hey, I'm just as good. I grew up here. Part of the family. Did all I was supposed to do, won here, been loyal. Why don't I get some of that money they're printing?"

It creates a "me" attitude. It opens the door for an attitude of "I want mine, too. I deserve it." It leads people from my generation to think that Generation X feels entitled—when they're not. This is a part of the game that we all wrestle with, ownership, players, media—but especially the fans.

I put the fans in a special place, because I feel as though we constantly stretch their loyalty to the game. It's a fragile bond, the love affair that we all, as fans, pass on to the next generation.

Playing through this time of transition as I did, I absolutely noticed a change, an increase in the number of fans thinking that players were greedy. It was most of the fans thinking the players were greedy—not the owners. Fans believe that owners are entitled to profits, most of which are never disclosed by these privately held entities.

In our world of entrepreneurship, business, and commerce, we've gotten comfortable with businesses taking profits. It all really gets down to your pool of selection. There aren't many millionaire owners in the world. But there are even fewer people who can hit .300, or hit forty home runs, or win twenty games at the major-league level. There's one LeBron, one Adrian Peterson, one Kareem. One Michael, one Mickey, one Verlander. It comes down to a basic business calculation. The skills that top professional athletes offer are very rare, and a lot of people want to see them perform. That means they will command a big salary in the marketplace. But that's cold consolation to a fan who must pay so much to take his kids to see a game today.

George and his Yankees brought players in to help the team win. There couldn't be as much concern about players' feelings. It's hard to keep our emotions out of it, but you have to make the decisions that will keep the team a winner. That was the calculation Steinbrenner made back in 1978. Goose was twenty-six going into that season, Eastwick was twenty-seven. Sparky was thirty-three. It's that simple, and that cruel sometimes. Because time keeps moving.

It's like that line from *The Godfather*: "It's not personal, it's business."

So it was tough on Sparky, but to his credit he got along with Goose. He did everything he could to help him fit in with the team. That's the kind of guy he could be.

It was tough for Goose, too. He got into Billy Martin's doghouse right away. Besides the guys he made dislike him, Billy usually had two or three guys he easily got into it with, for whatever reason.

I already knew what that was like. Goose was about to find out. Here's one of the premier relievers in the game, the Goose and his 100-mph fastball. One of the biggest free-agent pickups in the off-season. We started playing spring training games, and Goose is about to pitch to a young outfielder on the Texas Rangers named Billy Sample. From what I later learned after talking to Goose, the first thing Martin says to him is, "Hit this blankety-blank in the head."

I don't know why Billy had such a grudge against Sample, who was a rookie that year. I don't know if Sample ever knew why.

Goose said he wasn't going to do it. He didn't have anything against Sample. He wasn't just going to hit him in the head to settle some score for Billy. He told him, "Sample never did anything to me. I'm not gonna fight your fights. Whatever this is, I'm not gonna get involved."

Goose would take care of business if he had to hit somebody for the team, if we'd had a guy beaned or something like that. He wouldn't hit Sample for nothing—and Billy never forgave him for that. He told Billy, "I hit Sample in the head, I could kill him"—which was true, as hard as Goose threw. Billy told him, "I don't give a s—t if you do kill him!" He called Gossage every name in the book. A really vile tirade. But Goose just wasn't for it.

Gossage always said he thought it was a test of loyalty on Billy's part. I don't know. I never knew another manager who needed a test of loyalty. But then, I never knew another manager like Billy Martin.

I'd say events proved Goose right. Martin never got over him refusing to hit Sample during a spring training game. It's hard to believe. From then on, Goose and Billy had no relationship. Goose used to say, "I can't stand the blankety-blank." I understand that.

I think all of the nonsense in spring training and the pressure he was under already as the big, new free-agent signing got to Goose a little early on. I knew what he was going through.

We opened up on the road, in Texas. Guidry pitches a great game, gives up one run in seven innings, but we wasted all kinds of base runners. Goose comes in, gets the side out in the eighth; Richie Zisk hits a homer off him leading off the ninth. Ball game.

We went to Milwaukee next, and Billy brings Goose into a game we're leading, 3–1, in the sixth. Gives Kenny Holtzman the quick hook. First batter, Goose gives up a two-run homer to Larry Hisle. Tie game. Next inning, Nettles of all people boots a ball. Goose gives up a single to Lenn Sakata and a double to Don Money. We lose, 5–3.

A few days later, against Baltimore, Martin brings him in to relieve Catfish in the fifth inning, in a game we're already losing, 4–1. Goose gave up a two-run homer to Doug DeCinces, takes us completely out of the game. Two days after *that*, we're up in Toronto. It's April, and it's cold. Kenny's pitching again, and Billy gives him an even quicker hook this time. He pulls him for Goose in the bottom of the fifth—bottom of the fifth!—with us down one run.

It was kind of nuts, even for those days. Bringing your top reliever in that early in the game, that early in the season, even with Sparky in the pen . . . But we battled back, Cliff Johnson hit a home run, and it was tied, 3–3, going into the bottom of the ninth.

Goose gives up a single to John Mayberry. Then Rick Cerone, who was the Blue Jays' catcher at the time, tries to bunt Mayberry over. Goose picks up the ball and throws it way wide to second, trying to get the lead runner. Almost threw the ball away. Two on now, nobody out.

Next batter lays down a bunt, too. Goose picks it up, looks to first base—and this time he throws the ball to me. I'm in right field, backing up first base. He must have tossed the ball six feet over Chris Chambliss's glove. It went all the way out to me, where I was running over to back up the play. The runner trotted home from second, and we lose the game.

That put us at 5–6 on the year. Goose had four appearances, no saves, no wins, and three of our losses.

That Toronto game broke his heart. He came into the clubhouse, and he fell into the chair in front of his locker so hard it broke. He was really sad, holding back the tears. Sitting there still in uniform—he must've sat there for an hour. Then I went over with Thurman and Lou Piniella and Nettles and Catfish. We just told him, "Look, you're coming to dinner with us."

That helped. He was all right after that. It was just bad luck, a bad start. Goose was enough of a veteran to shake it off after that.

But once again, it was the question of what was going on with the manager. Where was Billy Martin when one of our key players was struggling? Oh, was he still punishing him for not hitting Billy Sample in spring training? Some wonder, too, if that's why Martin was putting Goose out there so early, so many times—to pitch so many innings when it was still cold weather.

It didn't matter. We veterans took care of it. Thurman was great with him. Goose would come into a game, and Munson would go out to the mound and ask him with a straight face, "So how you planning to lose this one?" Pretty soon it got to be a ritual. Gossage would say, "I dunno, but get your puny ass back there and let me find out." Mickey Rivers, out in center field—when Goose came in, he would turn his back on the plate and get into a sprinter's stance, as if he was already set to race after the ball. Other times, he would stand in front of the golf cart they used to drive Goose in and say, "No, no, don't let him in! We want to win!"

Stuff like that is what you need to do to stay loose over the long season. We knew enough to do it—especially after everything that had happened the year before. We were, in many ways, a team that could run itself. We didn't have any choice sometimes.

Despite the slow start, none of the players were worried. Our worrier-in-chief was the Boss—he needed to win all 162. We'd started even slower the year before and ended up winning it all.

We were an outstanding team, and we'd made some improvements. Besides Goose and Eastwick, we picked up Jim Spencer, who was a Gold Glove and left-handed power hitter, to platoon a little with Chambliss at first, DH, and pinch-hit. We'd lost Mike Torrez to the

Red Sox as a free agent, but we added Andy Messersmith and a rookie, Jim Beattie, to the rotation. We had a lot of depth everywhere; we were strong through and through.

On Opening Day at the Stadium, we came off the road just 1–4, but it was one big celebration. They had Mickey Mantle and Roger Maris on hand to put up the world championship banner—first World Series title the Yankees had won since they were both in their prime, back in 1962.

Roger was there to throw out the first pitch. Both Mickey and Roger were always great to me. I remember Roger Maris came over to me when I was having a tough time once, laid a hand on my shoulder, and said, "Don't worry about it, Reg. You're all right. You're a great player. You'll come through the mess."

Just a very personal, confident conversation. I needed to hear that kind of stuff. Roger knew what he was talking about. He was a great player who got booed the year he broke Babe Ruth's home run record, just because some fans thought he didn't deserve to set the record. Now he'd come through it, and on Opening Day he got a huge hand. I could relate to what he was saying, to how hard it is to live up to the expectations some people might have for you.

Mantle was the same way. He was someone else who had been booed at Yankee Stadium just because people decided he wasn't what they thought he could be. Mickey was a Hall of Famer who won three MVP awards and led his team to twelve pennants and seven World Series titles, but some people felt he hadn't lived up to his potential. Yet these were two guys who were so gentlemanly. They were just good people, and all the stories you ever heard about their generosity were true. They appreciated the opportunity to play alongside each other and for a great franchise.

Everyone gets this chance at being booed in New York. You just need to play there. Save for Mariano the Great.

You know, for all the talk from people like Martin and some of the press about how I wasn't "a real Yankee," I always found the old Yankees from Billy's time very friendly, very welcoming. They couldn't have been more appreciative of my play. There was no feeling of "You're a hot dog or a showman."

I've got pictures hanging in my home of Joe D., with this inscription: "We're all so proud of what you did with the Yankees." Mickey Mantle would come and take me out to dinner—he came to my Hall of Fame dinner in 1993. I'll never forget the friendly blue eyes of Bobby Richardson. The welcome from Whitey, Yogi, Elston, Moose Skowron.

Through it all, I was still a fan. Still am to this day. I feel lucky to have been part of Yankees history. To have left a mark at the old Yankee Stadium. To have a plaque in Monument Park and my number still hanging on the wall, with all the other retired numbers. To have worked there and been able to watch, up close and personal, the greatness of the team from 1993 to this day. To have seen those Joe Torre and Joe Girardi teams, Posada, Pettitte. I saw Derek Jeter's first game in the big leagues, and I'll see his last. And to see maybe the greatest clutch performer in the history of sports, watching the great Mariano. I still get excited, 'cause I'm still a fan.

It's all fun, and all done with arguably the most recognizable franchise in history. That old, eccentric friend of mine, Gary Walker, was right after all about coming to New York.

When I was still playing in Baltimore in 1976, I said, "If I played in New York, they'd name a candy bar after me." I said it as a joke. That same year, I was in Milwaukee, and I said, "I can't come here. There are only two newspapers, and I don't drink." All in the spirit of fun.

When I went to New York, all summer Matt Merola kept calling every candy company he knew, asking, "Do you want to do a Reggie bar?" He called every company, and the last one he called was Standard Brands—and they took the bait! I got $250,000 a year for five years and a furnished apartment at Seventy-ninth and Fifth.

The Reggie! bar was a little less than two ounces of chocolate, peanuts, and caramel, I think. A little square in an orange wrapping, with a picture of me swinging a bat on top. A bargain at just twenty-five cents.

Opening Day 1978, Standard Brands hired a bunch of models and stewardesses to pass out seventy-two thousand bars to everyone coming to the game. Seventy-two thousand. We had about forty-five thousand people in the stands that day, so I guess some people got two.

After all the ceremonies, and Roger and Mickey raising the world championship banner, I came up to bat in the first inning with Mickey Rivers on second and Willie Randolph on first. Wilbur Wood was pitching for the White Sox. He was a very good pitcher but another knuckleballer, which was trouble for the White Sox. I took the first two pitches for balls, then hit the next one deep into the stands in right-center over the 408-foot sign. That put us up, 3–0—and counting the World Series from the year before, that made four consecutive swings at Yankee Stadium, four home runs. Nice.

I wasn't thinking much about that, though. I was just doing my job, rounding the bases—when all of a sudden I saw these little orange squares start to come out of the stands.

They said there was just one at first. It came out of the stands and landed near home plate. Then another, and another. Reggie! bars. You could really wing those things, the way they were packed into those tight little squares. More started to rain down, until, as Sparky Lyle put it, the fans realized "the beauty of the act."

Then it was a shower. A deluge. Little orange squares raining down all over the field before I could finish running around the bases. Thousands and thousands of Reggie! bars, fluttering down onto the field. Kids jumping down to help the grounds crew clean it up, stuffing the bars in their pockets.

I didn't know what was going on. I was worried. I thought they didn't like 'em.

Really, I was nervous. I didn't know it was a tribute. I didn't understand it at the time. I think the media did, and the PR people from Standard Brands. Afterward, it was in the news all over the nation. It was a tremendous coup. Standard Brands called me and told me how happy they were, what a success it was.

I didn't know. I was just glad I hit the ball out, glad we hung on and won the game. Afterward, the White Sox seemed pretty angry about it. I think they felt it showed them up.

I just told the press, "I figured they'd be coming out on the field"—which I admit wasn't true. Who could figure that? It never happened before. "I just appreciated it. It was a nice gesture," I said, which *was* true, although not an opinion widely shared.

"It was just a shame that something like that has to happen," Wilbur Wood said after the game. Bob Lemon, who was managing Chicago, said, "They should advertise it as the candy bar made to throw." He was pretty upset, saying, "It's not called for," and claiming somebody could have got hurt.

"Let them throw them when he's in right field, see how he feels," he told the writers. "People starving all over the world and thirty billion calories are lying on the field."

Until then, I had no idea we could solve world hunger with Reggie! bars. Even Catfish got on that, saying, "The people must have a lot of money here, to throw away all that food."

Catfish was just poking me, like a lot of guys. He had, I think, the best line about the candy bar: "The Reggie! bar. It's the candy bar that when you unwrap it, it tells you how good it is."

That's pretty good, I thought.

Yogi Berra said, "They wouldn't be throwing Yoo-hoo like that," which was also a pretty good line. Lou Piniella was waiting in the on-deck circle while they cleaned up all the bars. He picked up a couple and tried to hit them. Afterward, he told the press, "Hitting a Reggie! bar is very difficult. The flat bottom side makes it tough, and even if you'd meet one square, I don't think you'd drive it very far."

That was pretty funny, too. In fact, the whole thing was pretty danged funny. And, you know—really cool.

I never minded guys making fun of me like that. I always appreciated that line I think Darold Knowles had about me, back in Oakland: "They call Reggie a hot dog. There's not enough mustard in the whole world to cover that."

I could always take that sort of ribbing. That's one of the great things about playing major-league baseball, spending so much time with guys who could tease you like that, guys you got close to and who soon became family.

I could understand the White Sox being sore. They'd never seen anything like it. I'd never seen anything like it.

But when you thought about it, it was kind of fun . . . Like something out of, I don't know, a bullfight, more than baseball.

Isn't that why people come to the ballpark, to see something they've never seen before? There were a lot of new things going in baseball just then. Players having a little power, getting to play where they wanted to play. People changing teams, owners taking risks . . . and some great ball being played.

Wasn't it a pretty good time? Weren't we all having fun?

19

HERE WE GO AGAIN

THE REALITY IS teams that win have fun. Teams that don't . . . don't.

We were playing pretty well once Goose got straightened out like we knew he would. Just like the year before, we turned it around. Near the end of May, I remember, Andy Messersmith and Rawly Eastwick combined to pitch a one-hitter against the Indians, and we won, 2–0. We were 29–15 after that and playing well. Messersmith hadn't allowed an earned run yet; Eastwick had a 1.56 ERA.

Billy wasn't happy with it. He wasn't happy those two guys were on the team. He used to call them "George's guys" all the time. The fact that they were doing well didn't matter. It was the same thing with me from the year before: He hadn't been consulted about signing them, and as a result he didn't want them. It seemed he had to find something to chew on.

Then we started to lose again, and that brought on stress. Billy didn't do stress.

Unlike the year before, the reason we went on the slide again was pretty evident. Our pitching broke down. It quickly became clear that Catfish still wasn't right. He said his arm felt better, but he was diagnosed with diabetes, and he still struggled. He just wasn't himself and went on the disabled list.

Andy Messersmith had that good game for us, but he'd separated his shoulder in spring training that year, and he was never the same. He went on the DL as well and never pitched for us again. Don Gullett's arm hurt so bad he had had two cortisone shots by June. After that, he just tried to gut it out and pitch through the pain. He won his first four decisions. Then he lost two games, went on the DL, and never pitched for us again. Never pitched for *anybody* again. That was it, his career done at twenty-seven.

Dick Tidrow tried to pick up the slack the way he had the year before when Billy put him in the rotation, but he jammed his thumb. We still had Kenny Holtzman, and he had a couple good starts early. But he was still in Billy's doghouse. Billy wanted to put him on the disabled list, too, but Kenny said loud and long there was nothing wrong with him, so Billy just kept him on the bench until he could trade him. Kenny just needed to pitch.

That was embarrassing for the whole organization, but nothing was done about it. It wasn't just me. Roger Kahn had the guts to write about it in the paper. Graig Nettles said right out about Kenny: "It must be something that's not happening on the field. Because he should be pitching."

As the season went on, the rest of us started to get dinged up, too. Willie Randolph tore up the cartilage in his right knee. He played through it pretty well, stole thirty-six bases, but he missed twenty-eight games that year. Bucky Dent had a bad hammy all season; he missed thirty-nine games and had to go down and rehab in Florida.

And Thurman was finally wearing down. He'd caught more than a thousand big-league games by then, which is a lot for any man. His right knee was very painful all year. He couldn't hit for as much power; his arm was bothering him. Even so, he made adjustments and played through it. He still threw out almost half the guys who tried to run on him, even though he had to throw the ball to second almost sidearm. Still only missed eight games. It wasn't his best season, but it might have been his gutsiest, and he set an example for all of us.

What we missed most of all, though, was Mickey Rivers. He'd been such a catalyst for us the year before, getting us everything we needed, when we needed it—a stolen base, a home run, whatever. But in the first part of 1978 he was just *absent* a lot—for whatever reason, we were never sure. I know his hammies were bothering him some, his legs were achy. He had a hand fracture as well. But it seemed to be more than that.

Mick was always hard to figure out. He would kind of go on these little sit-down strikes when he thought he wasn't being treated right or when he needed an advance on his salary. Sometimes it worked; sometimes it didn't.

He had a great outlook on life most of the time. He used to say something like, "I don't worry about the things I can't do anything about, because I can't do anything about them. And I don't worry about the things I can do something about, because I can do something about them."

That's almost Zen—or Yogi. When you think about it, that's sort of beautiful. That was Mickey to a T. That's the way he lived his life.

I thought most of the players made fun of Mickey. They made out like they were laughing with him, but really I thought they were laughing at him. He had some problems with betting on the horses, some problems with a few different wives.

At one point, I believe he was married to two or three women at the same time. Down in Florida, he used to go by the Latino version of his name, Miguel Rivera, and he married a woman I think under that name while he had a wife in New Jersey.

She caught up to him finally. He was sitting in the parking lot in Yankee Stadium before a game with his Florida wife, in his Cadillac Coupe de Ville. His other wife came driving up in his other car, a Mercedes 450 SL, and she ran it right into him. Then she backed it up and ran it into his Caddy again. And again, and again, and again. Put it in drive, back to reverse. In drive, back to reverse, in drive, back to reverse. Incredible . . . I was parking my car at the same time, and it was painful to watch. Funny at the same time.

Mickey was devastated afterward. He was just slumped over the steering wheel. But you know Mickey. That was the morning. That afternoon, the game started at 2:10. Mickey came into the clubhouse and just sat in front of his locker until about ten of two. Then he got dressed, went out, and got four hits that day.

He was a lot of fun. He was very witty. He used to get on me a lot in the clubhouse and on the bus. He had that famous line where we were going back and forth on the team bus, and he says, "Reginald

Martinez Jackson. You got a white man's first name, a Hispanic man's middle name, and a black man's last name. No wonder you're confused."

I laughed my head off. He could be hilarious. But while what he was saying was in the spirit of fun for him, so many of the other guys enjoyed anything that would come back negative toward me. What he was saying became a big joke for players who didn't have the guts to say it directly to *me*.

Too often, Mickey was used as a court jester for the team. I felt there was a racial component to it. Sure, Mickey could hold his own; he was very witty. Mickey Rivers could hold his own with anybody. But other guys made fun of him. They made fun of the way he spoke, the English he used. And when he'd go at it with me, I was laughing, but I don't know if they were. Or put it this way: They were all laughing a little too loud. Egging him on. Pitting one of us against the other.

I think it was hurtful for both of us. We got by it. To this day, Mickey and I get along very well. But I regret what happened then.

Early in May, in a game in Kansas City, Billy got mad because he thought Mickey didn't hustle after a double Amos Otis hit in the ninth that scored the winning run. When he got to the ball, he didn't bother to make a throw to the plate, and Billy didn't like that either. Mickey had no shot at the runner, but that didn't matter to Billy.

It was a tough loss, a back-and-forth game where we blew a 6–3 lead, then battled back. You don't like to lose those games, but it was mid-*May*. We were 17–12 at the time, just three games out of first.

But Billy let it get to him; he couldn't really help himself by then. We had a long plane ride home, and Billy never did too well on long plane rides after a tough loss. They gave him too much time to think and too much time to fuel up.

It was all starting up again. It was like a forest fire that couldn't be doused. But then, what fire *can* be doused with alcohol?

He started yelling at Lou Piniella for playing cards with Rivers. Then he got on Thurman for letting his music play for a little while with the headphones out. When we landed, Billy even went back and started yelling at Munson, calling him a "bad influence." *Thurman Munson*—a bad influence!

Where was he going with that? Thurman had carte blanche.

Thurman gave it right back to him, told him the only reason Martin was saying that to him was that there were too many guys in between them. That enraged Billy; he made out like he was really trying to get to him then, just the way he had with me up in Boston the year before. Somehow, the same coaches managed to get in the way again.

I think even Billy was genuinely shocked by how he acted. He issued a public apology to Thurman the next day. I was still waiting for mine—not. But you know, for him to go after a guy like Thurman, to me it showed how much he was coming apart.

George Steinbrenner tried to smooth it over. He told the writers, "A ship that sails on calm seas gets nowhere. You have to have some turbulence." Al Rosen, who was the new president of the club, came out and said, "Ballplayers fight. What do you think our ball club is called, the New York Choirboys?"

Which was a good line. But I think we were missing Gabe Paul by then. Rosen was very smart; he was a good GM and would make some good moves later on down the line. Later he took the Giants to a pennant. And the Yankees certainly had plenty of other smart people in the front office still, guys like Cedric Tallis.

But Gabe had been in the game so long he had a way of seeing the bigger picture. He had a way of not letting anything get to him—at least not for very long. He had a sense of humor about things, with all his little sayings, and he was pretty fair, I thought. He made for some good grease between the big wheels, people like George, Billy, and the stars of the team.

However, after the 1977 season, Gabe had had enough. He packed up and went back to Cleveland, to run the Indians again. I think it was a loss. Because he had known George for years, he knew how to keep him calm, how to advise him. He understood just how much he should take from Billy.

I don't know why Gabe left. Probably sheer exhaustion. He had a bad heart by then, some health issues. But I think, too, it might have been how he had this minor stroke the year before, one that left his speech a little slurred. Lots of people made fun of how he talked and how he sounded after that.

Gabe was plenty tough, so I doubt if he cared. But who should have to put up with that? There were a few players on the team who had something to say about everything. They'd be sadistic about it—about George's style, Billy's style, my style. Anyone who was different. They were the same ones who would make slurs and anti-Semitic remarks. They would mock everything. That's pretty normal in a clubhouse, but we seemed to have more of them.

Without Gabe, there was nobody to really rein in Billy, nobody to give the Boss some perspective. When we started to slump, George started to let his football side come out, expecting us to win every game.

He needed to understand we had all these nagging injuries. And we were also playing against the most competitive division I'd ever seen.

The American League East Division in 1978 was unreal. It wasn't just Boston. You had Milwaukee, which came out of nowhere to win ninety-three games. They had an amazing team, amazing depth. A pair of Hall of Famers up the middle in Robin Yount and Paul Molitor. My old teammate Sal Bando, who was still one of the best third basemen in baseball. Great all-around hitters like Cecil Cooper and Ben Oglivie. Larry Hisle had a monster year, must've beat us three times that season with home runs, just putting that ball in the right-field bleachers. Gorman Thomas hit thirty-two homers; you had Sixto Lezcano, Don Money, who hit more than twenty home runs a year. Their pitching was a little weaker, but they had Mike Caldwell, who had a breakout year and won twenty-two games and was always lights out against us.

You had Baltimore, which won ninety games again under Weaver. They had a Hall of Famer in Eddie Murray, guys like Ken Singleton, Lee May, Doug DeCinces, who were terrific players. They had that great rotation of Jim Palmer, Mike Flanagan, Denny Martinez, Scott McGregor. They finished *fourth* with that team and those ninety wins.

You had Detroit, which already had Alan Trammell and Lou Whitaker. Ron LeFlore, Lance Parrish, Steve Kemp, Jason Thompson, Rusty Staub, who had 121 RBIs that year. Jack Morris was on the staff already, one of the dominant pitchers of his era—in my opinion, a Hall of Famer. They won eighty-six games with all those guys—and finished *fifth*.

Every one of those teams, the Brewers, the Orioles, and the Tigers, would make it to the World Series over the next six years—and each with the same cores they had already put together by 1978. This was the sort of competition we were facing day in and day out, and never mind the excellent teams you had in the West Division, like Kansas City, the Angels, and Texas. Almost every day, you had another tough game against a team that was tough in a different way.

And the Red Sox were better than ever. Maybe they didn't have quite as much power, quite as much hitting, as they had the year before. But they were a much more balanced team.

They'd gone and got Jerry Remy, who was a very good glove and a decent bat at second base and who gave them a little team speed for a change. Most of all, they'd improved their pitching, which was always their Achilles' heel. They signed Mike Torrez away from us, who was a proven big-game pitcher. They'd brought Dennis Eckersley over from Cleveland, who was just coming into his own. He had a breakout season, won twenty games and pitched us very tough. That gave them a lot of depth in their starting staff, and it let them move Bob Stanley to the pen when Bill Campbell's arm finally gave out.

Boston started putting together some serious winning streaks. Won eight in a row in April, another seven in a row in early May, still another eight in a row at the end of the month. Jim Rice was having an unbelievable year for them, hitting everything out, hitting for average. By the time we went to Fenway to play them for the first time in mid-June, they had just run off still *another* winning streak, nine straight this time.

Going into the series, they were seven games up on us, which was beginning to get serious, even for June. Standard rule of thumb, it's almost insurmountable when you get ten games behind in the loss column, no matter what time of year it is.

So we were concerned. I wouldn't say we were panicking. At least not the players. I couldn't speak for other people associated with the team.

The first game, a Monday night game, was just a typical, wild Yankees–Red Sox game. We were down to starting Ken Clay against Luis Tiant by then, but Thurman hit a home run, Roy White homered, and we managed to get up by 4–1 going into the bottom of the fourth.

Then the roof fell in. They strung together a bunch of hits off Clay, and Willie Randolph, who was hurting, made an error down at second, and they tied the game. Billy was playing it like it was the seventh game of the World Series. He brought Goose in during that fourth inning. Think of that today: bringing in Mariano in the bottom of the fourth inning. Forget June—anytime!

Goose really pitched very well and shut the Sox down until the eighth inning. More than four innings of shutout relief! But in the eighth, the Sox caught up to Goose, batted around against him and Sparky, and broke the game open.

We kept our composure as a team. Don Gullett went out the next night, gutted it out. Pitched a complete-game win despite allowing five hits and seven walks. We got down early again, 4–0, after Butch Hobson hit a three-run homer for them, but like I say, nobody was panicking, and we came back on Mike Torrez, who didn't have his best stuff. Chicken Stanley, our backup shortstop, hit a grand-slam homer off him, which you might say was a sign of things to come.

We ended up winning, 10–4. And that would make you wonder why Gullett, who was in constant pain from a sore arm, was left out there to throw nine innings and 154 pitches. Just as there was no need to wear out *both* of your best relievers the day before.

But by that time, I don't think anybody with the team was thinking very clearly. The next night, in the rubber game of the series, we had to throw our rookie, Jim Beattie, against Eckersley, another future Hall of Famer, who was pitching very well. Beattie only lasted a couple innings. He walked a few guys, threw a couple wild pitches, and the Sox stomped us.

Billy capped off the night by putting Catfish out there for the ninth, even though we were already down 7–2 and he knew his arm was killing him. The first two batters he faced, Freddie Lynn and George Scott, hit home runs off him. They loaded the bases then, before Yaz struck out.

A lot of people thought he struck out intentionally at the time. I wouldn't be surprised. That might have been a nice gesture on his part, but having Catfish out there pitching mop-up in the first place was an insult to a great pitcher. I thought it demeaned the whole organization.

It was an ugly game and a bad loss. Boston was eight games up on us after it was over, and they were going great. I even said afterward, "If they keep playing like that, we won't be able to catch them with a race car."

But you know, they'd only taken two out of three from us. It wasn't some beat down like it had been the year before. They just got us when they were hot and we were banged up.

Nobody had any perspective anymore. Immediately after the game, the Boss in his two-fisted style had Beattie sent back down to the minors, telling the media that he looked scared stiff. He said Beattie and Ken Clay had "spit the bit" in that series, which is a horse-racing term for choking and wasn't anything any young pitchers needed to hear just then. This was all in the press.

We'd had nine starters or potential starters at the beginning of the season, including six former all-stars. Now we were down to two.

When we look back now, it's pretty easy to understand the health problems of the pitching.

Well, what a surprise: a Billy Martin team where the wheels came off the pitching staff a couple short years later. That happened nearly wherever he ever went.

The Boss's reaction to the situation just made everything worse. I think it was the end of that series George came into the clubhouse and ran right over Billy, telling him, "Okay, this is how it's gonna be. If we keep losing, I'm just going to back up a truck and unload the whole team over in Jersey." He was going to make trades or do whatever it takes, telling everybody, "I'm not gonna stand for this. We're gonna win or else."

We all knew George got excited. That was because he cared. We all had to put up with it.

Billy was a beaten warrior by this time. The drinking got bad again. At times he was sleeping over in the clubhouse. Dick Howser was back to running the team a lot by that time. Billy was stressed by all the pressure being piled on him. And when Billy got stressed, he ran away, and rather than hit the issues head-on, he looked to put the blame off on others.

I was the star of "others."

2 0

FORCING THE ISSUE

I'D BEEN HAVING an okay year. Not as good as I wanted—yet. I figured I would get going. I didn't think there was a big problem. I was still hitting about .265–.275, with some power. Had something like fourteen or fifteen home runs, about fifty RBIs with less than half the season gone.

Going into July, I'd been slumping a little, struggling some against lefties. But nothing terrible. I knew I'd break out. I just didn't realize I wouldn't be given the chance.

About a week after the series in Boston, the Sox came to New York for two more. Eckersley beat us in the opener, and then in the next game Ron Guidry had one of his very, very few mediocre starts of that whole year, lost a 3–0 lead on a rainy, foggy night in front of a big crowd.

Billy was starting to mess with me again, batting me sixth in that game. But I had three hits, drove in Thurman to tie the game again in the eighth. Goose and Sparky both pitched outstanding ball, *eight innings* of shutout relief between them, and Nettles had a huge hit, a two-run homer in the bottom of the fourteenth off Dick Drago that might have saved the season for us.

We were running on fumes by then. We had Fred Stanley and a rookie call-up named Domingo Ramos playing short for Bucky. Dámaso García, another rookie, was playing second for Willie, Gary Thomasson was in center for Mickey. We had our bench players everywhere, names that were not recognizable like we all were used to with the Yanks back then. We had Dave Rajsich, Bob Kammeyer, and Larry McCall pitching in important ball games for us. We brought up another guy from Double-A, Paul Semall, who Billy was actually planning to pitch against Boston. Guys nobody heard of before or since.

It got to be so you couldn't walk through the locker room without a scorecard. We were a patch team.

We went to play in Boston again on July 3, and they started Eckersley against Figgy, who had a sore arm, too. He had to go, though, because we didn't have much else.

By that time, we'd traded Ken Holtzman because Billy wouldn't pitch him. We got Ron Davis for him, who would become an outstanding reliever for us but who was still a minor leaguer. We'd traded Eastwick because Billy didn't like him. We got Jay Johnstone and Bobby Brown for him—a pair of backup outfielders who helped us off the bench. By that time, we were down to guys like Paul Blair and Jim Spencer—an outfielder and a first baseman—warming up in the bullpen. But we were still trading pitchers because Billy Martin didn't like them—or because of whatever his personal issues were.

The game in Boston was a travesty. They just sort of cuffed us around. Figgy was done by the fourth, and Billy put in Sparky for one inning—I was wondering what Sparky thought about how he was being used in games, with the year he had in 1977—then Bob Kammeyer pitched the rest of the game.

I don't know who we would've pitched the next night: McCall or Paul Semall—pray for rain. Fortunately, we got it. And as it happened, that rainout really helped us.

We couldn't compete with teams like the Red Sox when they were healthy and they were playing well. There's no secret formula. You just won't beat top major leaguers playing a combination of your bench and guys who aren't ready for the major leagues yet.

Yaz said it at the time. He told the press, "We're getting a well-pitched game every time out there, while the Yankees are getting a new guy on the disabled list every day."

It was true. The Sox were getting pitching like they never had before. I remember sometime around then, Eckersley was 11–2, Bill Lee was 10–3, Torrez was 12–5, Tiant was 7–2—their top four starters were 40–12. We were throwing an unknown Bob Kammeyer. I remember running in the outfield before a game, looking at the scoreboard when they put up the standings: The Red Sox were 51–19.

But of course, there was an additional explanation, closer to some people's hearts: It was my fault. Particularly my fielding.

All of a sudden, it was like last year all over again. As if our stretch drive never happened. As if the World Series had never happened. Billy kept me hitting sixth. He started pulling me out of the lineup more and more. He almost never put me out in the field anymore. Then sometimes, after I'd been sitting for a while, he'd DH me against a tough lefty. Anything to show me up, I guess.

We started losing more, got down to just five games over .500. I *thought* the low point came right after the All-Star break, in mid-July. Right before the break we lost five of six, including getting swept three straight in Milwaukee. I was benched for the last two games—one of which was against a right-handed pitcher.

We lost both those games, and when we came back from the All-Star break to play the White Sox in the Stadium, the Boss had a big clubhouse meeting and announced there were going to be major changes. Mickey Rivers was back in center, so now Gary Thomasson, who'd been filling in, was going to start in left field, over Roy White. Mike Heath, a rookie we'd just called up from the minors, was going to start behind the plate. And Thurman . . . Thurman would be moving to right field to rest his knees.

Oh, yeah, where did that leave me? As the designated hitter—against right-handed pitching. Because supposedly I couldn't hit lefties anymore. Against lefties, the DH would be Lou Piniella.

Less than half a season after I had one of the best World Series in history, I was going to be a part-time player. Less than two years after becoming the highest-paid player in the game, I was going to be a platoon player.

The Boss told us we had no choice: "You're some of the best-paid athletes in the world, and I'm the man who signs the checks. If you don't want to do things my way, then you can go somewhere else. This is my team. I pay the bills. I'll do what I want to do."

I understood George's frustration. We all did. It must've been exasperating to watch us play and slip further behind. But this was his football background talking again. Lou Piniella said it at the time: "George thinks it's all just a matter of mental toughness, and it's not true."

Lou was right. It's a long, long season, baseball. You have to pace yourself, and you can't go out there and knock somebody down when you get mad.

You can have all the desire, all the mental toughness in the world—and you're still not going to win if all your pitching staff has arm problems, and you're throwing unproven kids against some of the best arms in the game. You're not going to turn double plays, you're not going to get big hits if you have to have minor-league fill-ins playing up the middle. Desire alone won't beat talent.

The trouble was also that the changes George wanted didn't make a lot of sense. Gary Thomasson was a good ballplayer; he made some nice contributions for us, especially in the field. He also got some timely hits. But he wasn't the all-around player Roy White was; he didn't have his experience. Hadn't been in two World Series the last two years, the way Roy had been. Mike Heath went on to have an outstanding career as a catcher in the American League, but he was just a rookie and wasn't ready to do much more than play part-time, to grow into the position on this level.

Thurman needed a rest, all right. But the place to get it wasn't the outfield when he'd lost a lot of his speed, couldn't cover much ground. He was going to become an outfielder at the age of thirty-one—thereby making *two* positions less than they should be.

It didn't make sense putting Lou on the bench that much, cutting down on his at-bats. Lou was a productive hitter. It made even less sense to not play me every day. I'd shown I could do the job, I already had four rings, and I had too big a paycheck to sit. They were going to make me a part-time player?

With all due respect to the Boss, it wasn't a good plan. I thought that if Billy had built up some trust and reliability, he might have been able to make George see things differently and talk him out of the whole idea. But Billy wasn't about to do that. He was too worn down, too beaten by then, on the edge of losing his job as manager. And I think he enjoyed seeing me get benched.

By then, I didn't even know what to say. I couldn't believe how fast all the goodwill, all the accomplishments from the year before, had dissipated. I was so discouraged. I was honestly wondering whether it was all worthwhile. I was mentally back there again!

After the meeting, the craziness continued. I went to the movies with a girl I was seeing. A woman came up and asked for my autograph. I told her no—politely—because, as I pointed out, then I'd have to sign for anyone who asked. I just wanted to enjoy my date, enjoy my night out, and see a movie.

This woman started getting angry, started yelling at me. She started screaming at my girlfriend. I tried to get between them, and the woman fell over and started shouting that I hit her, which of course I didn't. I really don't know if it was all some sort of a setup or if she was just crazy.

It became such a scene they ended up having to clear the whole theater. The next day it was all over the papers. They made it sound like a riot had broken out—and they made sure to say that my date was white and the woman who wanted my autograph was black, injecting race into it.

Before I knew it, the woman had filed a lawsuit against me. On my attorney's advice, I sued her back. Eventually, it went away and got thrown out of court. But it all just seemed crazy to me. As I told a reporter the next day, "When you're me, nothing surprises you. I went to the movies last night and got sued."

With that coming on top of my demotion to part-time DH, I had just about had it with everything—the Yankees, the Boss, and Billy. New York. I was just getting numb by then. When the writers wanted to know what I thought about our big realignment, I just told them, "George owns the freaking team. He can do what he wants."

That was how disgusted I felt by then. My only real hope was that George as a businessman—not as a fan—would recognize how foolish me being a part-time DH was and trade me somewhere else.

I kept trying to get through to George to tell him this. Back when he signed me in 1976, he made it clear I could always talk to him. So I tried to schedule a private meeting with him, say what I needed to say away from the press.

He wouldn't see me. I had already been trying for weeks to see him, but he wouldn't make the time. When George knew what you were going to say and it wasn't what he wanted you to say, he avoided you. That's something we've all experienced.

I tried to take it all in stride. I tried the things that had worked for me the year before: talking with my dad and my brother Joe. Praying with Gary Walker. I'd made some more friends around the clubhouse by then, and it was good to talk with them.

I had comfortable, calming conversations with the gentlemanly Roy White. We got along well. I'd talk to Fran Healy, who had retired but who George had made a broadcaster. Had some good conversations with Gene Monahan, who was one of the trainers and who would be with the team until just a couple years ago—forty-plus years.

I had some great talks as well with Pete Sheehy, who was the equipment manager with the Yankees going all the way back to 1927—the year they had that great team. He was a legend and had already seen so much. He was the guy who Lou Gehrig flipped his glove to when he realized he was too sick to play anymore and said, "I'm done, Pete." It was Pete Sheehy who gave Mantle his number 7.

When I had tough times, he'd come over to me while I was still at my locker and everyone else was gone. I'd be slumped down in my chair, half-clothed or whatever, sitting and staring. I'd be picking my Afro; I had a nice head of hair. Back then, anyway.

Pete would sit down next to me and put his hand on my shoulder. He'd look up at me and say, "You know, Lou Gehrig used to locker here. I used to say to him in difficult times, 'Just let the river flow.

Tra-la-la-la-la. Let the river flow.'" He'd say, "Sometimes, Reggie, you just have to go out and play and get out of your own way. Don't worry. You've got a lot of ability. I used to say the same thing to Lou."

That was a moment I'll never forget. Every time I would see Pete, he was very quiet. He would just kind of look at me in a very fatherly way. A gentleman who knew the path I was on, knew the road I was traveling. I'll never forget that! And today I still own that same locker; it's in my car garage. Got it from Steiner Sports Memorabilia, after the Yankees left the old Stadium.

Older people look at you in a knowing way. They see what's going on—but they are reluctant to tell you that. Older people know the answers. They don't say much because they know you have to go through it yourself—unless you ask them for help. Then they'll tell you. They know like I know the answers for my daughter, Kimberly—but I have to let her figure them out herself.

I was good friends with Ray Negron, talking to him all the time. I spent a lot of time with him; I was a big brother to him. If you think about it, it was an awkward yet unique situation. I think Ray was nineteen or so then, but he managed to have a relationship—strangely, yet fortunately—with Billy and me. We both respected that. I never got a message from Billy through him, and I never sent a message to Billy through Ray. We respected that.

But because I knew Ray, I knew Billy's girlfriends. They were always nice, and I always got along with them. Said hello, stuff like that, when I'd see them at the ballpark. Always a smile, never had any kind of thing against them. There was never any kind of bitterness that translated between his girlfriends and me; that was never a factor. That was how crazy a situation it was. I couldn't talk to the manager, but I was friendly with his friends.

After George benched me, I finally said it straight out to the press. I told them, "I'm not gonna DH for three years. I won't ever be a full-time DH, not until it gets to the point where I know I can't do the job in the outfield anymore."

I believe I said, "I'm still a baseball player, not a DH."

I knew I'd had a rough time in the outfield the year before. And that May, there was a play that got a lot of coverage. It was in Kansas City, and we were leading by a run with two outs in the bottom of the ninth. Martin brought in Goose, and Amos Otis hit a long fly ball off him, almost to the wall. Paul Blair and I were both going for it, and we ran into each other. Otis got a two-run, inside-the-park home run off it that changed a likely win into a loss, just like that.

No excuses, it was my fault. The center fielder is the captain out there, and he calls the shots. But that sort of thing just happens sometimes. It wasn't indicative of the year I was having. Overall, I cut my errors down from thirteen to three. To make out like my fielding was the reason we were in fourth place was ridiculous. To make out that Thurman Munson, a lifelong catcher, with his bad knees, could do a better job was even more ridiculous.

But once I finally got in his office with George, he told me right off that I just wasn't a good enough outfielder to be out there. That irked me, and we started to get into it. I think I told him something like, "Look, I still have the desire to play my heart out for you. But if you're not going to play me—if you're not going to treat me like a complete ballplayer—please trade me."

That seemed reasonable enough to me. But George got angry, started going on about how I should decide whether I really had the desire to play in New York or if I wanted to be traded. Essentially, he was ignoring what I'd just said, and he was getting madder and madder.

He stood up and shouted at me, "You better get your freaking head on straight, son!"

I could not believe it. Here it was, a year later, another meeting with the owner about all the turmoil on the team . . . and once again somebody is telling me I'd better get my head on straight? Like it was my fault?

I was so angry. I stood up, too. I told him, "Who the hell do you think you're talking to?"

He still wouldn't back down. He just said, "I'm talking to *you*!"

I was furious. I told him, "I'm not your son! Don't you ever talk to me like that again as long as you live."

Al Rosen, who was there, tried to calm us both down, but we

weren't having any of it. George told me, "Jackson, get the hell out of my office!"

I told him no. So *he* walked out instead. I had just chased George Steinbrenner out of his own office, which I think must be the only time that ever happened. It was pretty funny, in retrospect. But nobody was laughing about it at the time. You couldn't believe the crap that went on.

Later, I realized that George had completely diverted the conversation I was trying to have about him trading me. Now that I think back on it, I think that was probably the purpose, and he was good at it. I know George respected people who came back at him. He would go away and think about it. If you didn't stand up to him and battle back, he'd steamroll you . . .

We still had a game to play, against the Royals at the Stadium. Another Monday night game, about mid-July. Why so much always seemed to happen on these national broadcast games, these Monday night games, I have no idea. Kansas City had beat us in the first two games of the series, and we were just trying to salvage one—just trying to hang in the race.

Frankly, I think most of us believed that was already beyond us. We were thirteen games down by then, in fourth place. You don't come back from that far behind. Or so many of us thought.

Billy still wouldn't put me in the field that night, but he did write me in to the number four spot. We were facing Paul Splittorff. Remember him? I suppose this was another one of Billy's little games, his attempts to show me up, putting me in now against the guy he wouldn't start me against in the playoffs the year before. I couldn't keep up with how he was thinking, it made no sense.

We got off to an early lead, got up 5–1 on them. Catfish was pitching for us, and you know, suddenly he didn't look half-bad. His ball had movement again. But he hadn't pitched much, and he was tired out by the fifth. Sparky had to come in and take over for him. Lyle got out of the fifth, pitched a one-two-three inning in the sixth . . . then came in and told Martin he was done for the night.

Sparky told him, "I'm not a f—ing long reliever." Then he walked back down to the clubhouse, took a shower, and left the Stadium. Just like that. I loved it.

For Sparky, it was the last straw in what had been a humiliating season. He had a good point: He wasn't being used properly. Almost nobody on our staff was being used properly. Sparky was not a three-to four-inning pitcher. But you know, when Sparky said he wasn't playing anymore, his manager didn't cuss him out on national television. Nor did he "try" to take a poke at him.

Goose had to come into the game in his place. He pitched well, struck out Freddie Patek with two outs and the bases loaded in the eighth to end a threat. But then Willie Randolph, who was in and out every other day, playing hurt, made an error in the ninth, and the Royals tied it.

Martin just kept Goose in there, playing the game like it was the World Series—again. Gossage got through the tenth, and in the bottom of the inning Munson led off with a single for us. The Royals had their own closer out there by then, Al Hrabosky, "the Mad Hungarian." He was a lefty, threw some pretty good heat. Used to do all kinds of antics on the mound to try to intimidate batters, fume and bounce around, turn his back on the hitter when he came up.

Whatever. I came up, ready to hit—and Billy Martin gave me the bunt sign. Just like he had given me the bunt sign against Boston near the end of the 1977 season.

That was it. That was enough.

I was just so fed up with the entire scenario. I wasn't going to play right field. I wasn't going to play against left-handed pitching. I wasn't going to play against right-handed pitching, sometimes.

I just turned around and looked in the dugout, hoping I hadn't seen the bunt sign from Dick Howser, our third-base coach. I was almost making a silent appeal to Billy. I was thinking, "I'm your cleanup hitter. Now you're asking me to bunt? What other humiliations would you like to tack on here? Would you like me to wear a court jester's hat?"

But Billy still had Howser signaling bunt to me.

So I squared around and tried to bunt. Hrabosky wasn't fooled; he threw one in tight and hard so I couldn't get it down. The next pitch,

I found out later, Billy took the bunt off, signaled me to hit away. It didn't surprise me that he took the bunt off. I saw George Brett move in at third and knew the Royals were alert to the bunt now. But I didn't know for sure, because I was through looking at signals just then. Billy Martin wanted a bunt; he was going to get a bunt. I was tired of all the crap.

Hrabosky came in again, and this time I nudged the ball foul. Dick Howser called time and ran down to make sure I hadn't missed the sign. Because I suppose it was obvious that I was giving a half-assed effort at bunting. Dick came down, made sure I knew Billy wanted me to hit away.

But I was past that now. My conversation with myself was, "What am I doing here? If you want me to bunt, why would you hit me cleanup? Why would you do it? Put someone else in here."

Dick Howser told me, "Billy wants you to swing away." And I said to his face, "No, he told me to bunt. And no offense to you, but I'm going to bunt." Dick said something like, "I hope you know what you're doing here," and went back to third base. Which was exactly the right thing to do, and why Howser was a good man. He wasn't going to get in the middle. He was going to let us play this out.

I fouled off another one from Hrabosky, for strike two. Then I popped up a third one, which the catcher caught. I was out. Thurman was still on first.

I walked back to the dugout, ready for a confrontation. Ready for anything. It wasn't like all of a sudden I had gotten hot and angry and flew off the handle. I had had enough. Enough of all of it. I said to myself, "All right, here we go," and I went and sat down. Sat my helmet down, took my hat off. Took my glasses off, too, just the same as I did in Boston the year before. Because I knew with Billy, he's a guy who would probably try to blindside me if he decided to take a punch.

I was ready. I *hoped* I had done something to create a spark, to create a confrontation. I was *looking* for it this time!

Gene Michael came down to me on the bench and said, "You know, Billy wants you to go inside"—go inside the clubhouse. And I looked at Gene, and I said, "Gene, you said that kind of rough and kind of rude."

I'd always gotten along well with Gene. I always would. But I wasn't taking anything from anyone at this point.

Gene told me, "Reggie, it's not me. Billy wants me to tell you to go inside." I said, "If he wants me to go inside, tell him to come here and tell me himself."

I sat out there for another inning before I went in. Top of the eleventh, Goose was in his fifth inning of work. He would've got through it, too, but Thurman dropped a fly ball out in right field, where he was playing in place of me. The Royals scored four unearned runs, went up 9–5. We almost came back in the bottom of the inning, Willie hit a home run, and Thurman drove in a run.

In fact, the game ended with the very same situation we'd had the inning before: Thurman on first, me due up. Two outs, the Yanks trailing, 9–7. Billy *could* have let bygones be bygones, thought in the best interest of the team, and put me up there to swing away. I would've still been in the game.

My forced confrontation ended that possibility. Pretty honest, huh? Instead, Billy had to send Cliff Johnson up to pinch-hit for me. Cliff was a terrific hitter, but he was having a horrible year. At the time, he was hitting exactly .190.

When Billy sent him up, I headed for the clubhouse. I walked right by him and went inside without saying a word. Cliff flied out to left. Billy came down to his office, picked up his clock radio, and threw it against a wall. Then he picked up a beer bottle and threw that against the wall, too.

I was out by my locker, still in my uniform. Ready for anything. But Billy never did come out to speak to me.

It was the writers who came over and told me I'd been suspended. Billy never did tell me. The Boss had already issued a statement, backing Martin, before he had exchanged so much as a word with me: "What is paramount is a sense of command and discipline. If you don't have it, forget it. Forget the whole organization."

What nobody on the Yankees was willing to talk about was that Sparky Lyle had already told his manager to go to hell and walked off the field back in the sixth inning. Nobody said boo to him. I think it was Fran Healy who quietly let Henry Hecht know about it, or the story never would've got out.

I had my problems with Hecht at times. I'd got mad at him over that piece he wrote about me in the hotel room in Boston the year before. But he was willing to listen at least, and he went and checked what happened with Sparky. He discovered it was true, he got the facts, and I have to hand it to him: He wrote a story for the *Post* about how there was a double standard on the Yankees.

When that came out, the front office got very upset about it. I heard that guys like Al Rosen and Cedric Tallis even sat Henry down and told him they didn't want it coming out. But you have to give him credit, he made sure the truth got out. Our front office was trying to deny it, but Henry told the Boss, "George, I smell a rat!"

He could do that, because Fran tipped him off to the real story. It was all around then. I think George even liked that, because it was so much PR for the team. It was what Fran used to say: "It's better than Broadway!" Or Sparky calling it "the Bronx Zoo" in his book, or I think Nettles said something like, "Some boys want to grow up and play major-league baseball, and other boys want to run away and join the circus. I got to do both." Loved it!

I gotta say, great lines. But I signed up to play ball.

The truth was that Billy had already lost control of his team, even before he tried to humiliate me one more time. He'd lost control of it back in 1977, I thought, but nobody truly realized it because of Fran Healy patching things up and because of Bucky not saying anything about almost leaving the team.

He lost control of it again in 1978, I felt, because he was literally wrecking the arms of our pitchers and because they wouldn't put up with it anymore. Sparky Lyle never was a top reliever again after that season. I continue to believe that Martin lost control of his team because he would not put his personal feelings aside and do what was best for the team.

However, at the moment that wasn't what anybody in the media wanted to hear. Nobody said anything about Lyle—the American League Cy Young winner the year before—defying his manager and disobeying orders. Somehow, that wasn't a story. Just as nobody said anything about Bucky Dent trying to jump the team the year before. Instead, it was all about me again.

Maybe some of the writers didn't know about it. But there aren't a lot of secrets that don't get out on a ball club—or anywhere else. As Benjamin Franklin said, "Three men can keep a secret if two of them are dead."

My defiance of Martin was newsworthy and punishable by suspension and fine. Theirs—Bucky's and Sparky's—wasn't. There was definitely a double standard. Those are the facts.

I tried to defend myself a little at first. Told the press that I thought the way I'd been hitting recently, a bunt was the best idea. I said, "If I get it down, I'm a hero. If not, I'm a butt."

You know, I was still hoping to defuse the situation. But my heart wasn't in it. I was tired of covering up. I knew I couldn't win. No matter. I should just take it all, no matter how unfair it was. I would still come off as the outspoken black guy with the big contract who complained and couldn't handle the situation.

When the writers told me I'd been suspended, I said, *"Really?!"* And they said, "Yes. What are you gonna do?"

I remember being happy. I was glad. I wanted to bring everything to a head. I wasn't disappointed for a moment. I felt something needed to be done, no matter what. This was it.

All I said was, "I'm going to California on the first plane smoking tomorrow morning."

And that was what I did. I didn't say much else. I left the clubhouse, went back to my apartment, and packed a small bag. I made a flight at nine in the morning, to San Francisco. American Airlines. The press was waiting for me at the airport, but I was a very familiar flier on American, so they dropped me off on the tarmac.

This could never happen today, but when we got to the gate, they pulled up the unloading walkway—what they call the Jetway. They allowed me to go out the door, down those stairs, and go underground and avoid the press. It was so cool!

I went down through the underbelly of the terminal, connected with a friend who picked me up, and went home to Berkeley.

Here I was at home in California, "right back where I started from." I had no idea what was going to happen—and neither did anyone else. For all I knew, my career was over, and I was going to be vilified all over the country. And even knowing that, I *still* felt like a huge weight had been lifted off my chest.

"One's a Born Liar"

THE NEXT DAY, I was back on a plane. Off to Hawaii. I just threw another bag together, told no one I was leaving. Talk about tripping! Color me gone!

It was a surreal situation. The team was still in turmoil. There were all these big debates in the press about what the Yankees should do with me. Suspend me for the rest of the season. Try to cancel my contract. Whatever.

At the time, I was hoping to be traded. The day after I left, the Red Sox won again, and we dropped to fourteen games out of first place. In the whole history of baseball, just one other team had ever come back from that many games down or more, and that was the Boston "Miracle Braves" of 1914. (They didn't call them the Miracle Braves for nothing.) I was hoping the Yankees might trade me to some team that still had a chance to make the playoffs, and maybe I could show what I could do.

The more I thought about it, the more I didn't think I would be traded. George wasn't going to trade me. I'd tried to get him to do that before. I was a marquee attraction, regardless of whether I was a mess or not. George was not a quitter. When he set out to do something, he was going to do it, whether it was right or wrong. It was not going to just slip by. And after I'd brought everything to a confrontation, something *had* to be done.

By then, my feelings were, "While you're all discussing what's to become of me, I am, by the way, going to go to Hawaii for a few days and kick around." And that's what I did.

My thinking was, "Hey, here's what's going on, guys. You had a team that was coming apart." I thought, "You chose to ignore this before, even as the manager came apart at the seams, wrecking our pitching staff and putting some of his best players on the bench. Hopefully, I'm bringing this to your attention. I'm bringing this to a head. I'm not so wrong as you think.

"You're going to suspend and fine me? Okay. I expected that. At least everything is going to stop for a while. There's going to be some discussion about how it gets fixed. I'm not coming back the way it is, and I don't mind that." Of course, I never said that to anyone!

I knew the Yankees still wanted me, because pretty soon they called my attorney, Steven Kay, and wanted me to come back. At the same time, they were still saying I was suspended indefinitely. They told everybody, "As long as Reggie's not here, we're gonna fine him and suspend him without pay."

I said, "Fine."

I had a nice little savings, and I didn't have too big a house. I didn't have too many cars, I didn't have too many bills, and I could get through. At the time, I was doing pretty well.

I was not too worried about that fine.

I went to the hotel in Honolulu, and hung out there. Ironically, it was a place I knew from going there first with ABC for the *Superstars* competition—where I first met all my welcoming teammates.

I went there and just kicked around. Got lost. I knew a girl over there who was a friend. I had someone to talk to and have dinner with. The best part of it was she knew nothing about baseball. She said she had heard about my suspension, but she didn't care. I didn't give a hoot about going back or not. I didn't pick up a sports page. It was nice being away from it all.

The Yankees called and asked Steven Kay to get me to come back. This time they said they had rescinded the fine. They'd found out, too, that you couldn't suspend someone "indefinitely." Not under the basic agreement with the players' union—another thing we had to thank Marvin Miller for.

You had to make it a definite time. So Al Rosen decided I was suspended for five games. They asked me to come back right away, but I couldn't get back in time. I was in Hawaii!

Billy wanted to make it seven games, but Al overrode him. Billy was making all kinds of pronouncements since I'd left. He told the press, "If Jackson comes back, he does exactly what I say. Period." Note the "If." He said, "From now on, nobody tells the manager or the front office what he's going to do. Nobody's bigger than this team."

They asked him if he'd accept an apology from me. Billy told them, "I don't believe in apologizing. I won't talk anything out with him."

Fair enough, I said. I rejoined the team in Chicago, where we were playing. I did not have to pay a fine. I flew in and went to the ballpark in a cab with Fran Healy. I went straight to my locker to get dressed. I was ready to play. I got in too late to take batting practice, but I went out on the field, got ready. Played catch, stretched, jogged, got loose. I just told myself I should go in, shut my mouth, get it out of the way, do what you're supposed to do. Play ball.

That's exactly what I did. And I didn't know it at the time, but I understood afterward Billy was so perplexed that I didn't ask for a meeting to apologize to him and the team. But I'd seen how that worked out the year before, and I didn't really think I had anything to apologize for—to him or the team. I didn't need to go to Billy. Neither one of us wanted to see the other.

I probably should have apologized to the team, for creating a ruckus. I did go around to each player who I thought cared anything about me and apologized to him individually. Maybe a dozen or so guys who cared to hear anything I had to say. Some could have cared less.

Billy left me on the bench that afternoon. We beat the White Sox, 3–1, in the top of the ninth, when Chambliss doubled in Piniella and then Billy called for a squeeze play, a bunt by Nettles that caught them completely by surprise and scored an insurance run.

Afterward, in the locker room, the press all came around, and Fran Healy said to me, "Whatever you do, don't apologize." That was right up my alley. I didn't have to be coaxed.

You know, Fran was always a peacemaker, but he didn't really like Billy. Not very many people did. He told me, "Don't apologize, you don't have to do that."

Fran always had great advice. I don't know if he had great advice about me not talking to Billy—but I wasn't going to talk to him anyway.

All I told the press when they asked was that it was difficult coming back, but that I didn't have any intention of *not* reporting. I wasn't going to jump the team at that time and give Billy what he wanted. I told them I'd had a lot of time to think about the magnitude of the situation, the magnitude of New York. I admitted it was an uncomfortable situation.

One note here about using the word "magnitude." A lot of the writers at the time thought it was very pretentious of me to use it, particularly when I would say "the magnitude of me." They thought it sounded almost as if I were talking about myself in the third person.

I didn't mean it the way they thought. All it reflected was how crazy I thought the whole situation was—all this nonsense revolving around me, and the manager, and what was said about it. I didn't use the word to aggrandize myself, just to express how out of hand, how magnified, and out of proportion I thought everything could get.

How could I be such a big story? How could the manager and I not get along? It was crazy. I guess I was supposed to just go along with whatever Billy was trying to prove. To go through this at thirty-two years of age. I was too young to manage it. I was overwhelmed.

To have him not just put me in the lineup and get the hell out of the way—never speak to me. Just let me play ball. Why he couldn't do that—I just didn't get it.

At the time, it made me wonder, "Is it because I'm black and speaking my own opinion? Is it because I have a certain arrogance about me? The way I present things? Tell me what it is."

One of the writers asked me if I would bunt again in that situation if I had to do it all over again. I told him that if I'd known what the consequences would have been, I probably would have just swung away and avoided all the hassle! I admired the guts of the guy to ask me the question. I wanted to pinch his head off.

However, looking back on it now, I don't know if that's true. I was so upset at the time I don't think I was considering what the consequences were. And if I had, I still don't know if I would've backed down. I wouldn't have wanted to.

Something had to be done. Something had to be done to stop the team from coming apart any further. Something had to be done to keep the situation between Billy and me from getting any worse. I wasn't going to sit by and watch him ruin guys, including me. I wasn't going to sit on the bench and spend the next three and a half years as a part-time DH.

Maybe it was only my unconscious mind that was telling me to force the situation. I don't know. But if I had gone along and bunted just like Billy wanted, it wouldn't have done him or anybody else any good. If I had just meekly gone along with the changes George wanted, it wouldn't have helped anybody. We wouldn't have won anything that year, and Billy would've been fired pretty soon anyway. George (the Boss) would've torn the team apart.

Instead, as it happened, Billy took himself apart. He sounded very pleased with himself while I was out in Hawaii. The team won five in a row, and Boston finally ran into a rough patch. The Sox started suffering a few injuries of their own, started running into some hot clubs, and we cut their lead over us down to ten games—even if we were still in third place.

Billy was apparently saying to all the writers that this showed how right he was about things and how I was the problem with the team. He was really hoping I would just stay out in California, maybe get traded somewhere. And now I was back.

You know, one of the writers, I think it was Henry Hecht, had a theory from the year before that Billy was trying to "gaslight" me. It was a reference from this old Ingrid Bergman movie, in which her husband tries to convince her she's going crazy. Henry thought Billy was trying to do that to me, moving me all around the lineup, trying to undermine my confidence. Taking the bat out of my hand. Getting me to demand a trade and move *myself* out of there. If he only knew how much I was trying to be traded . . .

In the end, I was the one driving *him* crazy. Just by being there.

You'd think Billy would've been on top of the world just then. He'd just won five straight games without me. Just won a game playing Billy-ball, squeezing in a run the way he liked. You'd think he would've been happy.

Yet I don't think Billy was ever happy. Not then, anyway.

Then came the next unbelievable twist in the story. We were trying to get out of Chicago. We get out to O'Hare Airport, and our flight was delayed, and Billy starts fueling. Oh, Billy Martin and airport bars! He started pouring down the fuel with Art Fowler. Then Murray Chass of the *New York Times* came by and told him what I'd said after the game—about how it was an uncomfortable situation.

It wasn't much of anything to say, I thought, but Billy went off on it. He told Murray, "I'm saying, 'Shut up, Reggie Jackson. We don't need none of your s—t.'" He told him, "'We're winning without you. We don't need you coming in and making all these comments.'"

Billy told him, "If Jackson doesn't shut his mouth, he won't play, and I don't care what George says. He can replace me right now if he doesn't like it." He told Chass to go ahead and phone the story in, then he went back for more fuel.

Meanwhile, word was starting to get out about the sort of stuff he was saying. Henry Hecht went back with Chass to the bar, and Billy just kept running off at the mouth. When Henry told him what I'd said about what I would do if I had to do it all over again—how I guessed I would've gone ahead and swung away against Kansas City as ordered—Billy told him that was like "a guy getting out of jail and saying, 'I'm innocent,' after he killed somebody. He and every one of the other players knew he defied me."

Billy told them that I had taken off my glasses when I got back to the bench because I was getting ready for a fight. That was only half-wrong—I *was* getting ready just in case he thought I was going to be another in a long line of Billy Martin sucker-punch victims.

"He expected to get popped but good," he told Chass, and Billy said it took him "the most restraint it's ever taken in my life" not to hit me there. He said something about how he was going to kick my ass.

Uh-huh. He must've spent a lot of time in the off-season down at Disneyland, because that's where they got Goofy. He'd got real goofy if he ever thought he was going to kick *my* ass. I didn't want that confrontation. I knew I couldn't win in the public forum.

Billy just wouldn't shut up. Even as he was walking to the team plane with Hecht and Chass, he went on about how upset he was that I hadn't apologized. Then, when they told him they'd asked me and I said he hadn't spoken to me yet, he told them I was lying. Then he threw in George.

"The two of them deserve each other," he said about George and me. "One's a born liar, the other's convicted"—referring to how George was found guilty of making illegal campaign contributions to Richard Nixon.

Now he was comparing me to a murderer *and* saying I'm a liar.

Henry knew at once how big a story he had. He came back over to me where I was walking through the airport with Fran. Henry came up to me, and he said, "I think Billy's gonna get fired. Wait'll George hears about this!" He said, "He talked about George, and he talked about you, Reggie, and he was so upset that you didn't come and apologize to him and the team."

I didn't even *think* about it. I just wanted to be out of the way. I just couldn't believe I was getting tagged for Martin blowing up and calling me a liar. I hadn't said anything to him. I didn't even understand his comment. I didn't know who he meant. When I first heard that quote, I was honestly trying to figure out which one of us was supposed to be which. I was like, "What did I do?"

There's another thing a lot of people don't know about that quote. It wasn't even original. It was something a couple of guys on the team came up with. They'd been saying it about Steinbrenner and *Billy Martin himself*—not me!—since back in spring training. Billy picked up the line and used it about George and me.

Henry was excited because he had a story, and he was reporting it. He thought Billy was going to get fired. He didn't like Billy, either. Of course by that time, a lot of people were fed up with Billy. Even the players who *liked* Billy were uncomfortable with the way things were going.

The writers went ahead and called George from the airport and asked him for a reaction. He was stunned by it. Who wouldn't be?

The team had finally started to win—we won *that afternoon*—and here was Billy telling him off. For nothing. George hadn't said a word to him since we'd been winning.

The next day, after we got into Kansas City, Billy had that awful press conference at the Crown Center hotel. Standing on the balcony, sunglasses on inside the building. His hands shaking. He looked like a man ten years older than he was yesterday!

He told the writers he had a statement to make and he wouldn't say anything else, "now or forever, because I am a Yankee and Yankees do not talk or throw rocks." It was pretty late for him to decide that. He went on to say he was quitting to help the team win the pennant and for his own health and "mental well-being."

He apologized to George Steinbrenner for saying what he said about him—then said he didn't say it.

Surprisingly, he didn't mention any apology to me. He then went on to thank the front office, the media, the writers, the coaches, and the fans. Everybody but the players who made him a champion.

By the end he was sobbing. Not everybody was impressed. Roger Kahn wrote in the *Times*, "Babe Ruth and Lou Gehrig went out of the arena more quietly to face their death." Pete Gammons wrote, "Martin had to be led away from the news conference in tears, which was good for a few laughs."

I wasn't laughing. I can't honestly say I was sorry to see him go, but I wasn't laughing. Phil Rizzuto had to come up and lead him away, I think. I don't know if the Yankees even had anyone official there.

I don't know how I'd describe the whole scene. But it was fitting. Because once again, Billy was alone.

It was such a weird time. I didn't know all that was going on at the time. Fran knew more than I did, people talked to him, they didn't talk so much to me. I was suspended; I was back on the team. I was the problem; Billy was the problem. We're on our way to Kansas City, we're going pretty good . . . and Martin? He was getting fired? What happened? What did I do?

Certainly I understood it takes two to tango and I was one of them. I regret the way this turned out. I remember at the time Fran Healy was telling me how to handle the press, what to say. He warned me, "They'll blame you; they'll make you out to be the villain."

I basically remained quiet. Did whatever Fran told me. He would pick out a few things to say, and I would say them. Basic things about Billy, like, "This is his decision. I'm just going to go along with management. I don't have anything against Billy." It's tough to say things you don't mean.

I was very fortunate to have people around me who helped get me through the hard times, people like Fran, Gary Walker, my family, and others. I remember one of George's friends, Tony Rolfe, lots of times talking through all the nonsense that went on.

All these individuals were constantly giving me good advice, keeping my head straight, and pointing me toward what mattered most in life. I'm grateful to this day—I'll always be grateful—that they were there to help me.

I don't know that Billy was ever that fortunate. Throughout the time we were both on the Yankees, there were always people around him who kept telling him that he was right, and that George was wrong, and that I was the problem with the team.

Those people might have meant well. The fans meant well, siding with him through everything. They loved Billy as the underdog, and I understood that. However, ultimately, I don't think they did him any favors.

That helped to keep him from ever acknowledging that he might not be thinking clearly—that he might be wrong. And they did not make Billy face what had become a real problem in his life, which was his drinking.

Occasionally, someone said something. I remember hearing a

story about a day in 1977 when Billy was tying one on after a loss, and Gabe Paul looked at him and said, "You're drinking like we *won*." But those sorts of interventions were all too few and far between.

The reporters covering our team also didn't do Billy any favors by not writing about his drinking. Too often in our society, we celebrate public figures when they're on top and kick them when they're down, forgetting that the person involved is not just a picture in a newspaper or an image on a TV screen but a living, breathing, *bleeding* human being. A human being who could use our help before it's too late.

Being honest is a virtue. It hurts, as we all know. But sometimes it is a necessity.

Billy Martin was a human tragedy, in the real sense of the words. He defied long odds his whole life and maximized his abilities in the game. He helped the Yankees win five rings as a player and another one as manager. He fought hard his whole life—but too often, it seemed like he was fighting himself.

I was disappointed that we were never able to get along. I always felt we had some things in common, particularly a strong desire to compete, to win any way we could.

I never understood why he was so antagonistic to me from almost the moment I joined the team. Even though I understood the reasons intellectually—Billy was upset that he hadn't been consulted about signing me, he felt that I was the one who questioned his authority, he thought I would disturb the team chemistry, and all that jazz.

Emotionally, though, I didn't understand why he could never move past all that, in pursuit of our mutual desire to win. I couldn't understand why he was so determined to undermine me at every opportunity. It was as if he was trying to prove something that he himself didn't quite understand.

Billy once told some writers about me, "He's not a hater, he doesn't know how to hate. Raschi and Reynolds knew how to hate, I know how to hate."

I never had the privilege to play with Vic Raschi or Allie Reynolds, his old teammates. I'm sure they were great pitchers and fierce competitors. But I bet they knew how *not* to hate, too.

Billy was right, I was not a hater. When I heard about him saying that, I had and still have no comprehension of the thought process behind it!

I didn't hate Billy. I didn't hate anybody. If I didn't like someone, I just kept a distance. Still do. I just get away from them, or whatever it is that's agitating me. If you can't control it, prepare. If it's raining outside, take an umbrella. If you don't have one, wear a raincoat. If you don't have either, wait until it stops raining. Do whatever it takes.

"Reggie doesn't know how to hate"—he was trying to call it a weakness. But I would call that a strength.

Billy Martin went out on a winning streak. In his dream job, managing the Yankees. Managing the team the way he wanted, with me on the bench. And somehow it wasn't enough. He had let his demons take over.

That tells me that there was plenty more going on with Billy that we didn't see. It tells me that his problems went beyond whatever fracas he was having with George or me on any given day. He had everything he claimed to want—and then he was gone. That tells me that knowing how to hate makes no sense.

Billy was gone—and then he was back.

Just five days later, at our Old-Timers' Day, back at the Stadium, they made a surprise announcement that Billy would come back to manage the team in 1980.

It was probably the worst day in my baseball life. Nobody warned me about it beforehand. I didn't see Billy in the clubhouse; they were keeping him under wraps. Then there he was, running out on the field after all those Yankee greats, grinning from ear to ear. We had a big crowd, more than forty-six thousand, and they went crazy.

I asked George later why he didn't give me a heads-up. He said, "Well, I really didn't have to, Reggie."

Would've been nice, though. That's the short story on that.

The longer story was I think he really did it just to appease the fans, keep them quiet. And a couple days later, Billy was already spouting off, telling reporters, "I've always said I could manage Adolf Hitler,

Benito Mussolini, and Hirohito. That doesn't mean I'd like them, but I'd manage them." A few days after *that*, he told the press that he didn't have any malice in his heart toward me: "I've done everything I could to help the young man and now he has to help himself."

Yeah, that was Billy Martin, my mentor. Now I was a murderer sprung from jail, a born liar, and Hitler, Mussolini, and Hirohito, all rolled into one. It was a few days after that, I think, that he told the press that Fred Stanley, our backup shortstop, made more contributions to the team than I ever did.

You know, it wouldn't necessarily have been so bad to plan to bring Billy back in 1980—if somebody was going to use the next year and a half to get him some real help. But that wasn't going to happen. Instead, he was the same old Billy. He was just going to do what he wanted, say what he wanted, and come back anyway.

At the time, the Boss said, "All that happened in the past is meaningless." Which was just the problem. If you don't learn from the past, if you don't learn from experience, what do you learn from? How do you know the way forward?

Bringing Billy back, ignoring his past, meant the Yankees were just going to go around in circles. Which is what would happen.

But on Old-Timers' Day, we played the Twins. I had two hits and threw out Roy Smalley trying to take an extra base after a single. We won, 7–3. That was what we did. We were professionals.

"A VERY SIMPLE GAME FOR CHILDREN"

PRIVATELY, I TOLD myself that—one way or another—I would be gone by the time Billy Martin came back in 1980. I would *make* them trade me, somehow.

Then I just put it out of my mind. I think a lot of us were stunned that Billy was supposed to come back, but we just put it away. It was like what Lou Piniella said: "Nineteen eighty is a year and a half away. We can't worry about that."

It's too hard to play baseball and try to be successful—try to go out there every day and get hits—and have distractions. Those who've never played, you can't understand the difficulty of the daily grind and the demand for excellence. It is a struggle. It was hard to do for me. I chose to stay inside myself, it made it easier to be gruff because I felt it helped me play better.

I still had the feeling of being overwhelmed by the city. I don't blame New York. But sometimes when I was alone in my apartment, my mind would just get stale. I lived right across from the Metropolitan Museum then, at Seventy-ninth and Fifth, and I would look out over the museum and the park, and I would just drift. I enjoyed seeing the sun set to the west, over the Dakota building. I enjoyed the park, the trees and green, from where I was on the twentieth floor. It was nice and peaceful to look below and chill out, relax.

At the ballpark, it was bad at first, though not as bad as it had been the year before. Predictably, the fans blamed me for Billy's self-destruction. They hung up signs saying things like, "Billy's the One Who's Sane, Reggie's the One to Blame," and "Reggie, Are You Happy Now?" (Yes.) There were ones a lot worse than those, which security had to take down, they were so profane. When I'd come up, some of them would chant, "Bunt! Bunt!" for a while. (And much worse things.)

With all that pressure, there was a deep loneliness inside. That was the first time I ever really felt that. There was a need for help, and I recognized that. That forced me to go to the place where I had to go, to go to things that I needed as a human being. And those things were mainly God, Jesus, and the friends who supported me.

I had a girlfriend in California I could talk to and the other friends I'd made through the Boss in New York. Fran Healy was a great sounding board for me, as always; he'd help me with peace of mind. It was great as always seeing my brother Joe and my dad. They were still telling me, "Keep beating on the ball."

I probably saw my family three or four times a month that year. After the 1977 World Series, George wanted to do something special for me. He offered to buy me a car, because I guess he heard somewhere that I liked cars. I didn't need a car, so I got one for my dad. We bought it from our local dealer, Webb Cadillac, in Wyncote, Pennsylvania. My dad loved it. It had a remote start, so in the winter you could start it up, warm it up before you got in. He would drive up from Philadelphia to the game, or my friend George Beck or a couple of his friends would drive him up and back.

I really got back into reading Biblical passages and talking about faith with my friend Gary Walker. At this time in my life, I was having such difficulty, and Gary was very helpful. I didn't feel alone when I talked to him. I didn't have time to try to figure out Billy Martin. I had that need for guidance. I was in survival mode.

Faith is like a blanket. In life, I have learned that when I get up in the morning and get dressed, I need to put God on as well. I needed to ask Him to continue to stay close.

It's very much like the other things you have to concentrate on in the grind of a long season. You have to make sure that you have the right help as you go through life every day. The Bible for me became a guide. I didn't know where I was going, but I could see light, and I tried to keep going toward it.

On the field, when you're a professional athlete, you're constantly *adapting*. That's because your body is changing while you're also trying to adapt to the competition. What you rely on for that is your experience and your knowledge.

How to make up for the half step that you're losing. I would say that your body falls back 10 to 20 percent once you get to be thirty-three, thirty-four, thirty-five—and I was almost there by then. But you can keep going until you're forty and still be productive, as many of the greats have done. As Henry Aaron did. As Pete Rose has done—Molitor, Yount, Brett, Ripken, Yastrzemski, Williams. Frank Robinson, Mariano, and others.

Players make their adjustments to keep pace—to stay abreast. I wasn't feeling that so much yet when I came to the Yankees. But I was already adjusting. When I went to Baltimore and then New York, I went from a bat that was usually thirty-six or thirty-seven ounces to one that was thirty-five/thirty-five—thirty-five ounces in weight, thirty-five inches in length.

I tried to square my stance in Yankee Stadium, open up my front side a little. See the ball a little better, and try to maybe hit it to right field a little more. And I really couldn't. It *did* allow me to see the ball better, but I knew I just wasn't a pull hitter. I never was—and Yankee Stadium proved that. I ended up doing the same thing I'd done before, trying to hit the ball to the power alleys in left-center, right-center, the big part of the ballpark. After four or five years in the league, I knew what type of hitter I was.

It helps, in adapting—in making the adjustments you have to make—to have the clutter out of your mind and concentrate on what you have to do on the ball field. There were two things that are generally credited with enabling us to get away from that clutter, from all those distractions, and get back into the race that year. One of them really was a big factor. The other is overrated.

Replacing Billy Martin with Bob Lemon was a big change for the better. Bob was a wonderful guy, very easygoing. He was an old friend of Al Rosen's, which was where Al really helped us; he knew he'd be good for our team. Bob had been the pitching coach back in 1976, before he had to make way for Art Fowler. Then he'd made a good run managing a kind of patchwork White Sox team in 1977—got fired the next year when he lost half his guys to free agency. He knew baseball. He liked to have a drink after a game, but he used alcohol in a very different way from Billy. He used it, it didn't use him.

Bob Lemon also helped create a comfortable atmosphere in the clubhouse. He liked to call everybody "Meat" in a very good-hearted, affectionate way. He'd say, "Grab a bat, Meat," something like that.

I know the pitchers were delighted right away. For somebody like Goose, he was just ecstatic about the change. Bob had been a Hall of Fame pitcher (after breaking in as an outfielder), and he knew what he was doing. It was easy to see he was confident and comfortable with himself.

He also didn't overmanage. He liked to say, "Baseball is a very simple game for children that we grown-ups have managed to screw up." The first day he came in, he told us all, "I'm just gonna get out of the way, don't want to make too many decisions, and let you guys play." He said, "I hope I don't screw up too bad. Now go have some fun."

When the writers asked him about it afterward, he told them, "It went like every other clubhouse meeting. The manager talks and the players don't say a word. At least I wasn't booed."

I always got along great with Bob. What he told me was, "Meat, I'm gonna hit you cleanup every day. Sometimes you'll play right field, and sometimes you'll DH. You know what to do. Just hit some over the wall. I'm just going to let you have fun."

And it was fun. Bob Lemon made it fun again—as much fun as a job can be. He cut out the distractions, but beyond that he went back to letting us play the way we should've been playing all along. I was in right field and the cleanup spot. He put Thurman back behind the plate, put Roy White and Lou Piniella alternating in left and at DH again. That gave us a pretty strong bench, with all the guys we had there—Jim Spencer, Thomasson, Paul Blair, Jay Johnstone, Cliff Johnson.

Under Lemon, we put together one of the great stretch drives of all time. We went 48–20 for him, but 40–14 from August 5 on.

The year before, we'd gone 40–10 from the time Gabe—along with Thurman, Lou, George, and finally Gabe again—told Billy to cut the nonsense and hit me fourth to when we clinched the division. You look at those statistics, when we were playing for Bob

Lemon, or when we were playing for a Billy Martin forced to do what made sense . . . we went a combined 80–24. That's almost .770 ball, or almost 125 wins over a full season, which would easily set a major-league record. With Billy running the team the way he wanted to, we went 120–101. That's about 88 wins over a 162-game schedule.

In other words, doing things Billy's way, we were an okay club, finishing a few games over .500, good for maybe third or fourth those couple years in the American League East. Doing it our way, we put together the two greatest back-to-back stretch drives in history.

Now, that's not entirely fair. There are other factors involved. But without Billy we were just a much looser, more relaxed team—in a good way. Guys around the league knew it. I remember that Freddie Lynn on the Red Sox said something at the time, when he heard about Billy being fired: "Oh, s—t, that's the worst! With Billy they were fighting each other in the dugout. Now they'll come after us."

The other factor everybody gave for why we came back was the newspaper strike. On August 10, the big three dailies in New York—the *Times*, the *Daily News*, and the *Post*—all went on strike. Supposedly, because of the newspaper strike, we went on a winning streak.

I've got something I want to say about that. Please believe that while the power of the press certainly is valuable, and it helps the brand, it does not help you win a baseball game. It does not help a guy come out of a slump. It does not help a guy get a victory on the mound.

I would say it probably did help in getting rid of some of the clutter. But you have to remember, even with the big three papers in the city gone, we still had plenty of writers in the locker room every day. Guys from the Newark *Star-Ledger* and the Bergen *Record*. From the *Hartford Courant* and *Newsday*, and all those other papers from New Jersey, Long Island, and Connecticut.

The other thing you have to remember was that we won without a newspaper strike in 1977. Even with all the craziness, we still won. And by the time the strike happened in 1978? We'd already cut the Red Sox' lead almost in half, down to seven and a half games, and were in the middle of a six-game winning streak.

The real reason we won in 1978? Because we played great!

I think the fatherly hand of Bob Lemon helped. I think the easy hand of Al Rosen, who was the president, helped. I think you have to say, no matter what the owner did, he was helping. The ball club that was being put together by Gene Michael and his staff behind the scenes—that was working.

I'm more apt to give credit to the ingredients than to the sauce of the press. Most of all, that meant getting our team back. That's why it's not altogether fair to judge Billy Martin, either, purely by the statistics. The first half of the year, he had a badly dinged-up team. True, he exacerbated everything by just dumping pitchers he didn't like and creating a crisis every day. But we didn't have the horses.

In the second half of the season, our guys started to get healthy, and the Sox started to get injured. The game can be as simple as that.

Back behind the plate, Thurman hit over .300 for the second half. So did Willie. He also stole twenty bases in twenty-two attempts, played the great defense he always did for us when he was healthy. Piniella had a terrific second half once he could play all the time, led the team in batting again. Same with Roy White, he hit .337 in September. Mickey Rivers was back with us; he had a very good second half, had twenty-eight extra-base hits, stole fifteen bases in seventeen tries. I had a better second half myself, got my average up, hit another fourteen home runs. Hit .319 the first month and a half after Billy was gone.

What helped us most of all was getting the pitchers back and getting them healthy. Ed Figueroa's arm got well, he went 13–3 in the second half with a 2.46 ERA, seven complete games, two shutouts. Figgy went 7–0 for us in September, and that was huge for us.

So was Catfish. He got his arm worked on, let our team doctor do this new procedure where he put him out, then massaged the lesions on his shoulders to try to break up the adhesions. Catfish was saying by then he'd have let him cut the arm off if it would've eased the pain. Instead, there was the famous story about how when the doctor massaged them, the adhesions made this big popping sound, and his arm loosened right up. Suddenly *he* was back for us, went 10–3 in the second half with a 2.88 ERA, five complete games and a shutout—almost the Catfish from a couple years earlier.

Dick Tidrow settled into the number four spot in the rotation for us. Jim Beattie pitched a no-hitter down in Triple-A, came back up, and won four games for us in September, with a 2.70 ERA. Second half of the year, our rotation went 42–16.

But the guy who really did it for us all year long was Ron Guidry. He was the piece that couldn't be replaced. That year, he had everything going. A tremendous fastball. That slider that looked just like the fastball coming out of his hand, then it would fall off the table at the last moment. I've never seen a better one. He learned that from Sparky Lyle when he first came up, but he could throw it even harder, make it look more like a fastball than Sparky could.

Guidry was the most dominant player in the game that year. Jim Rice had his greatest year for the Red Sox; he was the MVP in the American League.

But Guidry was the dominant player in the game. He was every time he stepped on the mound. He was the one who kept us in it when everything was going wrong early on. Won his first thirteen in a row. He went 13–1 in the first half that year, with a 1.99 ERA. Tied the American League strikeout record at the time, when he struck out eighteen in a game against the Angels in June. That was the game where the fans at the Stadium first started the habit you see all the time now of clapping for a strikeout once you got two strikes on a batter. They started doing that, and the whole game it just kept getting louder and louder. The Angels just swinging and flailing up there—and they were a very good hitting team.

But you know, the second half, Ronnie was even *better*. Went 12–2, but with a 1.48 ERA. That's right, he already had an ERA under 2.00, and he *lowered* it by half a run. Finished with sixteen complete games, nine shutouts. More than a strikeout an inning.

His final record was 25–3. But that's not even the whole story. He lost a win on Opening Day when he held Texas to one run but we couldn't get anybody home, and then Goose lost it. He lost another game against the Orioles where he gave up one earned run and struck out ten—but Bucky made an error, Doug DeCinces hit a two-run homer, and we lost, 2–1. He didn't get credit for another game we won when Lou Piniella dropped a fly ball out in left against the Twins. In the thirty-five starts he made for us that year, we went 30–5. With a few more breaks, Ronnie could easily have finished the year at something like 30–2, 31–2.

I never saw anybody do what Guidry did that year. And I played in Oakland with Vida Blue, when he had that great year in 1971.

Guidry was such a great guy to play with, too. He was a real gentleman, but so laid-back, didn't let anything bother him. He gave us a real scare at the end of August when he got hit in the ankle with a line drive in Baltimore. Fortunately, the X-rays came back negative. He'd broken that ankle three times growing up.

"I got ankles like a racehorse," was all Guidry said about it. "If I break it one more time, they're going to shoot me."

There was one more factor in our comeback. Who was hitting in the cleanup spot when we went 40–10 in 1977? Who was hitting there when we went 40–14 in 1978?

Oh, yeah. Just saying. I wasn't the most important ingredient; I didn't have my best year in 1978. But when I was there, every piece was in place. We were a great team.

All of a sudden everything was the *reverse* of how Yaz described the situation earlier in the year. Now *we* were getting a well-pitched game almost every night. And almost every day, *they'd* lose somebody else to the disabled list. Yaz himself had a bad back; he was playing with some sort of steel corset wrapped around him. Dwight Evans got beaned late in August; he was never the same that season. Butch Hobson had elbow chips; he went from being the guy who hit thirty homers and drove in 112 runs from the nine spot to someone who had to take a running start across the infield to throw the ball to first. They left him in to make forty-three errors on the year.

Fisk cracked a couple ribs down the stretch; he was in pain every time he threw. Boomer—George Scott—hurt his finger. Burleson was injured, and Remy did something to his wrist, which was the key to their infield defense. They had to put Jack Brohamer and Frank Duffy out there, who were capable players—but not the same as having the second-best infield up the middle in the league, after us. (My opinion, of course.)

The Red Sox maybe—*maybe*—had better talent than we did, overall, when you look at every starting position. But I don't think they had our depth. That got exposed as their replacements just went south for them. Boomer was no longer the player he once was; that became evident that year. Bill Lee—a true Yankee hater—lost seven in a row, and Don Zimmer yanked him from the starting rotation.

And then, when they started losing some games, they started to have some controversies in the clubhouse. Which affirms what Joe Torre always likes to say about how you don't win *because* you have a happy locker room—when you're winning, you *get* a happy locker room. They had guys starting to complain and second-guess Zimmer. Controversies in the media. Clutter. I recognized that!

Meanwhile, we were finally what we should've been all along: a great ball club that was playing well, with everybody now being supportive of everybody else. We enjoyed playing well. We enjoyed playing with no distractions, no clutter. There was no more negativity about me or anything like it.

We were so far behind—fourteen games—that we weren't really concentrating on catching up to Boston. We were just trying to play well every game. It was connoisseur baseball again. But the funny thing was we weren't even getting that much luck, and we were still closing the gap.

We lost that game where Guidry pitched so well against Baltimore but Bucky made a miscue at short. Lost another game out in Seattle when Ronnie had a 3–0 lead, but then we made a big error, and Goose came in and lost on some freaky hits. Figgy lost a game in Baltimore where he gave up just one earned run and we came back from 3–0 down, scored five runs in the top of the seventh. But it was raining, and Earl Weaver made sure it took the grounds crew just about forever to bring the tarp out. When they did, they dumped more water on the field than they kept off it. They stalled enough to get the game called, and the score reverted to the last full inning, making it a 3–0 win for them. They went and changed the rule after that, it was so audacious. But that was Earl for you. He'd always find a way to win.

We thought we might have a chance to pick up some ground on Boston when they came to town for a two-game set early in August. There were still a lot of games to go, and we were only six and a half back now. We got up, 5–0, in the first game before a huge crowd of more than fifty thousand. But it was a rainy night and a sloppy game. Tidrow didn't have his good stuff, and we left eleven guys on base. Wasted a great *seven innings* of relief by Goose, another two by Sparky.

Those guys pitched the equivalent of an entire game and allowed just three hits and one run, but it was all wasted. They still had the curfew back then, where you couldn't start any inning after 1:00 a.m., and they finally had to postpone the game to the next day when it reached the fifteenth inning. We lost it in the seventeenth the next evening, then lost the regularly scheduled game, too, 8–1, to Mike Torrez. We just couldn't get to him.

There was another factor that night, too: I stunk. I had a terrible couple of games, went a combined 0–10 with five strikeouts. Made a bad play in the field. In that first game, especially, I had four strike-outs, kept killing rally after rally. Afterward, we were still in fourth place, eight and a half games out, with just fifty-five left to play.

But you know what? It wasn't a big thing. None of it was, at least not back in the clubhouse. Bob Lemon didn't *make* it a big thing; nobody else made it a big thing, not in his clubhouse. Nobody got blamed for anything that went wrong in any of those games. Nobody made a bunch of comments to the press about my hitting or my field-ing. Or about anyone else who didn't play well. Nobody changed the lineup all around, or seethed, or threw things against the wall. Nobody acted like we'd just lost the seventh game of the World Series. We won games and lost games as a team.

We just shook it off, went out and played the next night. We lost that one, too—a tough, 2–1 game to the Orioles. But we won the night after that, and then Catfish pitched a complete-game shutout against Jim Palmer, and we were in third place. Milwaukee came to town next. They'd been pummeling us the whole season, beat us some-thing like ten of twelve before that.

But now we kicked their butt. Tidrow pitched eight innings of shutout ball, beat Mike Caldwell, their best pitcher. Next night, we got down, 7–3, to them. Larry Hisle had another big night. But we got four good innings of relief out of Ken Clay, and this time we scored five runs in the bottom of the ninth off their two best relievers, Bob McClure and Bill Castro. Mickey Rivers hit a two-run homer, Chambliss hit a double to score another one, and I tied the game . . . by getting hit with a pitch with the bases loaded. We scored the winner on an error. That's all right, those things even out. Larry McCall, another one of our kid call-ups, got the win. Night after that, Guidry pitched another three-hit shutout, struck out nine. We won, 9–0. Now we were in second place.

Next we got off on a six-game win streak. Beat the Angels in eleven, when Blair hit a walk-off single. The next night, Guidry didn't have his best stuff against the Orioles, but he stuck it out, and we came back from down, 4–1, on a game-winning single by Cliff Johnson, who'd been having an ugly year. Then we took three of four against Detroit, and all of a sudden there we were: four games back with twenty-four to play—and the first four of them in Boston.

It was a second chance. We weren't a team you wanted to give second chances.

CATCHING BOSTON

FANS AND SPORTSWRITERS like to throw around words like "choked." "Oh, the Red Sox choked that year!" This guy choked, that team choked.

It's never that simple. Teams have ups and downs in a long season. The Red Sox went 19–10 in August. Was that a choke? They actually finished the month with a bigger lead than they had at the start of it, seven games instead of five and a half. The difference was that we were the team in second now.

From the first day of September, they started to lose a few more games they probably should've won. They dropped two out of three against Oakland, at home. Lost two out of three against Earl Weaver's guys, down in Baltimore. Was that a choke? Or those teams playing well?

By September 7, we had the lead down to four games, with a four-game series up in Fenway. All that August, guys kept saying, "If we can just gain a game a week on them, get the lead down to seven games, because we play them seven times in September."

That's how confident we were. Some of the guys on the Red Sox said it looked like we were looser, like we were having more fun than they were a few months earlier. I think that's because we'd been through so much already, over the last two seasons. Playing every day, with the balance of the pennant race hanging on whether you win or lose—after the year we'd been having, with all the issues, just playing baseball became relaxing, now that it was only the game we had to concentrate on.

I remember when we went to Boston, and people were saying we'd be doing all right if we could get a split. But Piniella was telling the writers straight out, "We're up here to win four." Thurman was saying, "We're going to kick their ass."

I'd had a virus that turned into back spasms. I'd missed the last three games, had spent two days in traction at Lenox Hill Hospital. But there was no way I was missing these games. We were ready to ride.

Those four games in Fenway, they never knew what hit 'em. "The Boston Massacre."

First inning of the first game, Willie Randolph reached on a throwing error by Butch Hobson at third. Then Thurman singled, I singled, Chambliss hit a sacrifice fly—just like that, it was 2–0.

Mike Torrez started for them. We put him in the showers before he could get four outs. Single, single, single in the second, it's 5–0. Third inning, three more singles, a double, a walk: 7–0. Fourth inning, another double, more singles, a throwing error by Hobson—it was 12–0.

Don Zimmer couldn't even sit down in the dugout before he had to get up and go to the bullpen for another pitcher. In the end it was 15–3. Thurman had three hits before the Sox went through their whole lineup once. Roy White had three hits, too. Willie Randolph had three hits, drove in five runs.

They couldn't stop us. We had twenty-one hits on the night—four doubles, seventeen singles, and not a single home run. That was the thing with us. We were great situational hitters. We hit .396 in the series. Outscored them, 42–9. Had sixty-seven hits to just twenty-one for them—and fifty-six of our hits were for singles. Just a couple home runs.

That to me is very indicative of what kind of team we were. We could adjust to anyone. We could beat you any number of ways, we came to play. It's an old cliché, but it's true. Like the great Yankees teams in the 1990s, and this past decade, we didn't try to do too much, just keep the line moving. Freddie Lynn called us "the pros' pros" when it came to hitting, and he was right.

Next night, they had another capacity crowd out in Fenway. We put it to sleep early. First inning, Mickey Rivers led off with a single, stole second, went to third on a bad throw by Carlton Fisk, scored on an error by Burleson at short. Later Chambliss singled in another run. Next inning, we pretty much nailed down the win when I hit a three-run bomb. Just like that, it was 8–0. This time Mick the Quick had three hits before the Sox were able to get through their lineup once. Lou Piniella had a double, triple, and home run. Fenway went silent as a tomb.

We ended up winning that game, 13–2. The Red Sox made *seven errors*, which led to seven unearned runs. I don't think I ever saw anything else like that in a major-league game. During the whole series they had twelve errors. Fisk's ribs were killing him; he was throwing everything away when we tried to steal. Dwight Evans, one of the best outfielders in the league at the time, dropped a couple fly balls in right field because he was still dizzy after getting beaned. Hobson, while injured, still kept going out there. It was tough watching him throw so low and wild because of the pain in his elbow.

Don Zimmer, I think, stuck with guys even when they were injured out of loyalty. That says something about him. It also says that guys wouldn't take themselves out of a game. It's a fine line and tough to do at that time of year. It becomes "Do you or don't you? Play hurt, or not?" Sometimes you're better not playing hurt. But sometimes 70 percent of you is better than 100 percent of your backup. Zimmer loved the effort Butch gave him, how he never complained, so he kept sending him out there to third. Same thing with Dewey Evans, same thing with Fisk. He stood by his players, told the press how hard they were playing despite their injuries.

But putting them out there when they can't perform isn't really doing them any favors. You just end up embarrassing them—and they're too tough to ask out. It isn't fair to the other players, too, who want to win. I know Zim couldn't have rested everybody, but . . . Well, who knows, I wasn't in his shoes. Fisk started 154 games as catcher that year, which I think is still the league record.

It was like we'd switched personalities as teams, from earlier in the year. Now *they* were the ones trying to plug holes and scrambling around for pitchers.

Third game of the series, it was a big, bright Saturday afternoon in early fall. They sent out Dennis Eckersley, who was killing us that year, against Guidry. Fourth inning, I hit a ball off Eck that I thought was gone, even with that big green wall they have in left. But the wind knocked it back down enough that Yaz could rob me with a spectacular, twisting catch in midair. Bounced off the scoreboard, then got the ball back to the infield in time to get Thurman going back to first for a double play.

Yastrzemski could still make plays like that at thirty-nine. It was just the sort of play that could turn a team around when it's in a bad slide. But there's an element of luck in baseball, too. Next batter, Chris Chambliss, hit a double, and they walked Nettles intentionally. Then Lou Piniella hit a little pop fly just back of second that should've been the third out. Instead, the wind blew it all around the outfield, it fell in, and before they get another out, it's 7–0. That was the final score. Guidry completely dominated them, only let up two chippy singles in the first inning.

I think it was Joe Gergen in *Newsday* who wrote after that, "The Yankees are a game behind and drawing away."

I think by then Boston *had* let the pressure get to them—the whole organization. After Munson got his three hits in the first game, Dick Drago hit him in the head with a pitch. Bob Lemon asked him if he could go the next day. Thurman told him, "Not for more than nine."

It was serious, though. I think Thurman was dizzy for pretty much the rest of the season. He played every game in Boston, got five more hits. But the next week he had to ask out of a game against the Tigers. He told us it wasn't a headache—it was just "tremendous pain" all through his head. He sat for two games, then got back in there—because he was Thurman. They weren't going to stop him by hitting him in the head with a baseball. Tough guy!

Last game of the Sox series on Sunday, Boston was so desperate they started a kid just up from Triple-A for them. Bobby Sprowl. He'd never won a game in the majors—and he never would. A lot of people were saying Zimmer should've forgiven Bill Lee, who he was feuding with, and started him. But it was too late. Zim was locked in. He'd just had Lee pitch seven innings of mop-up relief two days earlier.

Instead, we got to see Sprowl, who walked four guys in the first inning, gave up a single to me that scored Mickey Rivers, and left with just two outs and the score already 3–0. The final was 7–4, but it wasn't that close.

After 142 games, we were tied for first place with identical records with the Red Sox, 86–56. We'd come from fourteen games down, something only those 1914 Boston "Miracle Braves" exceeded, when they came from fifteen games down—though earlier in their season.

We almost couldn't believe it ourselves. It was like the dog catching the car. I remember sitting next to Lou Piniella in the locker room in Boston, after it was all over, and I looked at him and said, "Hey, Lou. Wait a minute. What do we do now?"

What we did was keep playing great ball. That week we went on to Detroit and took two out of three. Jim Beattie beat Jack Billingham in the second game, and we took over first place all by ourselves. First time all year, going right back to Opening Day.

Next weekend, the Sox had a return visit to us. I remember the Stadium was full of huge crowds. Just wild. Some fifty-five thousand every game, everybody going crazy.

First game, Chambliss and Nettles hit back-to-back home runs, and Guidry beat Tiant. He threw another two-hit shutout. That's how great Ronnie was that year—pitched two straight two-hit shutouts against the best hitting team in baseball. In the same week. Nice!

The next afternoon, they got up on us for a change, 2–0. But I had three hits off my old friend Mike Torrez, drove in Willie with a single. In the fifth, we were still behind a run, and I did a very foolish thing. Thurman, who was back in the lineup, hit a line drive foul. I threw up my right hand, to try to keep it from going into the stands and nailing somebody, and that ball ripped the nail loose on my thumb. Had blood running all down my batting glove.

Gene Monahan, our trainer, came out to tape it, and he asked me, "Can you hit?" I told him, "I have no choice."

He taped the nail back on my thumb, added some more tape over the batting glove, covering the thumb. I wasn't about to take myself out of that game, not with Thurman playing with a head full of pain. Instead, I went up there, worked the count to 2–2 off Torrez, then hit a home run over the right-field wall to tie the game.

The game went into the bottom of the ninth that way, when Yogi

Berra noticed how Yaz was playing Mickey Rivers in close and toward the line in left field. That's the kind of brain trust we had on the Yankees, with years of experience. Yogi picked that up and told Quick, and because Mickey was Mickey, he hit an 0–2 pitch right into the gap Yaz had opened up and ran it out for a triple. Thurman was up next, it was his first game back, but he already had two hits. Now all he did was win the game with a sinking line drive that went for a sac fly to right.

After the game, I remember just leaning against a pillar in the locker room, watching the blood run down my wrist, and not minding a bit. Catfish was there; he'd pitched a complete game for the win, only gave up two runs and struck out eight. He looked over at me and just smiled, and I smiled back. "That's the Reggie I always knew," he said, and I pointed to my hand: "Looks good, doesn't it?"

Then we just smiled at each other again. Not too bad for two former Oakland A's, playing in the big city.

We'd beat Boston six straight by then. We'd gone from seven and a half down to three and a half up in less than three weeks. We had just fourteen games left, and a lot of people thought the Red Sox would just fold and go away.

But that's when they really showed their mettle instead. They took the last game of that series at the Stadium against Jim Beattie, and then they made a run at *us*. That was when both teams really started playing some great baseball. Putting everything behind us now, just playing the great baseball we knew we were capable of. Hitting, pitching, defense, and clutch performances by everyone.

It was like walking a tightrope every day, a classic pennant race. It's so much fun to be part of that. Every game seemed like an epic. We had to score three runs in the top of the ninth to avoid getting swept in a doubleheader in Toronto. Goose came on to pitch three shutout innings. Struck out the last batter with the bases loaded.

Couple days later, we lost a heartbreaker in Cleveland when Figgy had about the only bad game he pitched in September, gave back a 3–0 lead. We staged another big rally, came back from being down 7–4 in the ninth to tie it on a hit by Piniella—but then we lost it on a passed ball, a wild pitch, and a single off Goose in the tenth. In a race like that, you remember every bad pitch, every key hit.

Going into the last week of the season, we went on a six-game winning streak. Getting a strong outing every start from our pitchers. They threw two shutouts and let up just one run in every other game. That's *four runs in six games*. They were dealing.

Ronnie pitched *another* 4–0 shutout. They couldn't stop us with our top guys on the mound. From mid-July on, Guidry, Figgy, and Catfish went 34–6 between them. Last Saturday of the season, Figueroa became the first Puerto Rican pitcher to win twenty games in the major leagues. He shut out the Indians, 7–0, and afterward he gave Thurman a big hug and started to cry. He told everyone, "I win twenty games for the people of Puerto Rico and Bob Lemon."

But the Red Sox still wouldn't go away. They were playing epic games, too. They lost a 4–3 lead in Detroit in the eighth, game went into extra innings, and the Tigers had men on first and third in the tenth, with Jason Thompson and Steve Kemp coming up. But they got out of it, won in eleven. Next night they came back from down 6–4, won when they got a great hitter, Rusty Staub, to hit into a double play in the bottom of the ninth with the bases loaded.

After that they went to Toronto, where they got beat 5–4 on a two-run single in the bottom of the ninth. Next day, Tiant pitched a complete-game win, 3–1, stranding twelve runners. Day after that, they scored two in the ninth on an error to tie the game, lost a chance to win it when they blew a suicide squeeze, kept the Blue Jays from scoring twice in extra innings with the bases loaded, and finally won it in the fourteenth inning. Next they swept the Tigers when Torrez shut them out, 1–0, in Fenway.

After the last game between us in the Stadium, we went 10–5—but they went 11–2. Going into the last day of the regular season, they'd won six straight, too, keeping pace with us every step of the way. It was like each of us was waiting for the other one to break, applying maximum pressure.

I say "pressure," but don't get me wrong. It's pressure because it's tense. Most important, it's big fun. Every pitch is important; every out is big. I was in a number of great pennant races in my career, but this was the closest one I ever took part in.

You love having something to play for down the stretch, and the games are exciting. You play better. It makes going to the ballpark fun, because you love the challenge. It's harder to play when there's nothing on the line. I was fortunate: There were very few seasons in my twenty-one-year career when I didn't have that. It gives you something to chase every day, keeps the blood running hot.

We *wanted* that sort of pressure—and it was there. The Red Sox kept chasing, and the last Sunday of the season they finally caught us. Catfish didn't have anything much that day, and the Indians finally snapped our winning streak, beat us 9–2. The Red Sox won their seventh in a row. We were going to have a one-game playoff for the decision.

The fact that we were there was part of an interesting decision by our manager, Bob Lemon. Catfish didn't have much, probably because he was only going with three days' rest. Until then, he'd been almost unbeatable. Went 9–1, 1.71 ERA since the beginning of August—as well as I'd ever seen him pitch, and I was a teammate for almost his whole career.

But Lemon had to make the decision about what to do if we ended up tied with the Red Sox and had to have a one-game playoff. So he had taken advantage of what was maybe Guidry's worst start of the season, when he lasted less than two innings in Toronto on September 20. Lem used that rare short start to pitch Ronnie on three days' rest for the remainder of the season. Guidry came through, beating Cleveland, 4–0, on September 24, and then Toronto, 3–1, on September 28, the last Thursday of the regular season. Even on short rest, the man was indomitable!

That meant we had to adjust the rest of the pitching staff and throw Catfish on short rest, too.

Was that the best decision to make? It's hard to say. When we ended up tied, we were very, very glad to have Ronnie available to pitch the one-game playoff. But would we have had to have a playoff in the first place . . . if we had pitched everybody with full rest?

Impossible to say. Not changing anything—keeping everybody on full rest—would've meant having Tidrow start that last game. Then, if we had lost, we would've had a rested Catfish Hunter in the playoff game—instead of a tired Guidry, starting his second straight game on short rest.

How that might've worked out is anybody's guess. The Sox had been hitting Catfish hard in Fenway, and even a tired Ron Guidry was like having the ace of spades. And in 1978, it was like having Sandy Koufax out there on short rest: How bad can it be?

It was one of those decisions that blows managers' heads up—if they let it. Fortunately, we had Bob Lemon, who could just have a cocktail after the game and forget about it. It was an impossible season, but it still wasn't over.

"I Hit It to the Prudential Building"

I REMEMBER VAGUELY the night before the playoff game going out to Daisy Buchanan's, which was a bar on Newbury Street, near the hotel, that a lot of the ballplayers went to. There were a bunch of us there—Lou, Thurman, Catfish, Goose, Sparky, Bucky Dent. We were there talking about the game, what it was going to be like. It was an early night. I don't really drink. Maybe I had a beer.

Just something to take the edge off a little. We were talking about how amazing it all was, once in a lifetime. There were no wild cards, no second chances, back then. This was only the second playoff in American League history, the first in thirty years. And the loser would go home.

There were some Red Sox fans there, taunting us a little, saying they were going to beat us the next day. It was the sort of thing you couldn't do nowadays; it would get out of hand. But it was all in good fun.

I think the atmosphere, the temperature between the Yankee players and the Boston fans, has usually been good. It's usually been one of respect, kind of "love to hate you." Especially then. For me, I admire the Red Sox franchise, always have. I'm a Yankee fan, but I have great admiration for John Henry and his group, who run the Boston franchise now. I think he's continued to keep the brand growing, on top or near the top. Ahead of us, chasing us, tied with us—it seems it's always been that way. It's been fun.

The Red Sox were getting better in the 1970s. I think they were held back by the fact that they were the last team to have a black player on their roster. Boston is a great city, and the Red Sox are one of the great franchises in sports. Certainly, the lack of color slowed their growth, but by 1978 things were starting to change.

Before we even got to Boston, Ron Guidry had already settled any possible issue of who was going to start for us. I remember talking to him on the last Sunday afternoon of the regular season, after we lost to Cleveland. I was asking him who he thought was going to pitch.

He said to me and a few other guys, "I am. I'm going into Lemon's office and telling him I'm going to pitch Monday in Boston with three days' rest." Lemon said, "Okay. Lightning, I can't say no to you." That's how Lemon had set it up for him to go, and we all thought he would, but Ronnie relieved any doubt and made it clear to us that he was eager to get out there.

Boston was going with Mike Torrez. I know a lot of guys on our team weren't too worried about that, because we usually hit him good. We'd beat him three out of four so far that season, hit over .300 against him as a team. Some guys held it against him when he asked out of a key September game against Boston the year before, with the score still 1–1 in the fourth. He said his shoulder couldn't get loose. Who knows? He said it hurt, I believed him.

We had a chance to sweep the Red Sox by beating them that night, which would've finished them. I do know that Martin and some of the others called Mike a choke in the papers—all without using their names, of course. That doesn't work!

Torrez went and signed with the Red Sox when they offered him two more years and another million dollars over what the Yanks offered. I couldn't blame him for that. Once he signed with Boston, he started running us down, telling the press they had a better ball club than we did. Telling them we all hated each other: "Graig Nettles hates Jackson. Thurman Munson hates Jackson. Jackson is not well-liked by many members of his team."

He started telling writers personal details about me, about how he helped get me through the season. Why he felt he had to do that, I don't know. All I know is that while he was on the Yankees, he was a good friend, and he was very supportive. Decay and garbage, why stop by and pick it up. Leave it lay, don't even kick it to the curb.

Torrez had been a very good big-game pitcher for us. Aside from that Boston game, he'd pitched very well down the stretch in 1977. Had that great playoff game for us against the Royals, coming out of the pen. Had two huge World Series wins for us, including the clincher. So far, in 1978, he'd had a bad second half with them, but he was coming around. He'd just shut out Detroit the week before. He was a big, strong pitcher, had a good fastball, a hard slider, a good curveball, and he'd be going on full rest against us. I knew he'd be very tough, and he was.

I didn't care who was pitching, I was excited. It's always a good feeling playing in a game like that. Be good or be gone, one game decides everything. I had some experience in that. I'd already played in the seventh game in the 1973 World Series. The fifth games in the 1972 ALCS, the 1973 ALCS. The fifth game in the 1977 ALCS—for one at-bat anyway. Later, I would get to play a deciding game in the 1981 division playoff against the Brewers, the 1986 ALCS against the Red Sox, when I was on the Angels.

I've been pretty fortunate, haven't I? Lucky? Remember, luck is when hard work meets opportunity.

It was a beautiful autumn day up in Boston. Cool, the sun was out. October weather. My time of year, Yankees' time of year. When the leaves turn brown, I'll be around.

I wish I had been able to play right field, but Lou was out there. I had that thumbnail that had been torn off my hand late in the season, so that was the excuse that was used to get me out of there. But at least Bob Lemon had the class to tell me to my face. Yes, he did. And of course, Lou played superbly that day.

It was a once-in-a-lifetime thing. We all knew, and we all enjoyed it. Even bigger than the World Series, and the league playoff series, which are played every year. They have a one-game playoff now for the wild cards, but it was nothing like this. We were both 99–63. We weren't wild cards. We weren't second-place teams. We'd *both* finished first; we were two great teams. That's why we were there.

We all wanted it this way. I mean, sure, we wanted to beat Cleveland the day before and just win, but at least we had the chance now to do it for ourselves. Before the game, our team at least was pretty loose. It was amazing how loose we were, really, everybody laughing and joking in batting practice.

Going to Boston, Lou Piniella was teasing Steinbrenner about losing the coin toss. Saying, "You didn't do your job, now we got to do ours." He was telling him, "You're the luckiest guy in the world. We're not only going to win it for you, but you'll get an extra gate out of it."

George tried to smile, but he looked a little airsick. "Lou, man, this is no time for humor," he said.

I wouldn't say it was just another ball game, but we were eager to go, we wanted to be out there. When you're trying to be a great champion, you don't get anything out of beating a bad team. If you're a champion, you *want* to play another great team.

The Red Sox looked and sounded very loose, too. They were ready to go. "He saith among the trumpets, 'Aha!' " We were ready for the battle.

The only regret you could have was that neither team would be at its very best. But then, you never really are at the end of a season. We were still both a little beat-up, but at least for once it was a pretty even match. Butch Hobson finally took himself off third because Zimmer wouldn't do it. He was the DH, and they put Jack Brohamer in the field instead. They finally had to sit Dwight Evans with that concussion, so they put Jim Rice in right field. Fisk was playing hurt, so were some other guys. But they were still a great team.

We had Thurman catching even after he'd got seven stitches in his right hand, when he'd accidentally put it through a window in the clubhouse sauna. But he was still playing. We'd lost Willie Randolph a couple days earlier when he pulled a hamstring. He was out for the season, which was a big loss for us. It would prove to be a huge factor, both in that playoff game and in the postseason—though not in the way anyone thought it would.

A game that big, everybody understood it. You knew the fans understood it, from how quiet they were most of the time, how quickly they reacted to things. How focused they were on the action. It was like 32,925 people were all holding their breath together.

In a game like that, I wanted to be part of the victory in any way I could. A hit, an RBI, a run scored, a stolen base. A great defensive play. A home run.

I came up in the first inning. Mickey Rivers on second, two outs. Torrez looked as tough as he had all year. I knew he would be. He had everything working for him. He had an extra few miles an hour on the fastball; his breaking stuff was good. First pitch was a fastball he put right by me, must've been ninety-five miles an hour plus. I swung through it, swung hard. Next he put a very nice slider on the inside corner. Missed that, too.

His third pitch to me, he tried to put one a little off the plate, threw me a fastball high and outside. Not outside enough.

I got hold of that ball, drove it to the opposite field. I knew I'd hit it good. I thought I hit it good enough to go out, but the wind was blowing in and knocked it down. I thought it still might go off the Green Monster and score Mickey, but instead Yaz caught it right at the foot of the wall, in left.

Just missed. Mike and I kind of smiled at each other after we watched that thing. We both knew what almost happened.

After that, Torrez settled in. He was giving us nothing, pitching very efficiently. Pitching better than we'd seen him all season. I had another good at-bat, came up in the fourth with Piniella on first. By now the wind was blowing out to left, but this time I hit his curve solidly and drove it to right. A hard line drive—but it was almost right at Jim Rice. Two good at-bats, nothing to show for it. That's baseball.

Nobody was doing much for us except Mickey Rivers, who had a walk and a double, stole a base. He almost got another hit in the shortstop hole in the fifth, but Rick Burleson grabbed it and threw to third, where he just got Roy White coming from second—knowing he would never have time to get Mick at first.

It was a terrific, heads-up play. It was a good, tight game all around. The sort of game we should have been playing against each other all year, if we both hadn't had so many injuries, hadn't played so many games in the rain.

Guidry was pitching well for us. I think if he'd had all his days he might've pitched another two-hit shutout. But going in his third straight start on short rest, he wasn't quite as fast, wasn't quite as sharp. In the second inning, Yaz pulled a pitch just inside the Pesky Pole in right field for a home run: 1–0. It was a great piece of hitting, but I don't know if he or anyone else could've done that against a fully rested Guidry that year. Next couple batters, Fisk and Lynn, gave the ball a ride, long fly outs.

You could see he didn't have his best stuff, but he still wouldn't give in. Sixth inning, Burleson hit a double off him, and then Jim Ed Rice just muscled a ball through the middle for another run, 2–0. He had a great year that year, Rice. Led the league in home runs, RBIs, even triples. Hit .315, was the MVP. But with all due respect, he couldn't touch Guidry when he was at his best.

Rice went to third when Yaz grounded out, and then we walked Fisk intentionally to pitch to Lynn with two outs. Set up the lefty-on-lefty matchup with Freddie Lynn. Ronnie was just missing; Lynn ran the count up to 3–2. Then Guidry got his slider up a little, and Lynn pulled it down the right-field line, just like Yaz did. It wasn't hit as hard as Yaz's ball, but it was higher, up in that tough afternoon sun out there, drifting into the corner.

You could tell right away it was trouble. Even from the dugout, it looked like it could go out for a three-run homer, or at least fall in for a double that would've scored two runs. That would've put us down 4–0, 5–0. It would've been tough even for us to climb out of a hole that big in the sixth inning.

But Lou Piniella was right there. Normally, he would never be over that far; he would never have had a chance to get there, not with Ron Guidry pitching to a left-handed batter. No way Guidry gets pulled like that. But Lou had been talking with Thurman the whole game about how Guidry's pitches were missing spots and he wasn't throwing as hard as he had all that year. Just before Lynn got in the box to hit,

Lou motioned to Mickey in center to move with him toward the right-field line, six or seven feet from where they'd normally play against a left-handed hitter, adjusting to the missing speed on Guidry's pitches.

Don Zimmer said it best later: "That's just the knowledge of a guy who knows how to play the game."

It still didn't make it an easy catch. Lou had to run over, battling that high sun all the way. He had to go into that tricky little corner they have down in right field in Fenway, with the fans right there screaming in his face. Had to stick his glove out and make what was almost an over-the-shoulder catch. Lou said later he actually did lose that ball in the sun, but he ran to where he knew it would be coming down—something that an experienced, skilled outfielder would know to do, someone who's played in the majors for ten-plus years.

He caught the ball in the top of the glove, bounced off the fence, and held on. Held it all the way to the dugout, where he sat down on the bench with it still in his glove. He wasn't letting go. In the park, it was like somebody pulled a plug on all the fan noise—just shut it off right away. Lou said later there was some big fat Sox fan out in right who'd been waving his arms practically in Lou's face when he was going after the ball, shouting at him, trying to distract him. When he caught it, when he bounced off the fence, then steadied himself, Lou said something to him before he ran back to the dugout.

After the game, the writers asked him what he'd told the fan. Lou told them it was "Take that."

What people say is that the momentum changed with that play. But in baseball, momentum is all about who's pitching. Doesn't matter what you do in the field if you still have to come up and face, say, Bob Gibson or Sandy Koufax. Or even Mike Torrez that afternoon. He was still throwing very well for them, and now we were moving into the tricky part of the afternoon in Fenway, with the shadows growing out of the stands between home plate and the mound and the ball coming at you out of the bright sunlight and into the shadow. It was all going to favor the pitcher now, and going into the top of the seventh, Mike had still thrown fewer than seventy pitches. We just had two hits off him. I was 0–3; he'd struck out Thurman three times. Our best hitter! We weren't panicking. That team never panicked. But it was getting late, bro.

With one out, Chambliss hit a single off his curveball, then Roy White hit another one off Mike's fastball, which was slowing down just a little. Another very professional display of hitting, from the great pros we had on our team—just hang in and take what he's giving you.

Brian Doyle, the rookie we had up playing second base in place of Willie Randolph, was due up next. Lemon sent Jim Spencer up to hit for him. Spencer was a great pinch hitter for us all year long, good power hitter, but Torrez cranked up that heater again and got him to fly out to Yaz in left.

That brought up Bucky Dent. An interesting decision. If Billy had still been the manager, no doubt he has Spencer hit for Bucky, not for Brian Doyle. Doyle was a lefty, hitting against the right-handed Torrez. Billy never really trusted Bucky; he pinch-hit for him when he could.

We had other bats on the bench. But with Willie out, we didn't have another infielder available, so you could only hit for one of them, Bucky or Brian Doyle. Fred Stanley was going to go in for Doyle now that he was out of the game. Fred could play anywhere in the infield and do a great job for us, he was a great defender. But there was really nobody else who could play the middle infield for us. Once Lemon decided to hit for Doyle, Bucky would have to hit for himself.

I can honestly say, "So what?" All the ifs and coulda, shoulda, woulda didn't happen.

Bucky didn't start out well. He went in there as usual crouched down, choking up on the bat—just trying to keep the line moving. Maybe drive in a run, or work a walk. Torrez started feeding him all fastballs. Missed with the first one, got him to foul the second one off the instep of his left foot. Ouch!

Bucky's legs had been hurting all year; that's what he'd been on the DL for. He'd just taken off the shin guard he'd been wearing most of the year, and now he'd hurt himself on the same spot. He was staggering around, trying to rub it off. Gene Monahan, our trainer, came out to see to him and spray ethyl chloride on the foot, to freeze it and numb it.

It had been like that all year for Bucky. With his hamstring injuries, he'd never really gotten started. He'd had a poor last month, though he'd driven in some big runs for us. He had gone 7–20 in the four games we'd had up in Boston—drove in six of the ten ribbies he had all month, including one with a single off Torrez. Maybe that's why Lemon decided not to hit for him.

But he'd been struggling again, so he'd tried a couple of lighter bats Roy White had loaned to Mickey Rivers and that Rivers had passed on to Bucky. They were just thirty-two ounces, thirty-four inches long. While Gene was working on Bucky's shin, Mickey noticed that the bat he was using was cracked. Just a little crack above the tape. He told Bucky, "Homey, homey, that's the wrong bat," and had the batboy give him the good one.

That was typical Mickey. He just had a funny way of making good things happen. He was like our carburetor. A great leadoff man. He didn't get enough walks, didn't get on base enough. But he hit for a high average, had some power, could steal bases, and covered a lot of ground out in center field. Above all, he would find a way to beat you.

Earlier that season, back in July, I remember he went up to pinch-hit with us losing, 2–0, to Detroit in the seventh. There were two out, Gary Thomasson on first. Rivers hit a ball out to the wall in right field. Mickey Stanley was playing there for the Tigers, and he went up for it but couldn't get it; the ball went off the wall.

Immediately, Stanley started arguing with the umpires that he'd been interfered with going up for that ball. Probably had been. Back in those days, they'd pull your glove right off your hand out in right field in Yankee Stadium. But you can't argue about it while the play is still going on. Stanley knew that; he was a good ballplayer, a veteran. He'd been on that world champion Tigers team back in 1968.

But while he stood there arguing, Thomasson scored, and then Rivers went all the way around to score. We tied the game, went on to win it by a run. Without that win, we might never have made it to the playoff. That was Mickey. He'd walk up there, carrying his bat on his shoulder like an old man carrying home a pile of wood. Looked like he could barely lift it. But he made things *happen*.

While Bucky was getting his ankle numbed, Mickey got him another bat. Bucky got back up, and Torrez tried to throw one more fastball by him on the inside corner. It got out over the plate, and Bucky got all of it. By that time, around five o'clock, the wind had changed, the way it usually did at Fenway in those days, before they started adding seats, and scoreboard, and other things onto the ballpark. It wasn't clear he'd got all of it at first. But that ball kept traveling, and you could see Yaz drifting back and back in left field, and then all of a sudden he looked up and it was going, going, *gone*. A huge, three-run homer. Yaz's knees just buckled.

Bucky did hit that ball very hard. That's the thing people forget. I know some of the Red Sox and their fans were saying later it wouldn't be a home run anywhere else but Fenway. Well, I seem to recall the Red Sox hitting a few Fenway home runs. Other people blamed Torrez. But it was a good pitch, and it was well hit. It went over the wall at 315 feet. On the way down, it makes it to maybe 350 or 360. That's a home run in plenty of parks.

I don't think it was a cheap home run. I think it was a timely home run, hit in a great spot.

Suddenly we were ahead, and the park was dead silent. Then Mickey struck again; he worked a walk on a full count. Zimmer pulled Torrez for Bob Stanley, who was their ace in the bullpen that year, and Mickey stole second again on his first pitch. Next pitch, Thurman hit a ball in the gap for a double, scored another run. That put us ahead 4–2.

That really spoke to how good we were. We were a really good team. Mickey Rivers was a great talent. He could rise to the occasion. Munson was a great talent. He was productive. He could get a base hit when he wanted to—could get almost any kind of hit he wanted.

Torrez pitched a good ball game that day, but now it was gone. Bottom of the seventh inning, Guidry finally ran out of gas, but Lemon got Goose in there quick, and he got the last two outs of the frame.

I led off the top of the eighth. I'd been confident I could hit Torrez, but I was just as confident I could hit Bob Stanley. At that time of year, I was going to hit you.

Stanley started me off cautiously. He missed with a couple fast-balls, got down in the count two balls and no strikes.

At that point he probably should've just walked me. I was looking to be very aggressive then. It was a free shot for me. I was leading off the inning; there was nobody on. I could just get up and swing, try to get us another run. He came back with another fastball, but I missed it, fouled it into the left-field seats.

Stanley was mostly a low-ball, sinker-ball pitcher. It was strength against strength. He threw a low fastball to a low fastball hitter. He didn't get it low enough. I got it.

He came right into my wheelhouse with it. And before it sank, I had airmailed it.

I hit it to the deepest part of center field. Went five, six rows into the stands. I stood and looked at it for a couple seconds, which I didn't usually do. I just knew I'd got all of that one.

As I said at the time: We needed an insurance run, so I hit it to the Prudential Building. Just a joke.

When I came in, I shook hands with everybody. I even shook George Steinbrenner's hand, where he was sitting in a front-row box. George was a friend, no matter what differences we'd had. He'd brought me to New York; he'd given me this opportunity.

I was lucky to have that moment, to just have played in that game. I wanted to be part of the victory.

We were up 5–2 now, but it wasn't over yet. Far from it. They came back at us, just like they did during the season. We were two great teams, going at each other. There was no quit in either one of us.

Goose was so stoked up he was overthrowing. He started falling behind in counts, couldn't finish guys off. Couldn't get his pitches where he wanted them. He was getting his ball up, and they started hitting him. They were such great hitters, that whole lineup. They strung together three straight hits and cut the lead to 5–4 in the bottom of the eighth. Yaz drove in another run; Lynn drove in a run.

Lem went to the mound and told Goose, "You're trying to make me an old man. But I'm already an old man." It was the perfect comment. Gossage settled down, got Hobson and George Scott to end the inning, but we had another one to go.

It was in the bottom of the ninth inning when Lou made another great play out in right. By then, it was the only part of the park not covered in shadows, and when he was back on the bench, he told Lemon that he didn't know what he would do if someone hit a line drive out there. That's how bright it was, how hard it was to pick up the ball coming out of the darkness and into the sun.

The Sox got Burleson on first with one out, and then Remy hits his ball there. Lou completely lost it in the sun. But he deked Burleson as if he were going to catch it all the way, made him hold up. The ball fell just to his left, so when it came down, he was just able to reach out with his glove hand and snare it. Made a great throw back to the infield that kept Burleson from going to third.

That made all the difference in the game. Rice hit a fly ball next, and if Burleson is on third, he scores the tying run.

But Lou made the play, he made all the plays out there. And afterward, he was very modest about it. He just told the media, "Look, when you play on world championship teams, *somebody's* got to make those plays. Whether it's me or somebody else—somebody's got to make them. That's how you become a world champion." He made them all.

Would I have made them? Would I have made that play on Remy? I don't know. Here's how it goes: You see the ball as it comes off the bat, then you lose the ball in the sun. You stay with the ball as long as you can, and then sometimes the ball will come out of the sun, and sometimes it doesn't. If it doesn't, it either hits you in the glove if you're lucky or gets by you.

Luckily for Lou and the team, he stayed with the ball through the sun, and it came out of the sun, and he happened to be in the right spot. But you know what I say about luck. Good defensive fielding, good instincts, were what enabled him to make that play.

Now, I know that the ball fell and jumped right up into Lou's glove hand. Lou's a righty; I'm a lefty. If I'd been in the exact same spot Lou was, the ball would've been on the side of my throwing hand, and it might've been hard for me to grab bare-handed.

Now, if I *had* lost it in the sun, would Burleson have gone for a deke from me the way he did from Lou—especially considering how much the media and Billy had been playing up my every fielding mistake? Again, there's no way of knowing. Like Lou, I had a good arm out there. Maybe Burleson would've run—and I would've nailed him at third.

We'll never know, will we? Let's just say, I stand on my postseason record. I was always "lucky" that time of year.

All I'm saying is, it's a case of "Oh, my gosh, what a great play Lou Piniella made." Which is all there is to say about it.

As it happened, Burleson had to hold up at second. It's just one of those things baseball turns on. Not that we were out of the woods yet. We still had to get past Rice, who was swinging the bat as well as anybody in the game at the time. He hit a ball that got out to right very quickly, but the wind out there was holding the ball up, and he hit it too high.

The crowd went nuts, they thought it was out, but Lou could see this one, and he made another nice catch. The crowd was still screaming, continuously now. Yastrzemski was up next, which wasn't much better than having Rice up there, but Goose finally made himself relax. He threw a fastball to Yaz that moved like only his ball could move: fast. One hundred miles an hour plus, I'm sure. At the last possible moment, it exploded on him, the way a great fastball will. Moved in on his hands and left him helpless.

Tough pitch to hit—even tougher to hit well. All Yaz could do was hit it weakly and hope it goes in the stands. Instead, he popped it up to Nettles. The sound went out of the place, with the exception of our dugout. We were all dancing around, you could hear us yelling on the field, it was so quiet. Even George came down on the field and was almost dancing a jig with us.

Those were great times.

"Finding a Prize in the Weeds"

I know that playoff game was one of the greatest baseball games ever. It had to be in the top five. There was the 1951 Bobby Thomson game, the 1975 Carlton Fisk, Reds–Red Sox game. Don Larsen's perfect game in the 1956 World Series. Koufax's fifteen strikeouts in the 1963 Series, Bob Gibson's seventeen-strikeout game in 1968. The famous World Series homers by Bill Mazeroski, Joe Carter, and Kirk Gibson. Babe Ruth's called shot.

Considering what was at stake in 1978, the history between the two teams, how much came down to that one game. How well it was played, how exciting it was all the way through . . . maybe, just maybe the best.

Afterward, we felt we could beat anybody. We had to play the Royals again in the American League Championship Series. They always played us tough, and it was the third year in a row we'd been in the ALCS against each other. Our winning wasn't at all assured. You play good teams enough, they'll find a way to beat you. We were physically beat-up, we were tired, and our pitching was in disarray. It didn't matter to the Royals that we'd just played one of the greatest games ever.

We had to go out to Kansas City the very next day and start Jim Beattie, our rookie, number five starter against their best pitcher, Dennis Leonard, who had won twenty-one games for them, sixteen of them at home.

But by then, we were flying. We all said it: After that pennant race, after that playoff game in Boston, the regular playoff games and the World Series were easier to play. The pressure was off now. We were in the postseason. We went into K.C., and had sixteen hits, beat them, 7–1.

I reached base all five times I was up, three hits and two walks. Hit a three-run homer to put the game away off Al Hrabosky—and my friend Billy Martin wanted me to bunt against him! They couldn't do much with Beattie; he gave up only two hits. When he ran down in the sixth, Lem brought in Ken Clay, and they could do even less with him.

Second game, Figgy didn't have his good stuff, and they tied it up. But then we went back to New York to face Splittorff. It was like a greatest-hits parade of all the pitchers Billy Martin thought I couldn't hit.

This time, I was in the starting lineup. And I got him. I homered off Splittorff my first time up, took him deep on a 3–1 count. Couple innings later, I singled in Thurman, then scored another run on Lou's hit. Third time up off him, I hit a ball more than four hundred feet to deep center. It was caught at the wall, but it scored Roy White for another run.

Hmm, I couldn't hit Paul Splittorff.

George Brett had a great series and a great game for them. He was batting leadoff that game for some reason, and he hit three solo home runs off Catfish his first three times up. They scored a couple more runs off Goose, and going into the bottom of the eighth, we were still down, 5–4. If the Royals had held on and won, they might've turned the whole series around, right there.

But Roy White got a base hit, and they brought in Doug Bird to face Thurman. He hit a ball off Bird that must've gone 430 feet, back among the monuments where they were behind the left-field wall then. It was the *shot* that decided the ball game. Munson was never known as a power hitter, but he had the ability to adjust his game to what was called for, many times.

That game, Ron Luciano had made a bad call on Lou a few innings earlier at home plate. Called him out trying to score on a fly ball when he obviously beat the throw. Piniella made sure everybody knew it, too; he ranted and raved and danced around the way only Lou could.

When Munson hit that home run, Luciano later said, he crossed home plate and just kind of growled at him out of the side of his mouth. Something like, "Pulled your ass out of the fire." That was Thurman.

The next night Leonard pitched much better for them. He only allowed four hits, struck out nine. Struck me out all three times. First inning, Guidry still looked a little tired for us, and Brett hit a triple off him and scored. But he hung in, pitched a great game. Nettles and Roy White hit solo shots for us, and Gossage pitched an inning for a save. One way or another, we were going to beat you.

Nobody told the Dodgers that, though. The World Series started tougher. I had another three-hit game in the opener and took Tommy John downtown. But Figgy got hammered, and we lost, 11–5.

Nothing like Dodger Stadium, far as I was concerned. The next night I hit a two-run double off Burt Hooton to give us the lead. That was enough for Hooton. He hit me with a pitch the next time I came up.

Ron Cey had a great game for the Dodgers in that second game of the Series, hit a three-run homer off Catfish to put them up, 4–2. I had another RBI for us, but by the ninth we were still down, 4–3. When we got two men on with one out, they brought in Bob Welch, who had come up to the majors in mid-season. He'd been throwing some serious heat for them ever since. Pitched three shutouts in thirteen starts, had another three saves coming out of the pen. He looked unhittable.

He got Thurman on a fly ball to right, then it was my turn. I saw eight to ten pitches, hit several foul balls. I had trouble catching up to that ninety-five-mile-plus fastball of his. He kept the ball up and in on me. The count went to 3–2; he came in with another fastball up and in. I was so focused on what he was throwing that I forgot the runners would be running. When they broke, so did my concentration, and I got beat. I took that bat and broke the knob off it right there, smashed it into the ground. I was amped up.

You know, then it was over. I gave it everything I had and left it there. I had no regrets. I was mad at myself in the moment. But by the time I got to the clubhouse, I was calm again.

"The kid beat me," was what I told the media. That's all there was to it. On this Yankees team you weren't getting second-guessed; you weren't getting shots taken at you.

The writers who were at the World Series—Roger Angell, Jim Murray, Steve Jacobson, Phil Pepe, Dick Young, Dave Anderson, all great writers—were talking about the classic duel in the sun I'd just had with Welch. Most of them had been around longer than I had. It was easy to respect them. I enjoyed listening to what they had to say. They treated it as a great moment. They were calling it one of the all-time great at-bats in a World Series. Everybody in the park standing for it, cheering on every pitch.

It was pretty cool, even though I struck out. I felt *grateful* to be part of that, just as I did for all the opportunities I had in my career.

I just wanted to square up that ball and hit it, and if I'd done that, it would've gone a long way. I wasn't trying to hit the ball out of the ballpark. I wasn't at home playing, saying, "Home run or nothing, here on Home Run Derby." I was not doing that. I was just trying to catch up to a ninety-eight-mile-an-hour fastball.

At the end of it all, when I looked back and saw the video, I said, "Boy, if I would have just cut my swing down a little bit, I could have squared that ball." Because I did have a couple balls to hit. It's one thing to lose because the other team is better or the other guy is better. It's another to lose because you didn't do what you should have done.

But hindsight's twenty-twenty. I was on my game, and there would be another day. I have to tip my cap to Bob Welch.

I think the Dodgers were pretty sure they had us then, up 2–0 on the Series. We were battered again, too. Chambliss aggravated a hammy, he was hurting, he'd miss a couple games for us. Mickey Rivers was hurting; Thomasson and Blair had to fill in for him some. But it didn't matter. We were headed back to Yankee Stadium and all our crazy fans, and we had Ron Guidry going in Game 3.

Guidry said later he left his fastball in the pen that night. Left his slider there, too. He wasn't sharp, couldn't hit his spots. He walked seven guys, and the Dodgers hit him harder than almost anybody had all year, got eight hits off him.

But that was the night Graig Nettles became a human vacuum cleaner. He put on a tremendous fielding clinic at third base. Maybe the best single fielding game anyone's ever had in the World Series. He was unbelievable. Ended four separate innings throwing guys out, all on spectacular plays. They figured he probably saved something like seven runs for us. I've never seen anything quite that good, not even Brooks Robinson with the amazing Series he had back in 1970 against the Reds.

The Dodgers kept pulling the ball on Guidry all night long. The right-handed power lineup they had was turning on him like nobody had all year.

Nettles saved that game for us. But it wasn't only him. Munson threw somebody out stealing. Guidry didn't have his good stuff, but he pitched a complete game. Rivers had three hits. We scored five runs, and five separate guys drove them in, including myself. We were really clicking as a team now. We had a dozen ways to beat you.

Figgy had a much better start for us in Game 4, but Reggie Smith touched him for a three-run homer in the fifth inning. Didn't matter. Tommy John was going very strong for them; he was just a groundout machine, the way he always was when he was on. Didn't matter. We found a way, just like we always seemed to.

It was our old pros again. In the sixth, with one out, Roy White managed to get a single through the infield, then Thurman got a walk. I hit a single into right field to cut their lead to 3–1, send Munson over to second.

That was when Lou Piniella came up and hit a liner to their shortstop, Bill Russell. He dropped the ball at his feet. I thought that he let it drop out of his glove deliberately. If he did, it was a smart play, because Thurman and I were frozen. We had no choice. If we'd run and he caught the ball, he could've just thrown to either first or second for an easy double play.

We had to wait, and when the ball hit the ground, it was too late. Russell picked the ball up right away and stepped on second. Munson was still running to third, but that retired me. I was still only a few yards off first. All Russell had to do was throw down to first and get Piniella, and the side would've been out.

Only trouble was his throw never got there. Instead, it hit me in the hip and bounced off into right field. Piniella was safe. Munson scored. Lasorda and the rest of the Dodgers went crazy. They wanted an interference call on me, which would've retired the side and kept the run from counting. But the umps put their heads together and ruled against them. Thurman's run stood, and we'd cut the lead to just one, 3–2.

It was the controversy of the Series. Afterward in the clubhouse, everybody wanted to know about the play. I just told them, "It was in my road, and it hit me."

You don't want to ever show the umpires up. But nobody was buying it. They could see on TV what the umpires couldn't see on the field. That was that my hip moved—just a little—and nudged that ball into the outfield.

Did I mean to do it? Let's just say it was what Roger Angell called it, "an almost unconscious reaction." I had started to second, but I had no chance to get there before Russell did. I saw the ball coming toward me, and I thought, "I'm going to get hit in . . . a highly sensitive area." So I just moved a little.

Now of course, if I didn't want to get nicked, I could've just hit the dirt. I could've jumped all the way to one side or another. But I thought, "I'm in my right-of-way. I'm in the baseline. I'm going to be out anyway, so why not just stand there and play stupid?" I thought, "I'm out anyway, so it's not so bad if I stay here and let it hit me."

It makes you think about the rule. I've made perfect throws before from right field and hit a runner while he was in the baseline running to third. A runner going from second to third is in the line of a throw from right field. If you hit the runner as he slides into third base on a perfect throw . . . it's called an error on the right fielder. The runner is safe.

The worst that could've happened was that they would've called Lou out for my interference. It would've been a double play, and the inning would've been over. In other words—no worse than what would've happened if I'd let Russell throw that ball on down to first.

Roger Angell called it something like "finding a prize in the weeds." He said the play had "street smarts," that it was just like the sort of thing we used to do on the A's when we were champions. Most others were making out that I wasn't that smart: "He couldn't think that quick." Well, they didn't know me. Roger knew what some of these Yankees were capable of.

The Dodgers were still ahead, 3–2. But in the eighth, Tommy John finally wore down a little, gave up a hit to Paul Blair, and then White bunted him over. They had brought in their closer, Terry Forster, but Thurman was such a great clutch hitter he doubled off him to left and tied the game. I was up next, fifty-six thousand people chanting, "Reg-gie! Reg-gie!" Forster hit me—which I guess was my payback for that little hip check.

They brought in Bob Welch again, who got them out of the inning. He got Lou to pop up and struck out Nettles, to keep the game tied. After that we brought in Gossage, and for the rest of the game it was two men throwing seeds. Just enjoyable baseball. Elemental baseball. Pure power.

It was a Saturday, so the game had started in the afternoon, but there was a long rain delay, and by now it was night and cold. Each of them went on through the ninth. Nobody going home, the crowd getting tenser. Welch struck out Chambliss and Spencer, who was hitting for Stanley. Goose fanned Reggie Smith and Garvey in the top of the tenth.

Bottom of the tenth, Welch got Mickey to foul out, but then Roy White—who had a great Series, was almost the MVP—worked a walk on a full count. Welch popped up Thurman, and then I was up. I stayed a little calmer this time, kept within myself a little more. Worked the count to 2–1. Welch threw me another fastball, and this time I pounded a single into right field. It wasn't a soft line drive, it was a bullet, and I said to myself, "Dang, if I had gotten that ball up, it would still be going."

The nice thing about facing Bob Welch was that he had enough pride in his stuff—fastball, curveball—that he was gonna give you something to hit. He had enough stuff to bury you, in the true sense of a power pitcher—a Gibson, a Koufax, a Seaver, a Palmer, a Jack Morris, a Guidry. Those guys had "I-dare-you stuff." Bringing it right up to today, a Kershaw, a Sabathia. Rivera.

You'd love to face a guy who had pride in his fastball. Nolan Ryan, the standard in the game for a long time, he would tell you at times, "I want to see if you can hit this." He did it to me: "I want to see if you can hit this."

Welch was in that category.

Piniella came up next, and the entire, sold-out Yankee Stadium was going crazy yelling his name this time: "Lou! Lou!" He swung at the first pitch and missed. His helmet came off; he hopped around a little and looked funny like only Lou could. Then Welch threw another fastball, and he hit it into right-center. Ball game.

You know, Lou said it best after the game. He said Welch reminded him of Jim Palmer. Which was a pretty apt comparison, as it turned out. Welch went on to have a great career; he won more than two hundred games. Won the Cy Young with Oakland in 1990, when he was 27–6, with a 2.95 ERA.

But Lou said, too, "We're all professional hitters here. You get nothing but fastballs, sooner or later you're going to hit one." That's true for even the fastest major-league pitcher. Even if you can keep it up over a hundred miles an hour. Sooner or later, major-league hitters will time it.

Bob would learn that. He would become an outstanding pitcher for many years. But now we were even on the Series. And the Dodgers just couldn't get it together to stop us.

The next day, they got up early, 2–0, but we came back on them again. Those two years, 1977 and 1978, we beat them eight times in twelve games, and in four of those eight wins they had the lead on us. Didn't matter. We just found a way to beat them.

That Sunday, we just pecked them to death. We had eighteen hits—two doubles, sixteen singles. Every starter in the lineup had at least one hit. Thurman, Mickey Rivers, Brian Doyle, and Bucky Dent all had three hits apiece. Thurman drove in five runs—he could just flat hit. We thought we had such a handicap losing Willie Randolph the last week of the season, but Doyle hit .438 on the Series and played a terrific second base. Bucky hit .417 with seven ribbies and was the Series MVP. Doyle could just as well have been the MVP in the Series.

Meanwhile, the Dodgers played a miserable game, especially once they got behind. They had three errors and too many wild pitches and passed balls. Jim Beattie did a great job, pitched his first complete game in the majors for us. Beat them 12–2 in the end, with eight strikeouts.

The Dodgers let themselves be distracted by the fans. By their frustration. Sometimes you just get your butts beat. You have to acknowledge that and move on. Instead, they started talking about how they hated the fans. How they hated New York. They bad-mouthed the whole area. Bill Russell, who had a bad Series in the field, was saying how New York was the worst. Rick Monday was criticizing the fans and New Yorkers' whole way of life.

They had the wrong attitude. They were a great team, with great pitching. But we were a great team, too. We were ornery. We had a meanness and a toughness to us. We were what they had to look out for—not the fans or the lifestyle. We were connected to our fans. Fans and players, we were one.

Those Dodgers were a well-bred, private-school group. And we were a group from Harlem. We were a group from Harlem, the Bronx, and Queens, all put together. With a Manhattan owner. You know what I mean? We had a top-hat owner. And we had guys who had come out of reform school, metaphorically.

With us you got your last chance to be on the Dirty Dozen. And this was your way out. We banded together as a group. Maybe this guy didn't like that guy, and that guy didn't like this guy, and that guy was jealous of that guy. You can have all those dislikes inside the family, but if anyone tried to come into our house, it was like, "No, no, no, we're not getting along *that* bad."

We could live together, and we could deal with it. We may not like each other, but you're not coming in here and kicking us around. We'll kick each other around, but you're not doing it to us. Be careful, because we're family, and together we will kick your butt.

One time, I might have sounded like the Dodgers did. But by then, I think I had learned to adjust to the city. I had come to understand it. I knew I fit here as an ethnically mixed guy. I had come to like the fast pace, the quickness, and the intelligence. There were ugly parts. It was a city not as free from anti-Semitism as it thought it was. It was not a city as free from racism as it thought it was. It could be a tough place to play. But that toughness made you tough.

We'd all gone through that. It made us the toughest team at the time. Probably because we were playing in and representing New

York City. We couldn't wait to show you we were different. We were the toughest team from the toughest town.

We still had another game to win, we had to go back there to Dodger Stadium, and that was all right by me. I'd always enjoyed playing there. They got out to an early lead again; Davey Lopes hit a home run. But the "Killer Ds," Dent and Doyle, got all over Don Sutton. They drove in our first five runs.

Top of the seventh, I came up with Roy White on first and us leading, 5–2. They had Bob Welch in again, trying to stop the bleeding, give them a chance to come back and stay alive.

That was the third time I faced him. He threw hard every time he came in, but the first time I saw him he was fresh as a daisy. The last time, you know the coffee had been on the stove a little bit. And I had smelled the aroma enough to be able to understand the taste.

I was waiting for my turn at bat, and Catfish, who was pitching for us, said to me, "Go get him, Buck."

I went up to home plate looking to hit the ball out of the ballpark—and did. Finally got my man back.

We won the game, 7–2. Won the Series, four games to two. Our second World Series championship in a row. Catfish Hunter was the winning pitcher in the last game, which was a fitting end to the tremendous comeback year he had.

I didn't have as dramatic a postseason in 1978 as I did in 1977. But overall, I had a better one. I was told I broke nine World Series slugging records in 1977 and tied five more. You put the Series games I played that year together with the championship series games against the Royals, I hit .306 with five homers and nine ribbies, in eleven postseason games.

In 1978, you throw in the one-game playoff in Boston, and I played in eleven games, too. And that year, I hit .400 in October, with five homers and fifteen RBIs. In twenty-two playoff games in the two seasons combined, I had ten home runs and twenty-four ribbies, with a .355 batting average. I also had eleven walks and was hit by a pitch three times, meaning my on-base percentage was .451.

That was a streak.

But I was only able to get there, only able to do that, because of the team I was on. When you include the postseason in 1978, we went 37–12 in our last forty-nine games. We were 17–5 against the Red Sox, the Dodgers, the Royals, the Brewers, and the Orioles—in other words, five of the best next six teams in the major leagues. After us, that is.

You don't do that alone. Nobody does that alone in baseball, and I was truly blessed to be with guys who could do it.

You just want to consider yourself lucky, you want to consider yourself fortunate being involved in it all, to be one of the players on one of the great teams of all time. Or in my case, counting those Oakland teams, *two* of the great teams. To be in that run from fourteen games out in 1978, to have played in the playoff game in Boston—to be part of all that is just immense good fortune.

Of course, it also took a great organization and an owner who understood the brand, the city, and how to build a champion at whatever the cost.

After we ended the season in Los Angeles, we flew back to New York for the parade. I didn't get to make my cross-country drive again, but I enjoyed the ticker-tape parade. How can you not enjoy it? New York City, in the Canyon of Heroes! It was a once-in-a-lifetime experience . . . and I got to do it twice!

It was a great time. I had adjusted to the city, and I think it adjusted to me.

New York has become a place I can call home on the East Coast because of my time with the Yankees in the Bronx. The people of Manhattan and all the boroughs have forever since treated me like one of their own. It's easy to see I'm one of them. It's a blessing I'm truly grateful for . . . I *love* being part of that city. If you can make it there you can make it anywhere . . . Oh, yes! I love New York.

"Nothing Gold Can Stay"

When I think back on it now, it was such an amazing time to have lived through. It was such an incredible thing to have experienced: both the great journey that the country made and the much smaller trip that I made, growing, learning, and changing.

It bears repeating. In the America that I was born into in 1946—the Jim Crow America that persisted through my high school years, 1960 to 1964, and beyond. We could not use the same drinking fountains, the same bathrooms, or eat in the same restaurants or sleep in the same hotels as whites. In some areas, the laws did not permit us to live in the same neighborhoods, or go to the same schools, or sit next to white people on trains or buses or streetcars—or even to remain sitting at all if a white person needed the seat. The laws did not allow us to marry a white person if we so desired. We were not even allowed to play ball with white people until Jackie Robinson, Branch Rickey, and Walter O'Malley had the courage to make a stand.

The laws were changed by the Civil Rights Act of 1964 and the Voting Rights Act of 1965, but prejudice and de facto segregation persisted in many of the places I passed through—Georgia and Alabama and Kentucky and the Carolinas and Idaho and even Tempe, Arizona.

Even in the supposedly enlightened North, if you were a person of color, you could not eat in some of the best restaurants or stay in the top hotels. You were banned by written covenant—by "CC&Rs," covenants, conditions, and restrictions—from living in many of the nicest towns and neighborhoods. (Even today, in some places!) And as I found, even growing up in a nice Pennsylvania suburb, full of what were truly some of the nicest people I've ever met, you were still liable to be subjected to all sorts of humiliations by white people who did not want you dating their daughter, or riding their kid's bike, or swimming in the same pool.

The laws changed. Black people, along with many courageous whites, made them change, often at tremendous cost to themselves. Those efforts opened all sorts of new opportunities.

Yet as it is written in Scripture, men must change before kingdoms change. The laws and the court decisions that secured our rights to vote, or to go to the same schools as whites, or to live anywhere we wanted were great achievements. But they did not change the hearts, or the attitudes, or the social prejudices of all too many people.

I have been a fortunate son. Starting with my dad, everywhere I've gone, I've encountered wonderful mentors, men who have helped guide me along the way. My time at Arizona State, with Frank Kush and Bobby Winkles. The minor-league managers who looked out for me, Bill Posedel, and Gus Niarhos, and especially John McNamara. The major-league managers I had the privilege to play for, people like Dick Williams and Earl Weaver, Al Dark and Bob Lemon, Gene Michael and Dick Howser, Gene Mauch and Tony LaRussa. The owners I had the good fortune to play for, Charlie Finley, George Steinbrenner, Gene Autry, and the Haas family, and so many others.

Even when I was down in Waycross, Georgia, having to live in an army barracks with the other black players on the A's because it was too dangerous to be out at night, I was grateful. Even when I was the only black player on my team in Birmingham for a while, trying to find someplace that would serve me a meal in the Southern League, I was glad for the opportunity.

Coming to New York turned out to be a great opportunity also. It happened at a time when the city and the country were still having to make vast social adjustments. Martin Luther King was just nine years gone when I first came to the Yankees. Jackie Robinson had been retired a little over twenty years.

Some still thought blacks being able to play major-league ball was a privilege we had been given. They thought of it as a favor we had to "live up to"—usually by staying quiet and subservient. It wasn't as though we'd earned it.

AMERICAN POETS PROJECT

I would not go along with that. When I saw certain attitudes and certain prejudices emerging, I spoke up about it. When I saw double standards being applied—to myself or others—I spoke up about it. You don't have to agree with all of it. I might have been wrong about some things. But you have to respect my right to say it—and the fact that I always put my name to what I said.

I have never curbed what I have to say. Speaking my mind even got me banned from the Yankees' locker room for a little while in 2012. But I will never start tailoring my opinions to what other people think I should say.

The fact is, as far as we've come as a nation, there is still a ways to go. There is still a double standard applied to some black athletes, such as LeBron—there is still resentment that never seems to be directed at white athletes, no matter what they do. There was a poll a couple years ago that listed "the most hated athletes in America." The top five were all black! And they were usually "hated" for doing the same things that white athletes do, that all of us do, like accepting a big new contract.

We have to recognize these double standards within ourselves. We have to recognize how much we pile on players simply for having a different skin color.

We have to do better. We can do better, and do better everywhere in society, not just at the ballpark.

For me, when I came to New York, I was still growing—more than I realized at the time. I was a young man, and I got blindsided by a lot of things I didn't expect. Things I had never encountered before.

I got through them, with the help of God, of my friends and family. It's the sort of thing you might call a learning experience, except the learning and the growing never stop.

I think I've learned to work my way through life, to keep the Man Upstairs top of mind every day. I think I've come to appreciate people more as I grow older, and I can't tell you how much I enjoy being with my family, my daughter, and friends all the time now.

It was a great opportunity to make the sort of money I made in the free-agent era, even though I had larger offers in other places. My agent, Gary Walker, gave me the direction to New York. I was afraid. But he wanted me to go to the Yankees to both compete against their great history *and* to be a part of that history. In the end, it was not about the money. I know that sounds hard to believe, but it's really not. It's pretty cool being known throughout the country as Mr. October. It's cool to stand in a sold-out major-league stadium and hammer a ball into the bleachers and hear fifty-six thousand people going wild, chanting your name. But you know, the chants end, the game ends, your career ends. And the same people might be booing you tomorrow.

What it is in the end is what my dad always drilled into us. It's being glad to have the chance to provide for myself and my loved ones. It's being grateful to have had the chance to compete at the highest level and show what I was capable of—not to be judged by the color of my skin or anything else but what I was able to accomplish. That to me is what we were all looking for.

I am grateful to have had my chance. I am so grateful for my time in New York, my time in the game. I need to remember to give thanks every day. I am eager to continue the journey. I can't wait to see what's around the corner.

Acknowledgments

I want to give thanks to those who helped me through this journey.

My dad, Martinez Jackson, and my mom, Clara Jackson, who were both there when it counted. My brother (Sarge) Joe Jackson, who helped with all his big-brother guidance. My sister Dolores Burton, a mom to me when I was in need. Beverly, Tina, loving sisters. Sluggo, a brother with all his support, of course, and Elissa, my lieutenant and a best friend. Ahhh, family.

I'd like to thank my friend and agent, Gary Walker, for his weekly word of prayer in 1977 to 1978. Bill Bertucio, for his friendship and loyalty.

Frank Kush was about toughness, he started me on my way at Arizona State University. Bobby Winkles, who taught me discipline and countenanced no back talk. Johnny McNamara, who was like a father. Charlie O'Finley, so tough, but he taught me the ways of the world to come.

My attorney and friend, Steven Kay, who worked so well with the Boss. And my *other* attorney and friend, Ed Blum, the "Sheriff," still helping me to stay between the lines.

The Boss, George Steinbrenner, was tough on me at times but always treated me as family. Fran Healy, a friend, on the inside, he told me things he heard people say that I couldn't believe, and kept things from me he felt would hurt too much. Fran was there every day, and stayed with me in the city. I now know Who put him in my space.

Dick Howser and Stick Michael, who always had an encouraging word. Kenny Holtzman, Catfish Hunter, from the days of the three world championships we won in Oakland and two more in New

York. We were still "we." Gator, Willie Randolph, and Mike Torrez, a thank-you to you all.

Tony Rolfe, a New Yorker, for helping me cross some bridges. Ralph Destino, my friend from Cartier. Jim and Trudy Woolner, friends who listened (RIP). Matt Merola, my New York agent and like family, always. Mike Lupica, a friend to talk to on rides home from the ballpark.

Jenny, for good memories; Betsy, a special person; and thanks to my friend Gara.

These were some of the people in my life during these periods of growth. And I'll tell you all the really neat part of what you just read, they're all still close to me.